PETER GREEN

FOUNDER OF FLEETWOOD MAC

The Authorised Biography

Cover design: The Whole Hog Design Co
Layout: David Houghton
Printed by: MPG Books Ltd, Bodmin, Cornwall

Published by: Sanctuary Publishing Limited, 82 Bishops Bridge
Road, London W2 6BB

Copyright: Martin Celmins. First edition, 1995. This edition, 1998

Photographs: Len Green and family, Martin Celmins, Redferns
Picture Library, Simon Lee, Terry Lott, Rex Features, Mich Reynolds,
Sony, Pictorial Press, Mike and Richard Vernon, the Marquee, Mark
Marnie and James Cumpsty

While the publishers have made every reasonable effort to trace the
copyright owners for any or all of the photographs in this book,
there may be some omissions of credits for which we apologise.

ISBN: 1 86074 233 5

PETER GREEN

FOUNDER OF
FLEETWOOD MAC

The Authorised Biography

MARTIN CELMINS
FOREWORD BY BB KING

FOREWORD

BY BB KING

Back in the sixties, Peter Green was one of a new breed of great guitar players, and during that time I spent a week touring with him and Fleetwood Mac. Sure, he was a very fine person; in fact he was the same person no matter who you were. Now that sort of guy is hard to find in this business.

It's funny, but I kind of remember him more after he left Fleetwood Mac, like when he played on my London sessions album. It was around that time, I know, that he became disillusioned, but it was also then that our friendship grew.

I could sympathise with him because there had been times for me too when I felt the same – sometimes maybe it seems like everyone else is doing better than you...looks happier...got the best ideas. But then things change – it's hard to know how, but they do. Years later when I played concerts in London Peter would still sometimes come backstage and say hello – and that meant something to me. It didn't matter that he didn't seem to want to say much – I was real glad that he bothered to come along.

People have told me that in his early years my guitar playing influenced Peter a lot. Now that's something I take as a great compliment, but I have to tell you that I don't get it myself. When I hear Peter Green...I hear Peter Green.

I'm happy to see Peter is back and playing, and I know his many friends back home are very happy about it too. Peter is the kind of guy who doesn't say much and lets the guitar do all the talking for him. Well, it's great to hear that voice again.

You know, I can understand his silence all these years: there are still many times for me too when I feel disgusted by the music I'm playing because I can't find the right notes and play the way I really want to. But that's a cancer I'll have to live with for the rest of my life because if you want to punish me for anything...then take away my guitar. I don't have to touch it, but let it sit in the room so that I can just look at it and daydream.

Peter is back with a guitar in his hands and is trying. That's a big thing for me.

BB King
Glasgow, October 1997

ACKNOWLEDGMENTS TO 1998 EDITION

The first edition of this book partly was born of sadness; namely, a bleak mood that took over as I sat and watched Trevor Dann's TV documentary *Fleetwood Mac At Twenty-One* way back in 1988, which included disturbing shots of Peter Green in Richmond. This second version is inspired by two positives – celebration of the recent past, and hope for the future. At the age of fifty-one – hardly old for a blues great – the man is back where he belongs: up on stage; immersed in music; and, in his own words, "This time I know I'll never give it up again."

The book's new chapter "Underway" is written at a particularly interesting point in Green's comeback. His band, The Splinter Group, have around a hundred-and-fifty gigs under their belts since headlining the Guildford Folk And Blues Festival in August 1996 and, now with Roger Cotton on keyboards and Larry Tolfree on drums, they are supporting BB King on his UK tour. After that the workload continues apace for Peter and his oldest friend and co-guitarist, Nigel Watson, who are recording a very personal tribute album to the delta bluesman Robert Johnson.

The original version of this book began to take shape in 1992, after guitarist and artist Top Topham took the time and trouble to supply me with my first list of names and telephone numbers. Thanks Top, because most other advice at that time – Frank Harding's excepted – told me I was barking mad to want to draw attention to a great though irrevocably obscure musical legacy.

That I secured a publishing deal in the first place, is largely down to Peter himself; and the patience and hospitality of his family – Gloria and Len,

Michael and Irene – whilst my interviewing disturbed the peace at Number Sixteen in early 1994. Best wishes to Mrs Anne Green, her spirit indomitable even in frail old age.

Listening to the thoughts of so many of Peter's friends and associates from the past has been a pleasure. Thanks to Peter Anderton, Peter Bardens, Lynn and Adrian Boot, Jenny Boyd, Bob Brunning, Cliff Cooper, Alex Dmochowski, Dinky Dawson, Sandra Elsdon-Vigon, Mick Fleetwood, Kris Gray, John Hammond Jnr, Jane Honeycombe, John Holmes, Madge Jones, Andrew Kastner, BB King, Dennis Keen, Dave Kelly, Danny Kirwan, Paul Jones, Bernie Marsden, Beryl Marsden, John Mayall, Phil McDonnell, John McVie, Zoot Money, Gary Moore, Paul Morrison, John Morshead, Roger Pearce, Huw Pryce, Keith Randall, Andy Silvester, Ed Spevock, Cliff Stewart, Bobby Tench, Mike Vernon, Peter Vernon-Kell, Charlie Watkins, Stan Webb, Chris Welch, Snowy White, Jeff and Dee Whittaker, Kevin Winlove-Smith and Judy Wong.

For excellent reference material, thanks to Charles Shaar Murray, Klaus Griesbeck, *NME* and *Melody Maker*. For good advice along the way "ta" to Harry Shapiro, Eddie Allen and David Mead at *Guitarist*, Mark Ellen at *Mojo*, Phil Scott, Ben Fisher, Douglas J Noble, Otis Grand, Mick Pini, Dusty Miller, Tony Elmore, and R Jim Greaves for his meticulous and exhaustive sessionography.

For this second edition special thanks go to Mich Reynolds and Stuart Taylor of Misty Music Management for their support in making this an authorised biography. Thanks also to Peter's new lawyer Cathy Fehler for ensuring that this update never gets so focused that it overlooks the bigger picture. I am also indebted to my editor at Sanctuary, Jeff Hudson, who has seen to it that we now have a book that Peter himself likes the look of.

Our collective thanks surely must go to Nigel Watson for achieving what only three years ago seemed forever out of reach – rekindling his uniquely gifted friend's passion for playing guitar. While Nigel, Stuart and Mich have been keystones bridging Peter's step-by-step return to the music business, Cozy Powell, Neil Murray and Spike Edney musically have laid down solid foundations...a class act, even on an iffy night.

Lastly, best wishes and thanks go to the artist himself as he resumes his journey on the Hard Road. Doubters – never a dying breed, alas – might say Peter Green's legend now has more to lose than gain: "Once a trailblazer, always a trailblazer – given space and time" would be my reply to them.

With love to family in Yorkshire, Sweden and Oz.

"Jet" Martin Celmins, Manchester, October 1997

CONTENTS

CONTENTS

INTRODUCTION

THEN PLAY ON

Today he's with a friend in Ealing, tomorrow will probably find him somewhere else – like Surbiton or New Orleans. Peter Green, now a wise old man in his mid twenties, is living out the lore of 'Rambling Pony', that primitive blues he wailed onto acetate six years earlier at Decca's West Hampstead studios during the summer of love: "Well I'm a ramblin' pony, just roamin' from town to town."

Around the time that he cut this Robert Johnson-inspired track – 1967 – blues music had seriously captured the imaginations of young English white boys cossetted in the cockroach-free comfort of mother and father's home in some safe part of town. From there these "Alans", as Fleetwood Mac jokily nicknamed the squads of "What guitar strings do you use?" obsessives who stalked Peter Green backstage, would get off on what amounted to stud imagery from dark and bygone times Stateside.

Images of the blues musician's low life were of wild whores, bootleg liquor and violence. A blues man was a real man – a homicidal roustabout banged up in the state penitentiary along with his guitar-playing prowess. And the glamour of raw, black blues was its danger; it was music for closet outlaws. There was really only one guy on the British music scene in the late 1960s who could disinter all of that remote Afro-American slave culture and bring it back to life before their very eyes. He was, of all things, a chirpy Jewish cockney.

Thus young Peter Green, former butcher's lad and French-polisher, the anti-star star, suddenly found himself exalted and in a creepy hall of fame. He could do without it – and now in 1973 he does. Instead, he's happily drifting from one friend's home to another, just figuring out how best to spend another day. Homeless, but with a stack of what he calls "unclean" money in the bank, the confinement of rock stardom has ended, only to be replaced by boundless freedom – itself pretty hard and soul-searching work.

Anyway, this particular day in early spring finds Peter paying Andy Silvester, former Chicken Shack bassist, a social call. Mild-mannered Andy takes up the story: "Peter came over one day and saw this big beast of a car parked outside my house in Ealing. It belonged to Dave Walker, Fleetwood Mac's new frontman, who had asked me to look after it for him while he was on tour with them in the States. It was a four-wheel-drive Jensen Interceptor FF – the Ferguson one – a monster that could do one hundred and forty mph, no problem. Dave had told me to use it each day – those machines can develop faults if they're garaged for any length of time.

"Of course, the moment he saw it Pete said, 'Come on, let's go for a ride. Can I have a go?' I said, 'No, I'm responsible for it so if we do go I'll drive.' Pete settled for that and so out we went cruising down Hangar Lane and on to the A40. Pete kept on at me to let him drive, so in the end I said, 'All right, just for a bit' and got out to swap over. He got in to the driver's seat and straight away his foot went flat down to the board...the tyres were screeching and Pete turned into a complete madman with absolutely no fear of speed.

"I said, 'For fuck's sake, Pete, slow down – it's not even my car!' but he wasn't having any of it. The car was virtually airborne. It took off around corners and, honest to God, I still don't understand how we didn't run out of road and get killed. He was absolutely crazy at the wheel. Soon I was hysterical and at last he mumbled, 'Okay...if I must,' and pulled over. As he got out and I took over he was laughing his head off. I just drove us back, stunned and very grateful that we were still here."

Right from the start, life-threatening situations for some reason just haven't worried Peter Green – they've intrigued him. For instance, there was the time when he was sixteen and came off a motorbike for the first time. He ended up lodged, but miraculously unharmed, under a parked car: "I don't remember coming off but I guess I must have done because next thing I knew, there were showers of sparks coming from where the handlebars scraped along the road." Peter now grins and even appears to relish the memory. "All I do remember were these sparks coming past my face, but being scared was not available to me."

Both these stories illustrate Peter Green's eccentricity and inability to live by rules that bind most people. He is, and will always remain, an enigma, and the whole point about enigmas is that they will not and cannot be pinned down. Spending chunks of time with the guitarist over the past two years and getting to know him a little better, only accustoms you to his unpredictability. The one thing that can be said with certainty about Peter Green, the man, is that he never reacts to a situation in the way you might anticipate. From day to day he will change his mind on many matters, and to some people this can come across as indecision. Equally likely, though, is that it is the constant re-evaluation of a perfectionist seeking out some semblance of truth, as opposed to sticking to glib, easy platitudes.

At any one time, Peter Green has trenchant views on topics ranging from white men singing the blues, to whose turn it is to fork out for the next round of refreshment. But they are trenchant views of the moment as opposed to fixed opinions or prejudice coming from a big, swanky ego. Two musical examples illustrate his open-mindedness – one from the old Fleetwood Mac days, and the other relates to his new band, The Splinter Group.

Peter is often amused by, and even scathing about, the huge success of his old band in 1969/1970: "We were a freak show", "We were like puppies, inexperienced musicians who just got lucky", "They were a bunch of out-of-work clowns" are a few of the things he has said. And yet in the context of discussing how a certain blues should be performed in 1997 – say Otis Rush's 'It Takes Time', for a moment lavishly he will praise the young Mick Fleetwood's drumming: "When Mick laid on that beat you really knew about it."

The second example has The Splinter Group working on defining their live sound and one recurrent flashpoint for Peter after some early gigs was Cozy Powell's forceful and exuberant drumming. "What am I doing in a band that used to play with fuckin' Black Sabbath?" Peter would ask himself out aloud, sort of joking, sort of not. Ever the pro,

Powell soon eased off on the heavy-metal pyrotechnics, but would still come up with the occasional very well placed explosion of skins. And when he did Peter Green was the first to acknowledge Cozy's flawless musicianship if it sounded right. For instance, in a taxi returning to the hotel after a warmly-received capacity gig at the Cork Opera House, Peter briefly broke his pensive silence. "Some of Cozy's drum fills tonight were just mindblowing...mindblowing," he remarked in awestruck tones.

So, a bigot he is not; if anything, Green comes across as aloof and even vague on first meeting. Perhaps this is invisible armour which at once distances those he'd prefer to keep at a distance. It was American friend Judy Wong who once described him as "a Scorpio with instant suss" who can check someone out before they've had time to say hello. However, any aloofness should not be taken as absentmindedness – he takes in everything, and cannot be fazed by sharp music-biz money men. Just when they think that they've dazzled him with fast talk and big figures he'll pull them up on some inconsistency, and leave them gobsmacked.

Green's conversational style can be a bit baffling: it is of the flow-of-consciousness variety in which many abrupt and sometimes hilarious tangents or digressions coruscate as if from nowhere. His creativity finds inspiration in the most mundane things. For instance, last summer, four hours before showtime at the Llandudno Theatre, promoters and crew were seriously anxious – one lorry carrying the PA had still not arrived and was presumed stranded by the roadside somewhere. "What's up?" enquired Peter, and was promptly told about the mystery of the broken down truck. On hearing this he began to smile and chuckle – a pretty weird reaction in amongst everyone else's palpable gloom and panic. "Broken down truck, eh?" he laughed. "That's a great new bit of cockney rhyming slang you've just come up with!" So, look out for the 'I Need A Broken Down Truck, Blues'...

But within this flow of consciousness, two related subjects crop up again and again: his legacy with Fleetwood Mac, and his experimentation with LSD. He knows – as do Mick Fleetwood and John McVie, presumably – that his massive creative input within Fleetwood Mac between 1967-70 in effect helped to set that rock institution of a band up up for life. Alas, this knowledge is tinged with some regrets and even bitterness on Peter's part – something he was quite open about in an interview with Tom Doyle in the August 1997 issue of *Q* magazine. "Those shadows come into your mind," Peter explains, referring back to the old Mac days. "John McVie's got his yacht and it's like, 'Where's Peter now?' It would kind of hurt him if I said to him, 'Ain't you a bit grateful to me for that yacht?'"

He's well aware that LSD may have initially opened up new vistas in his musical imagination – 'Oh Well Parts 1 & 2' is ample proof of this – but then soon led him down a long blind alley, spiritually: "Yeah, I do sometimes wish I'd never taken LSD...people say that I could've taken the shine off Eric Clapton in my time, and they're my, y'know, personal dark shadows."

Even so, Peter's whole LSD experience remains intriguing because somehow it just doesn't sit right. Why did this down-to-earth ex-butcher's lad transform in his early twenties from a completely dedicated and driven musician to an unmotivated spaced-out hippy? Well, forget the Munich conspiracy theories about being spiked with bad acid (see Chapter 9) and myths about so-called kidnappings. Peter himself chose to take acid and knew exactly what he was doing when he left the band, and why he was doing it. He succumbed to drugs at a time when the rock-star circus had caged him up – LSD was an escape for this wild spirit who, when the hits began to come, found that the business had dragged him a million miles from his natural habitat – a free creative state.

And yet "I took one LSD trip too many and never came back" is what he still emphasises in interviews which appeared in the national press soon after his return to the stage in summer 1996; almost as though he wants to live up to the acid casualty image that has stayed with him since the 1970s. So what does this tell us about him?

Psycho-babble aside, could it be that Green's assertion about never having come back in fact is surefire proof to the contrary – that he now really has come to terms with the damage LSD has done. Real acid casualties, tragically, are still out there in "ego-loss land", and as such certainly not headstrong enough to step outside themselves and reflect on their mental state.

Characteristically, Peter's definitions of being on acid vary – he's described tripping as "a hellish neutrality" or "like an electricity" or as "something that can't be described...perhaps that's the thing about it – you can't describe it". While drugs can magnify both fantasy and reality in a marvellous way, the downside is coming off the trip and then sometimes not being able to tell what was real about the experience and what was dope-induced delusion.

For instance, when he saw film of starving children in Biafra on the TV news he was high on Sunshine. In tears, he then hallucinated himself as one of those emaciated victims of famine on the screen. And so it was "compassion on acid" that prompted him to want to donate some of his large income to the War On Want charity. He simply wanted to contribute. But the press's built-in tendency also to blur reality and fantasy reported him as wanting to give *all* his money away. Peter now says that it was after he read those stories that he felt guilty and mean and so began to think on those radical lines of giving it all away. Weird scenes, or what.

He now also remembers with wry amusement some trippy conversations he had with name musicians in America where just talking about someone joining a new band actually "created" that band for the duration of the trip – and sometimes, spookily, this new line-up even went on to "exist" afterwards. (Some Greenophiles may remember some unlikely music press news items soon after he left Fleetwood Mac, where Peter reportedly was about to join pop groups such as The Young Rascals. Perhaps this was a case in point.)

The irony in all of this, though, is that it was Peter's greatest musical gift – his extreme sensitivity – which not only pushed him to seek freedom through drugs in the first place, but also meant that mental problems set in very soon after he started doing acid and mescaline.

For instance, there was one time while he was totally immersing himself in classical music masters such as Vaughan Williams and Leonard Bernstein, as well as learning how to play the cello. One morning he began work on his music and became absolutely convinced that he himself had composed the religious film epic pop hit 'Theme From Exodus'. What an awful thought that back in that summer of 1969 even as he drew inspiration from so many different types of music, and wrote and recorded several innovative gems for the *Then Play On* album, he was also feeling the first tremors of mental problems that would hound him for the next twenty-five years. Peter Green paid an extortionate price for that first shortlived creative peak – and our ongoing pleasure.

In 1997 it looks as though the musician's lifestyle is helping him deal with those past problems. He freely talks about voices in his head and how he now hears them less and less often. Perhaps this is because the daily practice sessions on guitar, banjo, bass or harmonica – as well as the frequent gigging – are improving his powers of concentration as well as musicianship. The way in which he approaches his playing today – free of drugs, medication, alcohol and, crucially, free from commercial pressure – seemingly makes music an anchor on reality. Back in 1969 it became more of a signpost to oblivion.

Even though there are these marked differences between Peter the working musician, 1997, compared with the late 1960s version, some attitudes remain intact from the old days. Perhaps drawing from BB King who once remarked that music to him can be nothing less than a "twenty-four hours a day job", back at the hotel after a show Peter often practises in his room, while next day's drive to another gig has blues and jazz playing on the in-car sound system. More significantly, in a throwback to the old days, for Peter soundchecks are more like welcome free rehearsal time, and not the chore many musicians see them as. Instead of trying to get through them as quickly and efficiently as possible, Peter actually looks forward to the chance they offer to experiment. New songs; new phrases tried on existing songs; new sounds and amp settings.

In Chapter 6, former Fleetwood Mac tour manager Dennis Keen explains how, over two years or so, he can only remember one pre-arranged Fleetwood Mac rehearsal. The rest of the time the new numbers were practised at soundchecks, "unplugged" in dressing rooms, and at band members' houses before the drive to gigs.

In 1997 things have changed. Peter still thinks soundchecks are useful opportunities to try out other things, but rehearsals are much more commonplace. At time of writing, The Splinter Group's new line-up – featuring Larry Tolfree on drums and Roger Cotton (ex-Larry Garner and Johnny Johnson) on keyboards – is locked away in a studio, honing a forty-five minute set for their forthcoming support slot on BB King's UK tour.

And so it certainly looks as though Peter Green has indeed come full circle: it was the music business that back in the late 1960s cruelly and selfishly pushed this artist into a scary darkness beyond the edge; and it is music – plus the support of old friends – which now is bringing him back to the light.

CHAPTER 1

BEFORE THE BEGINNING: ROOTS AND EARLY DAYS

It runs in the family: go-for-it Jewish *chutzpah*, a keen sense of survival and humour that shines through hard times. Generations of warm-hearted east Europeans ready to help anyone in trouble; except, that is, those with any airs and graces – they soon freeze.

Peter Green's grandfather on his mother's side, Mark Rachman, was by all accounts an accomplished self-taught violinist; while on the other side of the family, Grandfather Greenbaum was an impulsive and restless man who appears only to have felt settled when contemplating his next move. His son, Peter's father, Joe, could pick up any musical instrument and make sense of it in no time. And Peter's mother? Well, when eighty-year-old Anne Green speaks she still modulates her voice like a trained actress; she commands attention easily, and laughs at everything. She always did.

So, the Peter Green pedigree consists of two natural musicians, a free spirit and a homespun communicator. Not forgetting, of course, the Ukrainian, Polish and Jewish mix of blood: hardly the average Anglo-Saxon Protestant.

Mark Rachman arrived in England from Ukraine with his wife and daughter in 1913, just as the Great War was looming. Here were three Jewish *emigrés en route* to a new life in America, leaving quite recent memories of pogroms and the instability of pre-revolution Russia behind to start a new life under the watchful eye of Liberty.

In fact, the Rachmans' original intention was only to visit friends in London's East End for a couple of weeks; but during that time Mark was offered work and they stayed for good. He was conscripted into the British

Army as Private Richmond and Peter's mother, Anne, was born in 1916. After the war Mark started his own hairdressing business. Anne still has fond and vivid early memories of her father the musician: "When he came home from work each evening the first thing he would do was go to his room, pick up the violin and play his heart out. It was like a ritual in which he would forget all his cares."

As one set of Peter Green's forebears were laying down roots within earshot of Bow's church bells, his father's father had decided that the time had come to move. Of Polish Jewish descent, in 1920 Grandfather Greenbaum left wife Rachel, son Joseph (then aged four) and daughter Maory, and returned to his fatherland. This would have been around the time that the Polish Army were vowing to fight to the last man in order to beat back Trotsky's Red Army (the Bolsheviks) from the gates of Warsaw. Joe and the others never saw or heard from him again.

Anne and Joe were married in 1934 and the first pair of tiny feet to patter around the couple's home were Len's in 1935. They lived in Bullen House in Bethnal Green's Collingford Street. Singer Georgia Brown (then known as Lily Klotz) lived in the same block and was a childhood playmate of Len's in what was a predominantly Jewish part of the East End.

Then came the late 1930s and some awful, awful times. As Jewish communities came increasingly under threat in Germany and Poland, many in London were taunted and worse by Hitler clone Sir Oswald Mosley and his British Union of Fascists. Decked out as paramilitary stormtroopers, the Blackshirts flaunted their thuggery and anti-semitic prejudice through the streets of Bethnal Green and Whitechapel.

No great surprise, then, that Len's early memories include nasty incidents such as bricks being thrown through neighbours' windows, and anti-semitic slogans and graffiti daubed on buildings in Jewish housing estates: "When I was a kid the Mosley mob were marching around the streets. I remember a mate of mine, Danny Del Monte – he became an auctioneer – and two friends of his, Vidal Sassoon, the hairdresser, and a guy called Marksovich who was a tailor. When these three were about twelve or thirteen, they used to go down the East End, down the streets, wait for the mob to come along and then get into them and fight. Danny was only a couple of years older than me.

"Off the Commercial Road somewhere there were some blocks of flats and Mosley's lot knew there were old Jewish girls living there. So they'd come marching up at night and just throw bottles and bricks through the windows and paint 'Go Home Jew' on the walls.

"At school, kids used to blame us for starting the war because of Hitler. But now looking back, I think the real trouble was jealousy – even English people couldn't stand the fact that Jews were good at business. The English people were used to working in factories and going home at five. Jewish immigrants – a bit like Pakistanis today – would come over and in no time be starting their own businesses and be working twelve, fifteen hours a day.

"English working-class people just wanted to do their job, come home, get washed and dressed up and then go down the pub. They lived for pub life. All my mates' mothers and fathers would be in the pub Friday, Saturday and Sunday dinner, always singing. Kids would stand outside waiting for one of their parents to come out with a bottle of lemonade and a bag of crisps. And for half the English Christian boys that was their life every weekend – they just got used to it.

"My mother and father were never in the pub; they stayed at home. They were ordinary indoor people but, I tell you, we were the first family to have a television and first in the flats with a telephone. We were Jewish business-minded people. Neighbours would want to drop by and use our phone to place bets at the bookies!"

Today Len, in his early sixties and happily retired, looks back to those hard times with a resilient cock-sparrow's humour. From the word go, he'll tell you, he has survived mostly by "ducking and diving", but all of it "strictly legit...if you know what I mean". He's not even sure that they were the hard times many have made them out to be.

Peter's mother Anne agrees: "Looking back, I've never had any really hard times: we've always managed to get by. The children never really went without anything because life was a lot simpler in those days. I don't think that the working class expected so much out of life as they do now. I mean, it was only really the business person who needed and had a car – I don't think more than one in ten ordinary working men had a car to use for pleasure. It was mainly if it was a necessity for their work."

Peter's middle brother, Michael, arrived in August 1940, to the sound of ack-ack guns. He was born during an air-raid in the Blitz, as his mother well remembers: "We were evacuated from the East End maternity hospital – about twenty of us – down to a country house near Epping Forest. This

21

place, Hill Hall, had been turned into a maternity hospital; I think it's a women's prison now, so I can say I've been in a women's prison!"

Peter's only sister Linda (now a successful civil servant) came along in 1942, and Peter Alan Greenbaum was born on 29 October 1946, at home, which was still 27 Bullen House, off the Mile End Road. "Because Peter's birth was just after the war," Anne Green points out, "all the soldiers were coming home and being demobbed and so the birth rate was very high that year. There were no beds in the hospitals for all us ladies so if it wasn't your first baby you stayed at home."

Some two years later in 1948 Joe decided to change the family name by deed poll from Greenbaum to Green. He'd had enough. Michael now remembers some of the background to this decision: "I think my father in all probability did encounter some discrimination. Remember, he'd been in Bethnal Green quite a long time and at the beginning lived in the rough end around Brady Street and Whitechapel. He may have decided enough was enough when he heard some kids shouting 'Green bum' or something like that."

Fast-forward some twenty years to 1968: to a Lightnin' Hopkins-inspired Peter Green blues on Fleetwood Mac's second album *Mr Wonderful*. On the track in question 'Trying So Hard To Forget', Peter mournfully recalls childhood days when he was "nothing but a downtrodden kid". He refuses to talk about it nowadays, or makes light of it joking that, "I grew up to the sound of gunshots around my ears."

Fast-forward a further ten years to 1978, when Peter told a journalist: "When you're Jewish you can still create a lot of feel of your own. I was always a sad person – I don't really know why – and I suppose I felt a deep sadness with my heritage."

In the early 1950s in Bethnal Green, Peter was outwardly an ordinary and likeable lad with no hang-ups and no problems. Even so, opinions differ as to what he really felt inside. Was he himself ever the butt of anti-Jewish sentiment? Michael Green thinks not: "Because he was the youngest, Peter was protected from all of that. He went to Lawrence Road Primary which was a decent school – especially compared to Daniel Street Secondary which is where Len and I went – I only recently discovered, the Kray twins were there too.

"I think those kinds of sad, troubled feelings that he was later to write songs about came out of sympathy. He was always very, very bright and aware of everything that was going on around him – he always kept his eyes open. I can vaguely remember a couple of times in my early teens when local kids would throw stones at the window and then shout 'Yid'. But it never got to me because I don't think they actually knew what they were saying. Perhaps this did leave an impression on Peter because he was so very sensitive."

Sandra Vigon (*née* Elsdon) was a model and Peter's steady girlfriend from the John Mayall days. Her recollections leave little room for doubt that Peter was all too aware of those ugly incidents: "I think a lot of Peter's pain comes from his early childhood. Being Jewish, his parents and his family really had a terrible time. I remember one time, when he and I were all alone and talking, he burst into tears. He sobbed as he talked about how painful it was as a little boy being Jewish: he was teased and taunted and quite obviously the scars were still there. I could see then and there how he had absorbed the resentment shown towards his family. And to me those are Peter's blues: the blues for him are Jewish blues."

Michael Green distinctly remembers one instance of Peter's sensitivity. He had taken the seven-year-old Peter to see *Bambi* and they had both found the film moving. Later at home when Michael started to hum the tune, Peter burst into tears. He burst into tears because he loved animals.

Peter's sensitivity and awareness reached a peak when he was eleven or twelve about the time he started to learn to play the guitar: "You just couldn't pull the wool over his eyes about anything; he would ask questions and keep asking questions until he completely understood what you were talking about."

In the late 1940s their father, Joe, changed his job as well as the family name, leaving tailoring to begin a twenty-year career with the Post Office, at first working as a postman in Bethnal Green.

Despite persistent health problems, Joe Green, who died in 1990, was a colourful extrovert and prototype "looner", always looking for the funny side of life: whenever there was a Kodak Brownie camera in someone's hands, there was Joe pulling off some silly stunt just for a laugh. However, it was partly because of Joe's health problems that, in 1956, the family moved into a larger council maisonette in Lytton Avenue, Putney. As far as Peter Green, the embryonic guitar hero, was concerned (then aged nine, and yet to pick up his first Spanish acoustic), this most definitely was a move in the right direction.

Putney was just a short bus ride from Kingston and Richmond, and during the early 1960s the music-making in the art colleges and pubs of these two deceptively sedate London suburbs would shape the rock sound of the sixties: Jagger, Jones, Clapton, Beck and Page, to name just a few, were all rumbling and about to erupt from this unlikely epicentre. However, in 1956 young Peter was perhaps more preoccupied with making sure his pets were happy in their new home and settling himself in at Elliot Comprehensive, situated on Putney Hill.

The school was a whole new scene and not just for Peter, but for post-war Britain. Its futuristic building was equipped with every imaginable facility and was sited alongside a council estate made up of smart flats that some home-owners would have killed for. This blueprint for the socially classless 1960s would in time dispense with the eleven-plus exam that brought with it the humiliation of failure and rejection at a tender age. Instead there was a labyrinth of streams and grades which attempted to demarcate the bright from the not so bright tactfully. Peter Green, though reluctant and stubborn maybe, was unquestionably bright.

Ed Spevock was in the same year as Peter at the Elliot. After a brief spell in advertising, he went on to drum for soul band The Amboy Dukes in the late 1960s, followed by gigs throughout the 1970s with the likes of Babe Ruth, Chicken Shack and The Peddlers.

Both schoolboys were Jewish, both would-be pro musicians, and both the same age, but even so they weren't good friends, as Ed explains: "I was in the sporty fraternity and Pete wasn't. The school was one of the first experiments of the 1950s and 1960s comprehensives. It was a huge school with fifteen hundred kids and lots of sports facilities: five gyms opening out into a full-size pitch with an assembly hall that doesn't look like anything you can imagine – like a tank's wheels, an ellipsis – and it was virtually on stilts because right underneath there were piano practice rooms."

Pupils were graded using the name of a nearby council estate, Ashburton: A-S-H were the top three grammar school streams, B-U-R were sort of central, using old parlance, T-O-N were the secondary modern equivalents.

Ed recalls how "despite being shy, I think he [Peter] was well liked. You know, at school there were loud kids who you liked; loud kids who you hated; quiet swots who you didn't like, and quiet blokes who you liked, but they always kept to themselves – Pete was like that."

Peter Anderton, another contemporary of Peter's at the Elliot, remembers a more extrovert Peter Green. Anderton, then a fledgling drummer, was in the same class in the third and fourth years and played in a Shadows-type school band with Peter on lead and Michael Green on rhythm guitar. "We rehearsed," Anderton recalls, "at a flat in Walham Grove, Fulham, and at Peter's parents' flat in Putney. This would have been a bit before The Beatles broke through. I remember Peter playing 'Perfidia' by The Ventures and even as a skinny kid of fourteen he was obviously a naturally talented guitarist. I recorded a school concert we played at in that enormous assembly hall on this Elizabethan reel-to-reel tape recorder. There we were, the three of us, on this vast stage where you struck a chord and then heard it come back a second-and-a-half later!'

Peter Anderton stresses that Peter wasn't at all shy in his own social group: "He was a very popular guy – very laid back, with not a care in the world. He actually stood out because he was always courteous. I remember thinking that he was Italian Jewish because he had dark black hair and a very slim face."

Whereas Anderton's sensitivity and artistic character meant that he hated his time at that school, he remembers thinking how Peter was better at mixing: "Elliot was too big a school for me...there was an awful lot of bullying, and some really tough guys who would regularly have fights with their teachers. Then there was the Mods and Rockers thing, so the school was split. Peter most definitely was a mod in the Parka and Lambretta brigade. He was fairly streetwise – but not a hood or a toughie."

Despite being slim and about average height, other boys soon discovered it was best not to pick fights with Peter, as Ed Spevock points out: "He knew how to handle himself and I can say that because I remember once I walked into the toilets where Pete was having a fight with a guy called Jim Bryant. Jim was a big stocky fellow, the school's reserve goalie, and Pete was skinny. But I remember looking at Pete in action and thinking I wouldn't like to get on the wrong side of him. Nobody won, and nobody went down, but Pete definitely held his own and word soon got round the school."

Today Peter himself remembers several occasions when he got into an argument with somebody, wouldn't back down, and ended up challenging his opponent to a sort of schoolyard duel: "If you wanted to fight you could go to the headteacher, ask for boxing gloves and he would act as referee. I guess I had about half a dozen fights and won them all. I learnt how to move around and get the other bloke to open his guard – then get straight in there with a quick punch."

It was only years later (well after Fleetwood Mac) when an astonished Ed discovered that Peter was Jewish – it was something he would never have guessed while they were both at the Elliot. Spevock now emphasises widely differing attitudes to their faith at school: "I came from what I call a 'convenient orthodox' background and never cared whether or not people knew I was Jewish. Because of this I used to take a lot of flak. I remember playing football and a guy from Pete's class saying, 'Pass the ball.' I wanted to take it on my own, and he then shouted, 'Pass the ball, Jew!' It used to hurt but I never thought it was worth getting in a fight over. I remember after Fleetwood Mac Pete once said that the thing he admired about me at the Elliot was that I didn't care that people knew. I don't think the fact he was Jewish worried him at school, you know, being exposed or found out or anything like that – somehow then in his teens he just didn't have a Jewish identity."

Even so, he appeared to be uneasy about his background during an interview which took place at the height of his fame with Nick Logan of the *NME*. Logan asked him what his real surname was: "'Greenski?' I inquired, but Peter just smiled and wasn't telling."

So Peter apparently repressed his Jewish identity during his youth, and certainly Sandra Elsdon-Vigon (now a psychotherapist) felt that there was a lot of pain hidden deep down. But his faith appears not to have really bothered him until after rock stardom.

During the 1970s he over-compensated. First he worked on a kibbutz in Israel for a couple of months, then he wanted to form an all-Jewish band with Ed Spevock. Ed fondly remembers how he told Peter he was going about it the wrong way: "We don't need any more confrontation...We need integration!" He then found a nice Jewish girl to marry, but instead of religion being a cause of inner peace, as it had been for him with girlfriend Sandra when he explored Eastern mysticism, it became a cause.

Sandra's assertion that Peter's uniqueness is to be found in the Jewishness of his blues playing is an interesting one: take for instance, the beat away from the soloing in 'Fool No More' or the brooding 'Love That Burns', and it might just be a troubled soul wailing in a synagogue. Those blue notes and trademark trills could just as well be coming from a cantor.

Back at the Elliot around 1960, though, homework was the thing that was beginning to make him wail. Being in the top stream, Peter was obviously potential college material (like his sister Linda, a grammar school girl who went on to university), but after about two terms he began to lose interest in his studies. Academia's dull repetitive process of retaining facts to show off at a later date by committing them to paper, bored him witless, as would playing the same songs night after night in a hugely successful rock band some ten years later.

But there would be times later on when he regretted his lack of formal education, as he explained to Nick Logan of the *NME* in late 1969. Referring to the life-swap that resulted in him leaving Fleetwood Mac, Peter emphasised: "I'm not going to do anything until I've done some reading. There are a lot of books I want to read – history, general knowledge. I want to put something in my head because there's nothing there. I wasted all my school-days really, and it's a nuisance."

Despite good intentions, Peter never did get to be a "book person": his education has always come from the street, meeting people from all walks of life and listening to what they have to say. An offbeat and typical example of this comes from Peter Vernon-Kell, his second manager during the late 1970s, who remembers Peter gleefully recounting the time he spent in Brixton prison in the mid 1970s. He was there for so-called psychiatric tests after the notorious shotgun incident (see Chapter 14). "He told me how he actually enjoyed his time inside," Vernon-Kell smiles, "and was just as happy talking to a rapist or murderer, as a millionaire fraud. He had, and probably still has, a totally open mind."

Back in Putney in the late 1950s though he had more of a two-track mind; rock 'n' roll and girls, and in that order. The first single he ever bought was Jerry Lee Lewis's 'Whole Lotta Shakin' Goin' On', and his first steady girlfriend, according to brother Michael, was a young lady called Patsy Gregory. Once young Patsy was on the scene, he forgot the homework.

Peter liked the teddy-boy Edwardian drape-jacket look, fashionable just before Mods and Rockers were invented as a stylistic device enabling adolescent hyperactivity to kick the hell out of itself. So, during the mid-1950s, Saturdays saw the budding teddy-boy on his own outside British Home Stores in Putney High Street, listening to hit singles being played "on approval" by pop-pickers inside. The lad even cried his eyes out because his mother wouldn't take him to see the film *Don't Knock The Rock*, featuring kiss-curled Bill Haley.

Peter Green first picked up a guitar as a ten year old, but it wasn't really obsessive love at first sight. Learning chords proved something of a problem and, being bright, he had no time for problems. Brother Len had left home by then and got married, but on one family visit to Lytton Avenue he brought a Spanish guitar for young Pete to look over. Michael was there as well: "Len turned up one day to come and see mother and father and all of us, with a guitar under his arm. Apparently he'd had some lessons – about half a dozen – and could play some chords. Pete was obviously interested and Len showed him the three-chord trick – E, A and B7. Soon after that Pete and I got a guitar each and we started learning to play. Peter picked it up straightaway, but what he was good at were the single notes; chords he found difficult to remember.

"So, gradually after that we would learn to sing and play Elvis Presley and Pat Boone numbers. I used to play the rhythm and Pete used to play lead. The first instrumental we learned to play like that was The Shadows' 'Apache'. Pete must have been about thirteen. There were no books around then to learn from, he played it all by ear, and to me he was already sounding as good as the record, even though he was playing on an acoustic guitar with steel strings and no tremolo arm."

Michael and Peter then started to write songs together. One of them, 'Bandit', was recorded twenty years later for the *Little Dreamer* album.

Peter's solo playing rapidly improved, even though he never had a single lesson and it was evident immediately that Peter had a very sensitive ear. He and Michael were ambitious right from the start: Michael wrote songs, Pete did the instrumental bits and they'd send them to Norrie Paramor at EMI Records. None were accepted.

"We also used to sing Everly Brothers stuff and would sometimes entertain the neighbours," recalls Michael. "Pete had a terrific voice, especially before it broke. I remember he used to sing Laurie Landon's 'He's Got The Whole World In His Hands' and again it sounded just like on the record." Peter's parents even organised a spot for him on Carroll Levis's *Discoveries* television show, but he "chickened out".

Peter left school without any formal qualifications at fifteen after his fourth year. Peter Anderton went on to do "O" and "A" levels and couldn't understand why Peter was in such a hurry to ditch schoolwork. At the time Peter just said he was keen to go out to work and chip in with some money for his parents.

But he was clueless about how to get a job, even though these were the full-employment early 1960s when apprenticeships, labouring, and casual work were there for the taking. Len encouraged Peter to try trainee butchering: Len himself was in the fish market and was doing quite well. He believed the future was going to be computers and automation and that the only thing a computer or robots couldn't do was fillet fish or bone out a side of beef.

So Peter got a job as an apprentice butcher, earning five pounds a week, at David Gregg's in Fulham High Street and he did really well. Within a year he could break down a side of beef into cuts. He stayed there two years and then he got his music idea. The manager of the butcher's was disappointed about Peter's decision and predicted that Peter would only end up struggling like the rest of the many young people entering that field. "You're a good butcher," he said. "You've learnt really well and I don't want to lose you." But Peter's mind was made up and he left.

Some twenty years later, during a mid 1980s interview with Richard Newman published in *Guitarist* magazine, September 1993, Peter recalled his butcher's apprentice days: "In the end I didn't serve an apprenticeship, I just went as another member of the shop. I wasn't good at it at all. I couldn't master it. There's a feeling you had when you had mastered it, but I never got anything."

February 1994, and Peter's present recollections of his butchering days are hazy: "I think I left because the manager died – I may have handed my notice in before he died but I can't really remember." What's more, he is quick to correct a myth according to which he quit his apprenticeship because of an incident where the manager sliced his own thumb off whilst demonstrating some finer aspect of the art of butchering to Peter. The story continues with Peter, who looking on was stuck for words, only managing to deliver a well-meant but ultimately insolent inquiry as to whether it hurt or not. In reality, it wasn't the manager who hurt his thumb, but one of the other lads.

And so Peter, the future vegetarian, replaced brute force and the bloodied meat cleaver with a job requiring dexterity more akin to guitar chops. He found slightly more gainful employment as a trainee French polisher working for the television rental company DER, restoring and refurbishing television cabinets: "There's a great skill to it. I had to clean up old telly cabinets, fill in the chips and scratches, then polish it all over and spray it with lacquer." Peter hated it; he even had nightmares in which the skies were filled with old tellies and maintains that the only good bits of the job were the "tea breaks spent talking to this deaf and dumb bloke who use to load up the vans". Eventually, after about a year, his mostly successful attempts to converse with his handicapped colleague met with the foreman's disapproval and Peter the semi-pro bassist was sent "up the road".

Peter recalls walking out: "The foreman came wandering over to us and said, 'Come on, get on with your work and stop wasting your time. If you don't want your job – don't have it!' So I said, 'I won't have it then.' I'd already made up my mind that I wanted to leave and see what else was on the cards for me."

He now thinks this might have been some kind of divine providence guiding him towards a career as a full-time professional musician. His semi-pro days had begun soon after he left school, playing as bassist for a local dance band called The Ken Cats who later became Bobby Dennis And The Dominoes. "I switched to bass guitar," Peter explains, "because I loved the look of the thing. I was round at a friend's and he showed me this bass – I think it was a Gibson – and I really liked its solid meaty look. So my brother Michael lent me the deposit for a Star bass – not a Framus Star, it was just called Star. It cost me forty pounds and it was a really beautiful thing to play, with lovely action."

Peter started playing Beatles, Hollies and similar music as a semi-pro in pop groups. After Bobby Dennis's band broke up, the drummer played for another band called The Tridents. They already had a string bass player, although to Peter's mind he didn't play too well, and so he was asked to join. "I'll never know why I got in," comments Peter, "because they were a very professional group."

After The Tridents, he joined a band from Battersea called The Didlos, a Kinks-style group; then, in spring 1965, a rhythm-and-blues band from Richmond called The Muskrats: "I went along to see them play. The bass player looked good, but he couldn't play a note. So I got the job." Quite soon after Peter joined, he painted the name Muskrats on the side of his van in blue and yellow.

During his six months or so with them Peter must have started to realise his place in the overall scheme of things. He'd been listening to bits of blues for three or four years now, having been initiated round at a friend's place with a scratchy seventy-eight rpm pressing of Muddy Waters' 'Honey Bee', which he described as "very spare and together". Along with fellow Muskrat, guitarist Roger Pearce, he would go to local R&B clubs like the Zodiac, and Crawdaddy, eye up the competition, and then set himself what most would regard as immodestly high standards to work towards. This competition included The Yardbirds (featuring Eric Clapton) and even The Rolling Stones.

It's quite clear that from the word go Peter was able to discern what it takes to "make it" in the music business. He admired Eric Clapton as the English innovator of the guitar solo: as a song within a song approach to playing. And he liked the Stones' Bill Wyman for his unusual image, earnest and serious, adopting a serious, upright bass pose.

Roger Pearce saw Peter's talent surge during the time they played together: "Although he played bass in our group, he was already contemplating a move back to lead guitar. We used to go along to see Eric at a gig, and Peter often went up to him afterwards for a chat. Eric freely gave us advice and playing tips. I was a bit in awe, but I think Peter was quite able to take it all in, go home, and get stuck in to some very serious practising."

It runs in the family: just as brother Len had mastered the difficult art of butchering by strolling around Smithfield and using his eyes, so as a fledgling guitar star Peter thought nothing of going straight to the summit of modern blues guitar playing, knowing that there he would find out how the land lies. *Chutzpah.*

Roger often visited the maisonette in Putney, where the Greens lived and he remembers how Peter's parents' devotion and support for their son's musical efforts impressed him more than anything else: "Peter's mum and dad encouraged him at a time when most parents were praying that pop music was just a stage that junior was going through. Sometimes there'd be a hit playing on the radio and Pete's father would be going, 'That's a terrible guitar solo...Hey, Pete, you can do much better than that, can't you?' I really envied him for that."

During Peter's time with The Muskrats Roger remembers how Peter worked on developing strength in his fingers by playing intricate solos on bass. It was around this time that he began to realise that Peter was something special. On one song, The Yardbirds' 'I Ain't Got You', we played a guitar solo and a bass solo. I always used to make a complete mess of the solo break on guitar, and yet he could get it right...on bass."

The writing was on the wall.

CHAPTER 2

SERIOUSLY, A LOONER

Always in those semi-pro days Peter could apparently take the knocks – of which there were many. Progressing in leaps and bounds as a guitarist throughout the summer of 1965, Roger Pearce recalls Peter being much in demand as a ringer in other Richmond bands, as well as being The Muskrats' bassist. It was obvious, though, that his days with them were numbered and Pearce saw Peter's decision to play lead guitar as an early sign that he was determined to go pro: "He certainly had the right attitude: he was like a cocky barrow-boy who wouldn't take no for an answer. I remember one very rare instance when someone did manage to shut him up. It was during that summer just before he left, and we drove into town in a friend's sky blue open-top Ford Consul. We were driving along the Strand – you know, on a real lads' night out – and Peter spotted these dolly-birds walking along. As we drove up to them Pete yelled out 'Oi! Do you drop 'em?' and one of them instantly shouted back, 'No, I move 'em to one side.' Pete blushed and didn't know what to say. I think at that point he used to talk about doing it rather than actually doing it!"

Although Eric Clapton had already left The Bluesbreakers for his 'Magic Bus' Greek odyssey at the end of August, Peter didn't get his chance to play with John Mayall until the end of October which, as luck would have it, was just a week before Clapton returned, although that was still enough to help Peter decide to turn professional. Among the unsuitables that Mayall had hired and then fired were John Weider (of Tony Meehan, and Johnny Kidd And The Pirates) and Jeff Kribett (later in Dr K's Blues Band). Had it not been for Clapton's untimely return, Peter would have upstaged these other hopefuls and landed the Bluesbreakers gig and this must have given him the boost to go for it, even though he was bitterly disappointed at the time (see Chapter 3).

Peter's first pro experience after this was with a band called Errol Dixon And The Honeydrippers. It was a total disaster for him: "I got that gig because I'd told them I was a blues guitarist and they said they played blues. But at my one and only gig with them I couldn't really play anything. They were into jazzy blues with all these jazz chord progressions and I just stood there onstage not being able to play a note." After that little fiasco came a couple of months as an out-of-work pro who, on anxious Thursday mornings, would go through classified ads on the jobs page of the *Melody Maker*. He would also hang around the Gunnell Brothers' agency in the hope that something might turn up. In February 1966 it finally did.

To all intents and purposes, Rik and Johnny Gunnell were the London music scene in the mid 1960s: they owned the Flamingo Club in Wardour Street, an all-nighter venue at weekends, which attracted American GIs who loved their rhythm-and-blues, and blow. The Gunnells also owned the Bag O' Nails, and the Ram Jam club in Brixton, and had a big slice of any half decent live act going. They were very good at their job, commanding – and demanding – respect. Just as the Stax/Atlantic soul music invasion was being talked about, they put an instrumentals band together styled on Booker T And The MG's – as in 'Green Onions'. This me-too outfit was called Peter B's Looners, masters of "cool blue pop" according to the agency blurb, and at the start of 1966, they were looking for a new guitarist.

Mick Parker had left to join a palais dance band and Peter duly turned up at the Gunnells' agency to apply for his job. Judy Wong – who ten years later ran the Fleetwood Mac office in Los Angeles – was then friendly with Peter Bardens and remembers seeing this shy, rather serious-looking young man waiting outside the office, with long mutton-chop sideburns and a Liberty print shirt. "The first thing Peter Bardens said to him was: 'So you wanna be our new guitarist, do you? Well, those sideburns will have to come off right away.' Peter was speechless." But interestingly, on subsequent publicity shots the mutton-chops had survived.

The other Looners at that point were Dave Ambrose on bass, and Mick

Fleetwood on drums. It beggars belief that, when Peter did the audition, The Looners' rhythm section was unimpressed with his playing. Mick Fleetwood admits: "I just felt that he was too restricted as a guitar player, which is my biggest screw-up probably of all time. And to be perfectly honest, if it wasn't for Peter Bardens he certainly wouldn't have joined that band. He had a great sound and repeated certain phrases which were pretty cool: but then I thought, 'What else can he do?' So I took the cheap way out and said, 'Well, he's not good enough.' I remember Peter Bardens came straight back saying, 'You're both wrong. This guy's got a great talent. He's going to be great.' I was into John McLaughlin at the time and I just didn't think Peter had enough fire. Of course, that misjudgment has been a great lesson in life for me: Peter remains my favourite guitar player, so when I listen to anyone now I tend not to be so hasty."

Peter Bardens explains: "Pete played that very simplified, incisive, clean style perfectly. In a short space of time he changed from hacking out a few clichés to developing a style and playing with a lot of power, becoming a real contender. He had a raw talent and because we played so much in those days – too much, if anything – he really honed it." Each weekend the Peter B's played around six gigs; a Friday night evening session (seven-thirty till eleven pm), followed by a Friday all-nighter (midnight till six am), Saturday evening, throughout the night and Sunday afternoon (three till six). All this intensive playing was mostly on the London circuit – the Marquee, the Ram Jam and the Flamingo.

The band recorded one single before growing into Shotgun Express, which was also Peter's first time in a studio: 'If You Wanna Be Happy' b/w 'Jodrell Blues'. The B-side draws on a Ramsey Lewis jazz piano groove and features more guitar than the A-side. According to Peter B, Peter apparently took to the studio situation with no problems: "He was a very easy-going guy then, who would take things as they came. He didn't try to take over or anything like that. He was very retiring in a way, never got in your face and could take a joke. We used to take the mickey out him a lot in those days, but it was never malicious. I used to call him "pleb" because I was a bit of a middle-class snob, and he didn't take offence in the slightest."

Peter had a taste of how the other half lived when the Peter B's were together supporting American stars The Lovin' Spoonful at Tara Brown's twenty-first birthday party, held at a grand house in Ireland. Brown, heir to the Guinness brewing family fortune, was later to be another in a long line of Guinness family tragedies: he was killed in a car crash before he reached the age of twenty-two.

Despite Johnny Gunnell's hunch, the instrumentals-only idea didn't land them too much work outside London, so in May the brothers decided to expand the group's appeal by adding two powerful singers – Rod Stewart (fresh from Long John Baldry's Steampacket), and Beryl Marsden, who was already Liverpool's answer to Lulu and presently Peter's first real love interest. Soon this new band, Shotgun Express, were very visible sitting in Peter Bardens' black 1956 Cadillac limo, which according to Peter G, was too often to be found broken down on the hard-shoulder of the M1, Peter and Beryl snogging on the back seat. "We used to get a lot of stick," Beryl laughs, "because it is difficult, especially when you're starting a band, to be rehearsing and keeping that head on...and then the personal thing gets into it – playing on the same stage and giving your best when one of you has upset the other earlier that day." Then also nineteen, Beryl was already four years a pro when she joined Shotgun, and all this experience in one so young impressed Peter.

She began her career in Liverpool in 1963, when Merseyside was the centre of the pop universe and Beatlemania had broken out. As the fifteen-year-old singer with The Undertakers, a band who as a publicity stunt subsequently would drive around town with a coffin not too securely fixed to the roof of their van, she was too young to go with them on their first trip to the Hamburg Star-Club. She'd already had a deal with Decca, and a hit record, 'Who You Gonna Hurt?', which sort of got to Number Twenty-Nine. "I never classed that as being a hit," Beryl points out. "It was a bit dodgy. My manager I think had paid a few backhanders to a music weekly to place it in the chart, which went on all the time then, you know, the journalist just kind of dropped it into the Top Thirty! I didn't even know that at the time, and only got to know when the *News Of The World* did an exposé a few years later."

When Beryl arrived for Shotgun's first rehearsals, above a pub in London's Tottenham Court Road, Peter didn't make a huge first impression on her: "He was a little spotty-faced nineteen year old...it took a month or so before I got to know him and found out he was such a very gentle and deep soul. He'd come round to this house I shared with Jenny Boyd [Mick Fleetwood's future wife] and he nearly always brought me flowers. We'd have long talks about quite deep subjects – the planets, stuff like that – which was quite a change for me as I was a bit of a butterfly...a scousie-scallywag!"

Beryl was immediately taken by Peter's guitar playing and, looking back, she could foresee something new breaking through, not just with Peter but also the others: "I thought Peter was very talented but in a very different sort of way. We were all a good four years younger than many of the people who'd already made it doing soul, pop and R&B – people like Georgie Fame, Alan Price, and Geno Washington. What Peter G, Peter B and Rod did was to bring something a bit more poppy to the blues-orientated stuff that was already out. On nights when Rod and I were on target doing Sam And Dave numbers, I thought we sounded good together and a bit different. The trouble in the end was that we were gigging every night and it just got to be too much. We got a flat wage of fifty pounds a week, which wasn't bad, but we were going out for two-hundred quid a night and eventually I think somebody started asking the Gunnells questions. It ended soon after that."

Amidst all this pressure of work it quickly became clear that the romance between Peter and Beryl was not evenly balanced. She recalls: "I was young and up-the-wall then, and he was very serious about me, but I wasn't that serious about him." Peter now remembers: "It soon felt right to get married, and so I asked Beryl and she said, 'Oh, so it's all or nothing is it?' A bit later she turned me down."

By this time, summer 1966, Peter was living in Bayswater's Porchester Road in the same block as John Mayall. He'd already received at least one interesting offer from a name band to tour with them in the States. Together with Mayall he was also listening to a lot of straight blues, and was probably quite ready for a change. Following the break-up with Beryl, there wasn't a lot holding him in Shotgun Express, apart from his good friendship both with Mick Fleetwood and Peter B. Indeed over the following ten years he would record and gig with the keyboardist on several occasions. But there was something else on Peter's mind – Eric Clapton. Inwardly he was still priming himself for the challenge he knew would inevitably present itself: "Somehow to come alongside him [Clapton]," as Peter later put it.

Judy Wong clearly remembers one rather revealing incident during the Peter B days: she and Peter bumped into Eric at a bus-stop at

London's Notting Hill Gate as the Bluesbreaker was *en route* to Decca's West Hampstead studios to do some recording for Mayall's "Beano" album. Judy and Peter accompanied Eric to the session at which he put the vocals on a Robert Johnson track the band had recorded called 'Ramblin' On My Mind'. As Judy and Peter returned home afterwards Peter was silent and, Judy thought, put out by something. Eventually he spilled the beans: "Oh shit. He can sing too," groaned Peter.

Then, as luck would have it, Eric Clapton left The Bluesbreakers to form Cream in July 1966, which presented Peter with the opportunity to walk away from gnawing heartache and throw himself into another all-consuming love affair – playing the blues. He remained fond of Beryl for years to come, although the next time she saw him, the scenario was very different from their young and quite innocent romance. Peter had by then formed Fleetwood Mac and was outwardly basking in the success of his first hit, 'Albatross'. Peter wrote to Beryl (who by then was back in Liverpool) saying he was losing it, he didn't like what was going on and he was desperate to see her: "So, I actually travelled down and when I got to London I phoned his parents' place. They said they hadn't seen him for a day or two. I thought he might be hanging out at the Speakeasy nightclub, so that's where I went. He was there and totally off his face, with girls hanging around him. It wasn't the Peter I knew. I went up to him very briefly to tell him that I'd got his letter and was worried. He said, 'Oh that! No, don't worry I'm fine.' I could see it was a cover-up job, but it was awkward with all those girls crowding round him. So I just left." Beryl caught the next train back to Liverpool and didn't hear from Peter again.

Early July 1966, saw a bruised Peter hand in his notice to his boss of five months, after which Peter B brought in John Morshead. This replacement, formerly of Johnny Kidd And The Pirates, would go on to admire greatly and play with Peter in the late 1960s and early 1970s.

Once away from Shotgun and Beryl, Peter didn't stay forlorn for long. About a year earlier he'd met a blonde model called Sandra Elsdon, and once he was installed in The Bluesbreakers he gave her a call to ask her out. She accepted. Romance blossomed on their first date, spent at London Zoo in Regent's Park.

CHAPTER 3

A HARD ROAD TO EASY STREET: THE MAYALL SPELL

When John Mayall returned to Manchester in the mid 1950s, after a three-year army stint spent mostly in Korea, he chose to live in a treehouse. Later on, as travelling bandleader, he would make the most of what little sun Britain's summers offered, by sunbathing morning to night on the roof of the group's van – as it motored along highways and byways to the next gig, that is.

An expatriate, domiciled in Los Angeles since the 1970s, John Mayall was – and now in his early sixties happily still is – a shining example of an almost extinct breed: the great British eccentric. More than anyone else, it was Mayall who helped to form the character of Peter Green, blues man. Discipline, taste and songwriting skills were all things that a forceful nineteen-year-old absorbed from this equally forceful, sometimes dour artist from the north already in his early thirties. For a year or so they lived in the same house in Paddington's Porchester Road: a strange huddle of rooms on the top floor of a seedy block of flats. Daily the blues fell down one storey from John's flat to Peter's: old seventy-eights from John's wall-to-wall record collection, impromptu jam sessions and caffeine-fuelled conversations at all hours. Neither musician had the time to squander on alcohol.

On the face of it, theirs was an unusual friendship: an ex-art student of arty/bohemian stock, and a butcher's lad always a little wary of "college boys". Still, they hit it off in spades. The blues was a mutual and all-consuming passion: "While he lived at Porchester Road," John reflects, "we got very close. It was one of those instant things when you recognise your own kind. I guess from a musical point of view I was a kind of father-figure, but it wasn't like a schoolteacher; you know, write a five-hundred-word essay on JB Lenoir and the civil-rights movement. We just spent a lot of our free time talking and listening to blues.

"He'd just as often listen to stuff and play me records. You have to remember that records were nowhere near as accessible then as they are now with the advent of CDs and everything being available. So if you'd got a forty-five and nobody else had it then that was something really special and people would go out of their way to hear it. That's the way it was with musicians back then. I'd been collecting for about ten or fifteen years prior to that – seventy-eights and stuff – and Peter more or less wanted to hear everything!"

Peter's first contact with John was over the phone, when Peter answered an advert for a guitarist in a blues band. The ad didn't say whose band it was: "The guy on the other end of the phone asked me who I liked on the English blues scene and I said, 'John Mayall and Graham Bond,'" recalls Peter. "Then the guy said, 'Well, this is John Mayall.' He then told me he was looking for a replacement for Eric Clapton who'd gone to Greece." Mayall told Peter where he was playing that night and asked him to go along.

John recalls first meeting Peter during the interval of that Bluesbreakers gig in August 1965. Mayall was desperately looking for a reasonable replacement and by the time Peter approached him, he'd already been through six or so unsuitable contenders. Jeff Kribbett, was featured guitarist for the night: "Peter got up from the audience between sets and came up to me angling for the job saying, 'You let me play because I'm better than he is.' He kept on doing this each time getting a bit more forceful. My first impression of him was that he sounded very believable. I was pretty much open to hearing anybody: I hadn't a thing to lose really. But when Eric went off I'd told him that the job was there for him when he came back. Just before that he'd been getting very, very unreliable – not showing up, things like that.

"Peter was the last of about half a dozen replacements. As soon as I gave him a shot at it – that was it. He just sounded great and everything was all right again. But unfortunately less than a week later Eric came back and Peter's last gig was at the Mojo up in Sheffield. By the end of his week, Peter had really got into it and so he was bitterly disappointed that he didn't have the gig anymore."

This was to put John in a difficult position with Peter when Eric finally did leave The Bluesbreakers about a year later and John had to ask Peter back. However, by this time John had got the flat below his own for Peter and the two of them were friends, which made things easier. "But right at the time I needed him back he'd also got an offer from Eric Burdon, to join The Animals – or rather Eric Burdon And The New Animals because Alan Price had left – and go to America with them." This meant Peter had to make a decision: should he go to the States, the home of the blues, which he had always wanted to do, or should he stay in the UK and play the music he wanted to play?

Close friends or not, Peter force-fed John with dollops of humble pie before reaching a decision: "When I asked him back," John remembers with amusement, "it was no surprise that he played games with me, like I'd played games with him when Eric was away. He definitely wanted to keep me on the hook and make me have a hard time getting him back – so there was a bit of revenge there. He made me sweat for about a week before he accepted the offer!"

History has it that in his first few weeks as a Bluesbreaker Peter was frequently heckled at gigs with "Where's Eric?", and "He ain't as good as Clapton!". However neither John, Peter, nor Roger Pearce for that matter, who went along to many of those first performances, remember this being the case: "I was at a Marquee gig," Roger points out, "a couple of weeks after he'd joined and there was nothing like that. Peter already had a following of his own and I remember a group of girls right at the front by the stage. What I can still see vividly is Peter's beaming face when I went round to visit him just after he'd been asked to join. He was very excited; he had this advance copy of the 'Beano' album and was learning Eric's solos, as well as working out his own ideas."

Peter doesn't remember ever actually learning Eric Clapton's parts: "I didn't learn Eric's parts – I just enjoyed them. And then when I joined John I played things my own way." In the short term the main effect of Clapton leaving The Bluesbreakers was a financial one: Mayall was out of pocket. As a bandleader who paid his musicians a fixed weekly wage no matter how few – or many – gigs they got, what John remembers most about the Clapton-to-Green switch was an immediate and noticeable fall in audience sizes: "When Eric left, all the die-hard Clapton fans left with him anyway, so in other words the audiences went down by at least a third, but then quite quickly – in a couple of months really – we built up a following for Peter. I don't remember any jeering, I think all that's a myth. Maybe very occasionally one or two people may have said something, but as I say, Eric's contingent left with him, so they weren't even there at the gigs anymore."

Even so, in an interview with Norman Joplin for *Record Mirror* shortly after quitting Mayall in June 1967, Peter conceded that things had got to him when he first joined: "They [verbal taunts] weren't the kind of things which made me play better, they would just bring me down. For a long time with John I wasn't playing at my best. Only in the last few months with him could I really feel uninhibited." Whilst still settling in as a Bluesbreaker he told another journalist: "I just wish people would stop comparing me to Eric: I'd like them to accept me as Pete Green, not 'Clapton's replacement'. I've felt terribly conscious of this on stage. I can feel them listening for special phrases. It makes my job tougher and sometimes I try too hard and overplay. If I make a mistake when I'm doing this, I'm spoiled for the rest of the evening." So at this stage Peter's sensitivity as a performer often could work against him, but then again just a few years on he would berate himself for not trying hard enough on stage, and simply going through the motions.

There was always this keen self-critical tendency which could verge on the destructive and can only have been exacerbated by finding himself in a situation where he was forced to be a guitar hero. Without a doubt, it was the mid 1960s that saw the creation of featured soloists – guitar heroes. Up until then the guitar solo in pop singles was usually a perfunctory token gesture, slotted in after the middle-eight just for the record, as it were. Then John Mayall discovered a new market.

An astute judge of crowd reaction, Mayall noticed, first with Clapton and then with Green, how extended guitar solos got punters, men especially, hooked. As Peter recalled in an interview with Richard Newman, published in *Guitarist* magazine in 1993: "I was jumping the gun a bit, trying to play as well as Eric Clapton; I had to try because I had to fill his place. In The Yardbirds, when there was a solo break they all went in there and they all came out the other end. It was nice, the proper thing. But then Eric started taking too many solos. Maybe John pushed him into it, I don't know. John tried to push me forward. But I was just coming out of work, so I was pretty cold about going to the front if I couldn't handle it."

Pretty soon, however, he did learn to handle it and then, if audiences were so-so, would do what was expected of him: namely, scorch the fretboard in time-honoured Clapton tradition. This most definitely was a compromise, as Peter explained at the time: "The applause I get when playing fast – this is nothing, it is something I used to do with John when things weren't going too well. But it isn't any good. I like to play slowly and feel every note – it comes from every part of my body." This kind of restraint and minimalism, back in 1966/67, went against the grain: guitarists had learnt that flash, if nothing else, meant cash. It was Eric Clapton who first discovered this quite by accident and there were soon expectations which Peter did his best to ignore.

The improvisational, solo-orientated style with which Cream made their mark (most of which left Peter cold) was rooted more in panic and a dire need to pad out the length of their set, than in any grand musical vision. During a Radio One interview in the late 1980s, Eric chuckled as he recalled how Cream had a rather limited repertoire, in terms of quantity, with just days to go until the debut gig at Manchester's Twisted Wheel club in summer 1966. They had about half what the contract specified. Lengthy improvising was the band's hastily construed solution, and as accomplished musicians they pulled it off; necessity, as ever, being the mother of invention. Thus they unearthed a hit formula which also lent itself to studio albums at the time.

So in effect, Cream's unique selling proposition at the time of its launch was that they were a rock band with the attitude of a modern jazz trio – out to impress each other, and only then (almost begrudgingly) the audience. It was updated and highly marketable British *sang froid* and snootiness. Fleetwood Mac came from a totally different place. Where Cream emerged as a new strain, Fleetwood Mac was an offshoot.

Peter had been a Bluesbreaker for only a couple of months when Mayall could already see something new forming, a groove and style perhaps best typified by Peter's swing instrumental 'Greeny' (or as Peter liked to call it, "A Million Knobs"). As a bandleader, Mayall was understandably equivocal to such musical developments unfolding before him: on the one hand it was satisfying to stage-manage new and fruitful empathies between musicians, but on the other it was something of a pain, because almost inevitably they would up sticks and move on.

Mick Fleetwood's thoughts on John Mayall also articulate the fostering role of band leaders in general, and the fact that truly gifted ones are about as abundant as rocking-horse manure: "John had a natural authority: he was like a schoolteacher, and there were certain things you did do and certain things you didn't. In the short time I was a Bluesbreaker I was aware of Peter being extremely grateful to John, and respecting him a great deal. Obviously as a band leader he had an acute ear for talent, but what makes him really special is his generosity of spirit. Here you have a frontman who, if he admired somebody's ability, was quite happy to step back and almost become a backdrop for that talent. What often happened was that Eric, Peter, or Mick Taylor outshone or 'out fronted' the frontman, and yet John didn't mind at all. Now that's a rare quality and one to be admired." True enough: Little Richard and Jimi Hendrix, Diana Ross And The Supremes, Brian Jones and Mick Jagger, Bryan Ferry and Brian Eno, even Take That are just a few examples of there only being room for one ego of size in a group.

John Mayall had an objective view with regard to the extent of his own talents, an ego which allowed him to see that musically the whole is almost always far bigger than the sum of the individual parts. This enabled him to make the best of each line-up he brought together. "He knew and certainly taught me, that in a good band it's as if each musician plays vicariously through the others," remembered Mick Fleetwood. "In the short time John McVie and me were together in The Bluesbreakers, that's exactly the attitude he encouraged in us: to be a solid backdrop."

When Peter replaced Eric Clapton, John soon changed the repertoire to suit the new arrival's talents, and for some six months this worked out fine. *A Hard Road* sold as well as *Blues Breakers* the so-called "Beano" album. "As soon as Peter joined, we wouldn't play things that Peter didn't feel comfortable with. There's no point in trying to make one person fit someone else's mould. There were some favourites that we didn't carry on from one to another like Freddie King's 'Hideaway' which was the guitar solo at gigs with Eric. I don't think Peter ever played 'Hideaway'. We just picked another Freddie King instrumental, so Peter did 'The Stumble'."

By April 1967, when three-quarters of what would be Fleetwood Mac were assembled, John as band leader, perceived potential drawbacks as well as strengths. "When Mick came in the band," John reflects, "something did click: on certain numbers and certain types of rhythms all three of them obviously felt very much at home. But that posed a problem for me because the variety of what they could do wasn't really wide enough for The Bluesbreakers as I saw the band. Mick's drumming style was more the basic things like shuffles, rock 'n' roll, and some slightly Latin rhythms which ultimately became the Fleetwood Mac trademark."

So for Peter, the Bluesbreakers era was something of a baptism of fire. "Practising and developing technique, and delivering the required product and performance on the night, are two different things," he explains. "Delivering the product comes from experience, and John Mayall gave me a lot of experience: he used to let me play three choruses of a solo, if a number was going well, instead of one." John recognised these two apparently contradictory qualities in Peter – self-criticism and a deep-seated confidence – within weeks of him joining, and until they went badly out of kilter some three years later, these qualities actually fuelled his talent.

But Peter was sometimes just as quick to turn that aggression inwards, like the time he did his first Bluesbreakers studio session at the end of September ('Looking Back' b/w 'So Many Roads'). Experienced pro John was very happy with the outcome, yet newcomer Peter was not. "We recorded that single very quickly after he'd joined," John points out, "and he felt that he could do a better job. The blues boom was on and things were coming through thick and fast, so I wanted a single with Peter on it out as soon as possible. After it was released he told me how he wished we'd waited until he'd been in the band a little longer. But I didn't think so...it's got all the fire and intensity that was what Peter was all about right then."

Decca producer Mike Vernon, who subsequently set up the Blue Horizon label, was similarly and instantly impressed when he first met Peter at the 'Looking Back' session: "When John booked the studio some weeks earlier he hadn't told engineer Gus Dudgeon and me that Eric had left the band. So when Peter walked into the studio with that big black-and-red chequered lumber jacket and curly hair I remember Gus was a bit put out. When John casually walked over, told us who Peter was and that there was no problem about him replacing Eric, we were still put out! Once he'd set up his amp and guitar – similar gear to Eric's – within about five minutes we realised, to our absolute amazement, that John was right. His style was very different from Eric's but he had the same touch and conviction. What's more, he was affable and friendly, quietly confident, and easy to work with." 'Looking Back' was, in effect, Peter's second time in a recording studio.

A couple of weeks later, the band began to make *A Hard Road* and the new Bluesbreaker recorded his songwriting debut – 'The Same Way'. In the months before Peter joined, John shared his ideas about songwriting with Peter. "We had a lot of fun writing songs," John recalls, "and I taught him my way of doing it. If I write a song there's usually some memory-bank reference that will give me a mood that I'm looking for. And then I have to know what the story is going to be all about. It's usually a personal experience which is more in the abstract, or it could be a specific incident in life. You've got those two elements: you've got the story to tell, which tells you what mood it should be in and that will help you figure out the most suitable key. Then somewhere along the line from your vast memory-bank of blues references you get a starting point. Peter did that with 'Black Magic Woman': he started with a few notes and the feel of Otis Rush's 'All Your Love'. Everything in the blues is a borrowed thing: in its essence it's just a very basic and simple music, but one that lends itself to so many different offshoots and interpretations. It's really limitless."

Around the time of *A Hard Road* sessions in mid October 1966 the Mayall schedule was gruelling. "It was very exciting," John recalls, "to be in the scene at that time because there was so much work. With Peter in it didn't take long before we'd built our audiences back. A lot of the time we were doing eight, nine, even ten gigs a week, you know afternoons and evenings at weekends. The Flamingo was still the mainstay, because we were being booked by Rik Gunnell, and so on a Friday night we'd play a ballroom somewhere then come back to the Flamingo and do an all-nighter – same routine on Saturdays too!"

The *A Hard Road* line-up (John McVie, Aynsley Dunbar and Peter) got on well with two provisos: Aynsley's love of the spotlight, and John's love-like devotion to Scotch. Aynsley saw himself as a featured drummer in the jazz tradition and so would forever be hankering for solos, often to Peter's and McVie's annoyance. "Aynsley was a very wild drummer with a jazz and rock 'n' roll background and he started taking too many solos," John explains. "That was a case where giving a musician his freedom backfired. Peter and John, who were not from a jazz background, really didn't like just standing there on stage, arms folded across instruments and doing nothing! 'Don't like that...' Peter would say disdainfully. 'Too jazzy!'" the band leader chuckles.

John McVie's reputation for boozing through the years has been engraved on stone tablets and remains an endearing part of British blues mythology. Yet the fact that Mayall re-hired him more times than firing him speaks volumes about his bass-playing. The firings were variously for lapses, or impromptu displays of amateur gymnastics on stage (the alcohol-induced forward somersault into a bank of speakers, for a time, was McVie's speciality) and John McVie remembers them with wry amusement: "When I joined Mayall the drinking was a part of the scene. I never drank for pleasure, it was more an environment thing in The Bluesbreakers that started it off. I met a lot of people who drank and it snowballed until I'd be drinking half a bottle of spirits a gig." But Mayall was loath to let him go because "his playing was simple, not a front-line Jack Bruce thing; he had a good tone and could really swing, which is what blues bass-playing is all about really." What's more, the tale that ruthless disciplinarian Mayall once, when returning from a gig, left a loaded McVie on a roadside in the middle of the night to make his own way back, is somewhat exaggerated: "I left him on the Old Kent Road by a bus-stop. He was just totally out of control," Mayall laughs, "so we had to do something drastic before he threw up!"

McVie's aversion to sobriety was matched only by his dislike of brass sections in blues bands. "To me back then brass equalled jazz," the bassist remembers. It may seem such a trifling point now, but back amongst the blinkered blues purism of the mid 1960s the fact that Mayall used horns on *A Hard Road* was perceived by some as the most significant thing about the album. More important almost than Peter's contributions.

The four tracks he did during the sessions drew from a wide range of styles – from protest singer JB Lenoir ('Alabama Blues', which was not included on the album) to showman Freddie King ('The Stumble'). Peter's own instrumental 'The Supernatural' uses extremely controlled feedback to spooky effect. "That [composition] was Mike Vernon's idea," Peter now points out. "We were in the studio and he was playing this chord sequence on the organ which was really good. I did some guitar and the piece developed from there. Really it should have been Mike's, but he just said, 'Have it – it's yours.'"

Peter's rendition of 'The Stumble' thirty years on goes out on the English airwaves every week as the introductory music to Paul Jones's *R&B Show* on BBC's Radio Two.

It was through John, during his time as a Bluesbreaker, that Peter met and backed visiting blues men like Chicagoan pianist Eddie Boyd ("He came round to my parents' house...got on well with my dad") and white harp player Paul "Bunky" Butterfield with whom the Mayall band recorded an EP. It was Butterfield and guitarist Mike Bloomfield who together gave John Belushi the idea for The Blues Brothers; Butterfield may also have first given Peter the idea to go and live in Chicago and play alongside local black musicians (something he thought about doing when he left The Bluesbreakers in mid 1967). By 1966 this white American college boy had already achieved the very thing every white blues boy wanted to achieve – he was accepted in black clubs on Chicago's South Side as a musical equal.

Recording sessions took place at monthly intervals with Mayall. Although he never had anything approaching a hit single, as a former ad-man John could see the publicity value of issuing forty-fives regularly and at least having them reviewed in the music press. After the *A Hard Road* and Paul Butterfield sessions in October and November the band were back in the studio in January to record a sweet country blues, 'Sitting In The Rain'. Primitive, with gentle swing, it perhaps marks the four musicians at their tightest. However, Aynsley was getting very busy (witness that chunk of ego-rhythm, 'Rubber Duck', in which manic Scot Dunbar gives his kit some real *laldie*), John Mayall was increasingly into jazzy horns and all this served to make Peter rather restless.

Ironically, just as *A Hard Road* came out and went into the album Top Ten in March, things began to fall apart for this line-up of The Bluesbreakers and began to come together for Fleetwood Mac. In early April Mayall decided that Dunbar was out and after briefly rebounding into The Jeff Beck Group (at that point also featuring Rod Stewart, hotfoot from the defunct Shotgun Express) Aynsley formed his own band, Retaliation. The name is thought to have some bearing on how he felt about being dumped by The Bluesbreakers for being too flash. It was Peter who suggested Mick Fleetwood as a replacement and after Mayall agreed to give him a try, phoned him up and asked him to come along to a gig. At this point Aynsley was still in the band so it was all a bit sticky.

"It was a strange situation," Mick reflects quizzically, "because I basically had no idea why I was being invited in to John Mayall's Bluesbreakers. I drove down to this gig the night he [Aynsley] was fired. The thought of taking over from Aynsley, who to this day is an incredibly capable drummer technically and has played with everybody from Frank Zappa to The

Mahavishnu Orchestra, was awesome. He was a great performing drummer who had his own following at gigs. I never even remotely thought of myself like that. I thought of myself as a guy that has a lot of fun banging the drums: mine was a naive animal approach really. I think that's why Peter and John wanted me in because Aynsley was getting too clever playing a format of music which didn't warrant paradiddles every three seconds or drum rudiments during a blues shuffle. Even so, at the time I didn't understand and said, 'Why do you want to get rid of him? He's great!' So I went into it, and came out of it about a month later, with a sense of humour, to be quite blunt. I even had a graph in the van, a datesheet, like a calendar, and I remember one time ticking off the gigs: 'That gig drunk; that gig drunk; that gig fairly good – good drum solo' and then at the bottom it said, 'Fired for drunk and disorderly behaviour'. I showed it to John Mayall and everyone had a laugh, but practically that same day I was actually given my marching orders. In a way I was almost willing it to happen, often saying, 'I won't be upset if you fire me', so it was very above board and lighthearted."

London drummer Mickey Waller (formerly with Cyril Davies, Joe Brown, Marty Wilde, Brian Auger, Georgie Fame, Steampacket and others) stood in for a couple of gigs before Mick joined in early April, and almost straightaway the band was back in the studio to record their third single of that year, Otis Rush's 'Double Trouble' b/w Elmore James's 'It Hurts Me Too'. By the time this was released in June, the drummer and featured guitarist would be halfway to forming their own band named after another track recorded by the three "April 67" Bluesbreakers minus Mayall – "Fleetwood Mac".

Could Mayall sense dissent rising within the ranks? "I think as a band leader you always do. Peter had certainly expressed dissatisfaction with the more jazzy things and was quite open about wanting to do things that were more basic. Then on his birthday I gave him some recording time to use as and when he wanted, and a bit later he got together with Mick and John and did that 'Fleetwood Mac' thing. From then on I guess it was just a matter of time."

Even so, John's recollections about Mick's departure from The Bluesbreakers differ somewhat from those of the giant drummer himself: "The main thing I remember is not the drinking part of it, although he did get totally wasted here and there along with McVie and not necessarily at the same time! I remember that there were limitations. There were other songs that I needed to be able to do which required different rhythms. It was probably a bit of both; you know, the drink limited what he could play proficiently."

A no-nonsense pro, John wasn't upset by Peter's departure. Peter didn't defect when he left at the beginning of June, he left ostensibly to do nothing but go with the flow, possibly to Chicago. The bond between mentor and protégé remained strong as ever: "The rapport that brought me into contact with him in the first place and that made us so close," John proudly points out, "once you get that kind of friendship you never lose it. It's always there: you look into that person's eyes and it's all there, right to this day."

At the end of 1967 Peter was up to his neck in getting Fleetwood Mac's first album finished and gigging virtually every night of the week. Yet he still found time to do a session for his former boss. The product included Mayall's all-time favourite with his former guitarist, 'Picture On The Wall', the B-side of 'Jenny'. "It was about a girlfriend of mine, Rosalyn, a very sad love affair. It was just Peter and I who recorded that together. He was playing that beautiful Dobro slide guitar and I was playing normal guitar. It turned out a sublime piece. Every time I hear it, it tells me everything about Peter's music that I loved. The thing with Peter's playing, and people like Eric and BB King is that they have that touch – they can pick up a guitar and play just two notes and you know who it is. Now that's a very rare thing."

In mid July 1966, when Peter joined The Bluesbreakers, Mayall was effusive about the abilities of Clapton's replacement and told one interviewer how in his opinion Peter was "a young genius who will grow into something better than Eric". Reminded of this some thirty years later, and of Mike Vernon's generous praise, Peter now remains completely unflattered: "They had to say *something* didn't they? Especially as they were expecting a disaster."

CHAPTER 4

FLEETWOOD MAC ROLLS
ONTO THE TRACKS

Blues harp wailing like an express, cymbals clicking like steel wheels on rails and a percussive steam engine bass: that was 'Fleetwood Mac' the instrumental, the studio debut of Messrs Green, Fleetwood and McVie as a unit. The roots of Fleetwood Mac the band, though, take a little longer to trace. "The name just came to me," says Peter. "I thought 'Fleetwood' sounded like an express train and groups were starting to call themselves after musicians. Then, we were in the studio recording an instrumental that sounded like a train." Fleetwood Mac were haphazard, flukey and in complete contrast to the kind of world domination vibe that surrounded, say, the launch of Cream a year earlier in 1966. Some maintain that Peter formed Fleetwood Mac because there was nothing else to do. Others, like Mick Fleetwood, say he had no choice. After leaving Mayall, he was toying with the idea of an extended pilgrimage to Chicago, but came to the conclusion that life for a white boy might prove rather dangerous in a place once torn apart by race riots. So for a couple of weeks in mid 1967 (after his 15 June swansong with Mayall) Peter was gigless and, according to Mick, being pestered by producer Mike Vernon, who was hungry to establish one of his three independent blues labels, Blue Horizon, as Blighty's answer to Chicago's ultra-hip Chess Records.

Mike Vernon now insists that Peter was not coerced into forming Fleetwood Mac; it was something he wanted to do, initially as a three-piece in the Buddy Guy, Jimi Hendrix and Cream format of lead, bass and drums. "Being involved with John Mayall," Mike points out, "Peter was being pushed in one direction, because John did tend to rule the roost, give commands and people would jump. That's how The Bluesbreakers worked."

The original plan for Fleetwood Mac was as a trio, but Peter always thought it would be great to have a guitar player who nobody had heard of and who was completely different from himself. Six months beforehand Mike had done some demo tapes at Decca with a trio from Lichfield. He had thought the drummer and the bass player absolutely dire, but the guitarist, Jeremy Spencer, sensational, the nearest thing he'd ever heard to Elmore James. Mike gave Peter Jeremy's phone number and also called Jeremy to tell him that Peter Green was sniffing around for a guitar player and was possibly leaving The Bluesbreakers. Mike suggested that Jeremy should go to a gig to introduce himself to Peter. The next thing Mike knew was that Peter and Jeremy were talking and that the idea of a trio was completely wiped out.

Peter got out of The Bluesbreakers because he thought John Mayall was getting too jazzy. "John's material," Peter said at the time, "was less and less the blues. We'd do the same thing night after night. John would say something to the audience, count us in, and I'd groan inwardly." One of the last times Peter had to take orders and suppress the groan was up at the Birmingham club Le Metro where The Bluesbreakers played on Sunday, 11 June, 1967. The same week that Mayall placed an advertisement in the situations vacant pages of *Melody Maker* for Peter's replacement: "John Mayall requires lead guitarist to match the brilliant blues standards set by Eric Clapton and Peter Green (BB King, Otis Rush-style). Also, tenor player preferably doubling baritone for section work only. Both candidates must have an unswerving dedication to the blues." The successful respondent to the advertisement was future Rolling Stone, eighteen-year-old Mick Taylor.

Keith Randall, who later became a close friend of one-man blues band, Duster Bennett, was in the audience that night at Le Metro, and remembers how an informal audition took place afterwards between Peter and "a local Elmore James nut called Jeremy Spencer": "After the gig when the bar had closed we hung around for a bit and saw Peter and Jeremy jam for a couple of numbers – just the two of them without a band."

Peter's recollections of that first meeting with Jeremy are twofold: "I thought he played slide with conviction, and looking at him I could see he was a villain." So Jeremy Spencer was in.

What Jeremy couldn't have known was the role that Peter had in mind for him at the time. In effect, he was to be the warm-up man, something Peter had explained to Tony "The Duster" Bennett at the time, as Keith Randall recalls: "Tony said Peter had once told him that Jeremy was brought into the band as a foil for Peter Green, somebody to start the show off, do some up-tempo rock 'n' roll numbers, although what Peter called rock 'n' roll included Elmore James, and warm up the audience. So after he'd done three or four things he'd go off stage, not to be seen again for about an hour. Then he'd come back on, not very pleased, because Peter had hogged the stage all that time. A few times I heard him say very sarcastically, 'Thanks for bringing me back on stage.' Then they'd end the set with a rock 'n' roll finale."

Mick Fleetwood's involuntary rest from the music business (after being kicked out of The Bluesbreakers that April) was to last all of six weeks. Having just obtained a loan from his father to buy ladders so he might earn a living as a window-cleaner and decorator, Mick got a phone-call from Peter. So he too was in. "At the time I didn't have a lot of musical confidence," Mick recalls. "Peter knew that, but he also knew from the John Mayall days that he enjoyed playing with me. And from what he was planning to do with Fleetwood Mac he realised that I was the guy for the job. He didn't want to be Cream – he wanted to play the real stuff.

"To be quite blunt, that was the way I played naturally. I didn't learn that shuffling especially for Fleetwood Mac. A lot of it was just luck. The insight that Peter had was that he saw how he could utilise my style of playing and give me the encouragement. He would say, 'Mick, just stay as you are. You swing like the clappers, so just stay on the groove, and that's all you have to do.' I used to be very insecure about it and I'd say, 'I'm not that good, Pete,' and he'd say, 'Yes you are – you're great!'

"He went immediately for the human touch with me, and that's what Peter's playing has represented to millions of people: he played with the human, not the superstar, touch. And so I always listened to what he had to say, even if he was beating me up a bit."

In mid 1967, summer of love and celebrity drug busts, the blues in Britain were beginning to boom. It continued to do so for a further eighteen months until the novelty of raunchy, repetitive twelve-bars and lightning pentatonics began to fall on somewhat jaded, not to mention aching, ears.

While it lasted, though, there were literally hundreds of blues trios and quartets pounding the country's newly-built motorways in ridiculously broken-down old vans. This was before MOT tests were introduced to try and keep certain death off the roads. Happy to play gigs at the countless Hoochie Coochie blues clubs that had sprung up, most of these bands were appallingly bad, as Peter himself then observed: "There were a million groups making a mockery of the blues, and a million guitarists playing as fast as they could and calling it blues. I didn't want the music messed around with; I suppose I was possessive about it." Their leader was going to make sure that his band was a cut above, not only in ability but also attitude. Despite the laddish, insouciant image they affected, Fleetwood Mac were really purists on a mission, not just artisans on an outing.

By 1967, twenty-year-old Peter's blues guitar had already earned him a reputation that reached as far as Chicago's South Side. In March, whilst still in The Bluesbreakers, he had gone into the studio with veteran blues pianist Eddie Boyd, who praised him as a great blues man, later remarking: "He's a negro turned inside-out."

There is something in every sense funny, upside-down and inside-out about that whole 1960s UK/US musical exchange. In the United States negroes increasingly wanted to move on from their blues heritage. Ever since the 1940s, migrations from the rural south to northern cities like Chicago had produced a black urban underclass. By the 1960s successful blacks wanted to leave all this behind and be assimilated – something reflected in the visual style of artists on Tamla Motown's roster. With their western-style wigs or shiny mohair suits, the fashion statement of acts like The Supremes and Four Tops was "We too can dream the American dream".

Meanwhile in England the reverse was true: any snobbery amongst the young was radically inverted as cool, middle-class musicians, some with double-barrelled surnames, for a while adopted the Barbecue Bill style of the Mississippi cotton plantation. Dressing up entailed studiously dressing down in old jeans and hobo hairdos. The outcome of these bizarre transatlantic games of sociological snakes and ladders? Blues music prospered as never before – first in England and then later as it was reimported back into America. This is in part why Eddie Boyd, BB King and Otis Spann were so grateful to Eric Clapton and Peter Green in the late 1960s: in America English guys represented the acceptable face of the blues to sons and daughters of Republican apple-pie mommahood. What Fleetwood Mac then did was to unwittingly draw from the music in three ways: they parodied it, they developed it and they actually performed it. The result was a unique rhythm and blues, rock 'n' roll vaudeville show. Anybody who hammed up Elmore James today to the extent that Jeremy Spencer did then – he was, in effect, a blues Al Jolson without the greasepaint – might be dismissed as bad, politically incorrect and out of order. But in 1968/9 the illusion of a tiny white boy impersonating a big black man and his music was great entertainment.

In fact, one of the more ironic incidents of that decade relating to the transatlantic crossover of blues, did actually involve a bunch of white boys and a black man: The Rolling Stones and Muddy Waters, the man who gave that group their name. The Stones were in Chicago in June 1964 and were booked in for a two-day session at the famous Chess studios to record a cover version of The Valentinos' R&B hit 'It's All Over Now'. (Some five years later Fleetwood Mac themselves would record there.) "We were unloading the van, taking the equipment in, amps, guitars, mike stands, etcetera," recalls Bill Wyman, "when this big black guy comes in and says, 'Want some help?' We look round and it's Muddy Waters. He starts helping us carry in the guitars and all that! As kids we would have given our right arms just to say hello to him and here's the great Muddy Waters helping to carry my guitar into the studio."

Alas, the American blues legend was not at Chess cutting a new disc, he was redecorating the studios because he needed to earn some extra dollars. Over time, it was this kind of incongruity that gave English fans the blues about the blues, and a cool cause to fight for. (After all, what was on offer in the English folk tradition – Morris dancing?) And in the right hands, the blues about the blues moved the music forward, beyond faithful or even outlandish pastiche to the new black and white blues which surprises nobody today. Back then, John Mayall's blues about the blues related in particular to JB Lenoir: Mayall would later champion the late Lenoir's music so that his family would get any royalties due.

So by 1967, in Britain, it was all rather earnest. Before that, in the mid 1960s, The Yardbirds, The Pretty Things, The Animals and the Stones somehow managed to juggle pop with rhythm and blues, and to do so in a way that was quaint and very English. But presentation was still often rather straight-faced and moody. When Fleetwood Mac was being formed it was precisely because the blues pose was one of angst, that Mac set themselves apart: they would openly enjoy themselves on stage, shout obscenities, enjoy whatever the musician's life had to offer and then laugh all the way to the VD clinic.

Combine this image with guitar-playing that was outstanding in its authenticity and they soon became mavericks well ahead of the herd. Peter chose Mick Fleetwood as a drummer because his style was both simple and strong and his sheer strength as a shuffler – shi-boom...shi-boom – was really the band's calling card in those very early days. There were blues bands and there was Fleetwood Mac: or "Fleetwood Mack" as the *Melody Maker* first called them; or "Fleetwood Wing" as they were christened by *Record Mirror.* That June, in 1967, the music press got other things wrong.

The announcement of this new band, "Fleetwood Mack", took all of two-and-a-half column inches in *Melody Maker.* Entitled "More Cream?", the text read: "A new Cream-type group is being formed by ex-John Mayall guitarist Peter Green, and they will make their debut at Windsor Jazz Festival next month. The group includes Mick Fleetwood (drums), Gerry Spence (bottle-neck guitar, vibes and piano) and a bass player yet to be enrolled."

Jeremy Spencer "on vibes" was prescient: the guitarist's ribald humour would dominate the group on and off stage, often to outrageous effect. But the hack who wrote the piece could not have known how wide of the mark he was in comparing this new band to Cream, a "progressive" supergroup, whose very name spoke volumes about the testosterone-on-acid swagger of its members. A part of Eric Clapton's musical vision when he formed Cream was to adapt Robert Johnson's legacy to the second half of the twentieth century, something he did with the heavy-rock version of Johnson's 'Crossroads' amongst other things. But in direct contrast, Peter Green was a blues man who wanted to preserve blues music like a cherished antique.

Peter's Jewishness helped him identify with the blues' political roots – field hollers, persecution and oppression – whereas Eric Clapton, "motherless son", went more for notions of the blues man as an artist, stud and achiever against all odds, despite a painful childhood.

"I would try to picture," Eric once said, "what an ideal blues man would live like: I would picture what kind of car he drove, what it would smell like inside. Me and Jeff [Beck] had this idea of one day owning a black Cadillac or Stingray that smelled of sex inside and had tinted windows and a great sound system."

Peter explains how his early blues aspirations at that time were somewhat less hedonistic: "JB Lenoir was a symbol for me of African slavery – that high voice said something to me. And Sister Rosetta Tharp: I first saw her on telly when I was about fourteen. Just this woman with a guitar, her voice and the gospel – marvellous."

JB Lenoir and Sister Rosetta Tharp were both politically and spiritually aware musicians and perfect role-models. Small wonder then that around that time in 1967 blues "traddie" Peter even berated Eric for his modernity: "Eric sat in with us the other week and he isn't the same. He's lost the feeling. He could get it back but he's so easily influenced. He sees Hendrix and thinks, 'I can do that. Why don't I?' But I'll always play the blues."

Peter's launch plans for Fleetwood Mac ran up against a problem when John McVie, his first-choice bass player, refused to budge from what was a financially-secure gig with John Mayall. McVie had been with Mayall for many years and it was a very, very good job. What's more, Mayall put up with McVie's taste for drink, after all, he always put in the business and played very well. So Peter placed an ad in *Melody Maker*.

Bob Brunning replied to the ad: "It read something like: 'Bass player wanted for Chicago-type blues band.' But it had the wrong phone number because of a misprint. The *Melody Maker* gave me the right one and I got through and arranged to audition. When I arrived at a council flat in Putney I made a complete fool of myself: this guy introduced himself as Peter Green and I said, 'You've certainly got the right name for a blues guitarist. Do you know about your namesake who plays with John Mayall?'" Somehow the bass player recovered from this gaffe, did the audition and got the gig. So Bob Brunning was in.

The band began rehearsals in July at the Black Bull pub on the Fulham Road, during which time Peter naturally established himself as leader. "Peter formed Fleetwood Mac," Bob reflects, "because he wanted a successful band to play his own music. He did have a clear idea of what he wanted, but he didn't turn round to everybody and say, 'Here is the song: you do this, and you do that.' Instead he would explain the structure of the thing and then we'd play it and see how it sounded. The first time we rehearsed at the Black Bull I remember I went over to buy a pint and then about an hour or so later I went over to buy another pint and Pete said, 'Oh, Bob, you're not having another one of those are you?' He was very strict on people not being remotely drunk at gigs – he just wouldn't allow Mick to do that."

As Mick recalls, Peter had made his stance about booze and blues quite clear during the Mayall days: "He would find my drinking amusing, but only up to a certain point and then he'd turn round and say gruffly, 'Mick, you're pissed as a newt!' There was a cut-off point, which did happen more than once or twice in the Mayall days, where he felt compromised because John and me weren't playing properly. He most definitely wasn't amused by that and he would let us know. But still there were those moments, unfortunately, with me and John where the whole rhythm section was pissed as a newt and it was not right. Peter would then choose an appropriate moment to coldly say, 'You just don't do that when I'm on stage.'"

In the run-up to their Windsor debut, Peter and Mick looked after the practicalities of getting a band on the road. Although Peter was only eighteen months a pro, you couldn't put one over on him and in the four years since Mick first went on the road with The Cheynes he too had seen it all, relatively speaking. Both were wise to the dubious ways of Tin Pan Alley crooks and wide-boys who were all so adept at promising the world, and then delivering little more than ultimata and the odd threat to sue. "What we were trying to do," Mick explains, "with very little money, was to get to a situation where we didn't owe our souls to our booking agents, the Gunnell brothers, because what they seemed to do was get everyone in debt and then, for some strange reason, you'd never seem to be able to get out. So you were basically working for a small wage and yet were unable to leave when things appeared to be getting better. Peter had the savvy, being an East End lad, to call their bluff."

Peter decided the band would own their own van and equipment. So he and Mick went scratching around answering ads to buy old Reslo microphones and a few weeks before Windsor even went to an outdoor music festival near Alexandra Palace for the sole purpose of hustling amps and mic stands from the various roadies. "In that sense," recalls Mick, "it was stressful because we were getting in quite deep – I think my parents had even signed for some equipment."

So determined were they not to be owing to anyone, that Peter and girlfriend Sandra Elsdon moved out of their flat in Porchester Road and he went back to live with his parents at Putney to save on rent.

Sandra meanwhile got a flat with some girlfriends and Peter would spend a lot of time there. Although they talked about getting married and both going to Chicago so Peter could play with the blues guys there, Sandra remembers there was always something inside him that was restless. Getting the group together and developing was Peter's main focus. Their relationship was always important, but his biggest love was the guitar.

"Peter's music was an expression of his emotional and spiritual being. He is a deeply spiritual person and that was his main driving force – to express that spirituality. He wasn't out to be famous, and the responsibility of the power that goes along with that kind of position was not something he wanted," reflects Sandra. "Like any performing artist, he needed recognition but he didn't have a big ego in that sense. Purity is a word that springs to mind – he came from a solid working-class background and there was a certain refinement, which came across in his music."

On the big day of the Windsor debut – Sunday, 13 August – two small things happened which, though insignificant at the time, would prove prophetic for Peter Green and Fleetwood Mac. Bob Brunning well remembers while they were driving along in the van Mick suddenly started talking about investing money in property, initially buying a cottage in Wales, once the band started to earn a few bob. "Now for people like me who'd just been to college this was something I'd never even vaguely thought about. Even at that point Mick didn't care what material was being played: his aim was always success." However, in less than three years' time and right in the middle of a headlining European tour, it would be a more heated version of the same brief exchange between founders and bosom pals Peter and Mick, one which would prompt the leader's departure.

The second incident of 13 August is recalled by Stan Webb of Chicken Shack, whose group was also part of that Sunday's programme at the seventh Windsor National Jazz, Pop, Ballads And Blues Festival (forerunner of the Reading Festival). Stan was privy to a chat backstage between Peter and Eric Clapton which neatly illustrates the two musicians' somewhat different style and aspirations: "Peter and me were talking about the price of beer – Peter was wearing a white T-shirt and blue jeans – then Eric turned up and came over to us wearing a bedspread, rings on every finger his frizzy hair sticking out six inches, and said to Peter, 'Pete, you'll never be a star if you dress like that.' Peter just smiled. And that sums it up."

Fleetwood Mac were given an encouraging reception from the forty thousand *bona fide* and weekend hippies assembled on Balloon Meadow at the Royal Windsor racecourse, even though the sound quality of every band on the bill was by all accounts patchy. In today's age of one-and-a-half million watt outdoor public address systems, it's unbelievable that during that weekend in 1967 sound engineer Charlie Watkins (of WEM PAs) had all of a thousand watts at his disposal. With this, a whisper by today's standards, Watkins manfully tried to project the music, theatre and egos of acts like Pink Floyd and Arthur "although my hair's on fire there's a mile high angel watching over me" Brown.

According to Chris Welch of *Melody Maker*, every single performance featured technical hitches and embarrassing unplanned silences, and even at a thousand watts the noise levels were enough to drive some crusty locals to despair: "A host of guitarists," wrote Welch in his review, "like Peter Green, Eric Clapton, Jeff Beck and David O'List had their sound reduced to a near pathetic level. Peter Green's Fleetwood Mac made an impressive debut, while John Mayall was received with fervent enthusiasm. But Eric Clapton is still two-hundred-and-forty miles ahead of other guitarists in his field." Fleetwood Mac also played at a fringe blues event on the Sunday evening. The only person who had a bad word to say about their performance was the musician who would join them three weeks later: John McVie is reported to have found them "boring".

Huw Pryce, the band's first roadie who has since worked for Pink Floyd and Paul McCartney amongst many others, was then not long out of Goldsmith's teacher training college in south London. Seeing Fleetwood Mac at Windsor sealed a lifelong fate: "I got the job," Huw remembers, "through Stan Webb and Chicken Shack really. I went down to the festival from Kidderminster in Shack's J2 van and got introduced to Peter and the band backstage. They offered me a job there and then basically. Peter was a straightforward, sincere guy, but someone you obviously wouldn't want to mess about."

Being a roadie in those days wasn't very sophisticated: the roadie was usually the guy who had a van and was often better-paid than the band itself. When Huw started working for them they had already bought a van – a brand new light-blue, short-wheelbase Ford Transit. This was pre-Clifford Davis who at that point was a booker for the Gunnell brothers.

After the Windsor gig, Fleetwood Mac went straight onto the pub rock circuit. With four or more gigs a week, up and down the country, this "new and increasingly successful combo" as they were sometimes billed, had a strong following from the very start. Huw wryly recalls one gig where Peter was actually described on the flysheet as "the world's third greatest guitarist". The promoter presumably gave Hendrix and Clapton gold and silver.

"A typical pub gig would see us arriving about seven, setting up the gear, which didn't take long, a bit of a soundcheck then off to the bar until start-time at nine. Everyone was deadly serious about their careers, but while Bob was all right playing in a blues band, what he really wanted to do was be a teacher – you know, get a proper job!"

None the less, in the short time he was with them, Bob recorded four tracks with the band, two of which – 'I Believe My Time Ain't Long' and 'Rambling Pony' – were released as the first single. These recordings were respectful tributes to Elmore James, and Hambone Willie Newbern's 'Rollin' And Tumblin'': it was plain and simple roots music at a time when psychedelic trimmings – wah-wah, fuzz and prototype phasers – were the order of the day. The single went nowhere with a bullet.

Then *Melody Maker* announced in its 9 September issue that "former Zoot Money bass guitarist Paul Williams had joined John Mayall's Bluesbreakers replacing John McVie who is joining Peter Green's Fleetwood Mac. Tenorist Dick Heckstall-Smith has also joined Mayall." Brass instruments in a blues group was more than John McVie could bear. He now remembers, "In those times I was very blinkered and horns equalled jazz. Of course, in retrospect that wasn't the case. But there was this Bluesbreakers gig in Norwich or somewhere and during the soundcheck one of the horn players asked John what kind of solo he wanted in a section. John Mayall told him to play free form. That was it. I phoned Peter that night." So, after a three-week dither, John McVie was in.

In that same issue *Melody Maker* ran a feature on "The Magnificent Seven". Nothing to do with Hollywood gun slingers, this article gushed on and reminded readers who needed no reminding that this was the age of the guitar hero. The seven were in fact Eric Clapton, Jimi Hendrix, Pete Townshend, Jeff Beck, Jimmy Page, Stevie Winwood – and Peter Green, "the newest, toughest, and meanest of the guitar heroes".

Some time after this, another article in music weekly *Disc* nominated "Britain's new Fab Four": they were Eric Clapton, Alvin Lee, Peter Green and Stan Webb. But, as Stan now points out, this was all over-the-top media hype: "We were all ordinary blokes who, when we met up, talked about ordinary things. We didn't rush up to each other saying, 'I'm Number Two, you're only Number Three!' or whatever. Playing guitar was something we just did. To us it wasn't this big precious thing that lots of people wanted to make it into."

Even in those early days, Peter would become less able to shrug off all this attention. As he rose to fame people began to treat him differently and where others may have lapped it up, he grew suspicious. "Why am I now so attractive when just a couple of years ago as a butcher, nobody wanted to know? Why all that applause just for playing guitar?"

What Huw Pryce remembers more than anything else about that first autumn the band was on the road was the sheer enthusiasm coming from everybody in Fleetwood Mac: "Jeremy was absolutely fastidious about getting his Elmore James and Homesick James right down to a tee, and they'd sing their hearts out every night. They'd sometimes practise backstage and Peter always took his guitar back to his room. I honestly don't remember a single bad gig, or a poorly attended gig."

In the final weeks of 1967, the band turned its attention to recording their first album for Mike Vernon's Blue Horizon label. They were to quit the label early in 1969, which Peter later regretted, but in 1967 Blue Horizon was exactly the right label for the band.

It was a prototype independent label that oozed integrity,

rootsiness and every other wholesome non-capitalist quality, as its head Mike Vernon explains: "It had been set up as an independent, limited edition label, the product of which was sold directly through a blues fanzine called *R&B Monthly*. We had a limited edition single of Hubert Sumlin which I recorded in my bedroom at my parents' house with Neil Slaven playing second guitar. If you pressed just ninety-nine copies you avoided paying MCPS royalties, so all we had to pay out was for the pressing and a fee for the artist. We sold the lot in just ten days with one small ad. We did a couple of other limited editions on Blue Horizon which also sold out. Then we gallantly ventured into the world of MCPS by pressing a thousand copies of 'Lonely Years' by John Mayall and Eric Clapton on the Purdah label, another indie venture of ours. We could have sold ten times that amount."

So, in classic cottage industry style, studio producer Mike learned about the record industry by operating on a scale where novices' mistakes didn't break the bank: "I released a terrible thing by Jimmy McCracklin called 'Christmas Time, Parts One And Two' and also tested the market with another label called Outa-Site. In all, we brought out about a dozen singles before we concluded a deal with the major record company CBS, who would release and distribute material on Blue Horizon. Fleetwood Mac was our first signing – a one-year deal with the option on our side of a further year."

Fleetwood Mac's first album *Peter Green's Fleetwood Mac* (the sleeve for which featured a Soho back alley aspiring to be a Chicago slum) was recorded as part of a frenetic schedule. Huw Pryce remembers one gig up in the Midlands on 26 November, 1967: "We did the Union Boat Club gig at Nottingham and then drove straight back down to London to the CBS studios in Bond Street and started recording at three in the morning. As I remember it, the first and second album was an ongoing project and it was Jeremy who had the idea to play through the PA to get a live blues sound in the studio. The first album was mostly DIed [direct input into the tape deck] but for *Mr Wonderful* we had speakers and amps all over the studio and Mike Vernon positioning microphones."

"They must have been some of the strangest, weirdest recording sessions of the 1960s," Mike laughs. "To get an authentic feel of Chess Studios in the 1940s, Mike Ross, the engineer and I spent a lot of time manoeuvring amplifiers and speakers around the studio to get a muddy murky sound."

For the first month or so, Fleetwood Mac had no manager. Mick Fleetwood naturally slotted into this role: a born diplomat with what Huw calls a "posh services background". His sisters (Sally, and Susan Fleetwood the acclaimed Royal Shakespeare Company actress) would occasionally go to the London gigs and Huw remembers them as "charming daughters of the Raj". So although Peter was the leader it was Mick who right from the start organised the musicians, informed them of what was happening the following week and suggested doing certain radio shows and interviews.

The band did a lot of recording for the BBC at various studios around London: Maida Vale, Regent Street, the BBC Playhouse on the Embankment just by Charing Cross and the Paris Theatre at Shepherds Bush. The BBC of the 1960s was a far cry from the more streamlined enterprise of the 1990s Birtian era, which contracts out programmes to really slick production companies. It was then a musty, slightly decadent, and very overmanned civil service, employing jobsworths who had little else to do all day long but affect an officious manner.

So the average BBC studio engineer was hardly your hip freak with flares and attitude – more likely he was a pipe-smoker in grey-flannel bags, brown suede brogues, with a fondness for the Gang Show and Vera Lynn. These engineers were also particularly adept at putting Jeremy's nose out of joint.

Most of the sessions the band recorded were either for Alexis Korner, or for John Peel's *Top Gear* on Radio One, which had just been launched as the BBC's version of the pirate stations. For one session at the Playhouse Theatre the band even did a couple of numbers for The Joe Loss Bandshow. For their *Top Gear* debut on 16/17 January 1968 the band received a fee of thirty pounds.

Over the following two years these BBC sessions would include some rare Peter Green gems like 'Sandy Mary', a track featuring him in rock 'n' roll mode on a song which was shortlisted for possible release as a single. But at that time rock 'n' roll meant something quite different to Peter than to most people, whose definition was 1950s modern dance music. "For me," Peter said, "all faster tunes are rock 'n' roll songs. The blues has always been the slower tunes, and I put all my life and emotions in while I'm playing. Blues unchains all my emotions, but with rock 'n' roll I'm back on this earth again."

Journalist Chris Welch first met Peter that autumn. At the time the *Melody Maker* office was right in the middle of Fleet Street, a convenient place for musicians and artists to simply call in whenever they were visiting the papers: The Beatles, the Stones, The Kinks, David Bowie, Marc Bolan, Rod Stewart and even Bob Dylan. Chris recalls, "The Red Lion pub in Fleet Street was where musicians would hang out because they knew they'd meet lots of journalists and that's where I met Peter. He came with this god-like reputation, you know, a successor to Eric Clapton and I wasn't sure how he would be, but he surprised me. He was trying to shake off this tag of being King of the Blues: he felt that blues was black music and he didn't want to give himself too many airs and graces, he just wanted to downgrade his position. I liked him for that: he was a bit shy and down to earth when most musicians at that time tended to be quite full of themselves!"

The Gunnell Brothers agency, based in Soho's Gerrard Street, looked after the band's bookings from day one. Clifford Davis, who once worked for The Beatles' Brian Epstein, had recently joined Gunnells as a booker, although initially he didn't look after Fleetwood Mac, or rather "Peter Green's Fleetwood Mac Featuring Jeremy Spencer", which was the perfectly democratic mouthful the leader originally had in mind as the group's name. Not long after Davis arrived, Peter went to see him at the office to complain that Mac's booker wasn't getting them enough work. The problem was sorted.

Once he knew Clifford a little better, Peter told him how Rik Gunnell was leaning on him to sign an exclusive management deal. Either that, Gunnell warned, or Fleetwood Mac would find themselves looking for a new agency. Davis was a martial arts instructor and reacted swiftly, decisively, and in a way that must have impressed and reassured a vulnerable Peter. He confronted Rik about the matter in a West End club that same night, and just to show that he meant what he said, he reportedly floored Johnny Gunnell before leaving.

According to Huw, Clifford Davis made the first move to become Fleetwood Mac's manager as they were travelling to a gig at Guildford Civic Hall a month or so after their Windsor debut. Clifford put the question to Peter about managing them and, although reluctant, Peter agreed he would sign, although he didn't sign then and there. Huw vividly recalls to this day how Peter later confessed to not trusting Clifford Davis: he knew he had to sign for the band to get on and further their career.

Clifford Davis's reputation as Fleetwood Mac's "big bad manager" is apocryphal, but this, it must be said, has more to do with bitter disputes that took place between him and the band after Peter left. Without a doubt, he was a crucial part of the band's early success, booking them into much larger venues as soon as the hits started to come.

What no one could have known at that stage is that the job Clifford was there to do, and was best at doing – making money for himself and for the band – would eventually become such a contentious point in Peter's eyes. Lots of bands have fallen out with managers who turned into devious money syphons, but few managers found themselves reprimanded for making money in the first place.

Len Green at one point suggested that he should run his brother's group, but Peter had his doubts about this. "When Pete cracked it and they'd suddenly become popular," Len says laughing, "I said to him, 'Want a manager? This is going to be a moneyspinner.' Pete said, 'Len, I wouldn't have you as a manager, you're too dishonest.'" Looking back Len now freely admits that working in London's Smithfield market, everybody had to be a "tea-leaf" to some extent, just to get by. Still, he was a bit hurt by his younger brother's attitude: he'd taught Peter to play. "So what I'm saying," continues Len, "is that when he took over, Pete really liked Clifford."

In addition to their new manager, there was another crucial player who, for the time being, was waiting in the wings – a young guitarist blessed with perfect pitch who would spur Peter on to some of his best work.

In the autumn of 1967, Danny Kirwan was seventeen going on twelve. Not long out of school and armed with six "O" levels, he worked as an insurance clerk in the City. Danny set his heart on joining Fleetwood Mac the first time he saw them and he eventually did so in classic fairy-tale fashion.

The ending, however, was far from happy. In 1994, forty-five-year-old Danny is to all intents and purposes a homeless alcoholic. Divorced, with a son he hardly ever sees, he lives in a men's hostel near London's Covent Garden. The experience of stardom at such a young age has left him with a very tenuous grip on reality. As Mick Fleetwood achingly reflects, "Danny just wasn't cut out for the world of showbiz." Peter himself adds, "It was Mick who asked Danny to join, not me. I preferred his playing before he joined us – he should have stayed with Boilerhouse. Then he started to overplay...I think Mick and I are responsible for where he is now."

In the late 1960s Danny's wild, precocious talent made him a catalyst for the band's rockier music. However in 1967, a year before joining, he was a Clapton/Green fan who loved it all, and fronted Boilerhouse, his own three-piece blues band. Peter first spotted Danny ("he had a marvellous finger-vibrato") when Boilerhouse supported Fleetwood Mac at the Blue Horizon club at Battersea's Nag's Head pub. Following that, Danny's band – with David Terry and Trevor Stevens on drums and bass – often supported Mac at London's Marquee. It was clear to Huw Pryce that Danny was angling: "When we had gigs in London Danny would often turn up in the afternoon, hang around, and offer to help me carry the gear in. He and Peter would jam after the soundcheck and before the doors were opened. Peter really enjoyed that." Danny's subsequent fate is the most cruel blow the Mac story dealt anyone.

Back then, the music press often busied itself defining "the blues", that is when it wasn't arguing the toss about who was the world's third greatest guitarist. In typically brusque form during one interview Peter remarked, "There is such a sick thing about 'What is blues?'. Some people think that it is just a way of playing guitar, but it isn't. The blues really is having the blues, and if you haven't got the blues, forget it, you cannot play or sing the blues."

Fast-forward to October 1993, and a chilling snapshot of what he meant. In a Soho pub where downwardly mobile bohemians kill time and liver tissue as they rub shoulders with low-lifers and smacked-out aristos, Danny Kirwan is being interviewed by a reporter from *The Independent* newspaper: "Yesterday, looking cheerful but dishevelled, he [Danny] told of five years living as a hermit in a dark basement flat in Brixton, south London and his time with Fleetwood Mac: 'I was lucky to have played for the band at all. I just started off following them, but I could play the guitar a bit and Mick felt sorry for me and put me in. I did it for about four years, to about 1972, but... I couldn't handle the lifestyle and the women and the travelling.'"

This, in the 1990s, is Kirwan's story of the blues – a hobo who, thanks to substance abuse, has strayed a million miles too far. But in 1967 at a Christmas gig at the Marquee, as Peter Green, Mac and Boilerhouse saw 1968 fast approaching things couldn't have looked brighter. Their mission, musically, was to bask in the light of that blues horizon.

CHAPTER 5

FINDING A NEW,
TRUE BLUES HORIZON

In early 1968 Peter Green had a very low boredom threshold. Just six months into Fleetwood Mac, he already felt that the band musically was marking time, even though they were playing to packed houses every gig. The size of their following was reflected by the debut album's sales that year: released on 24 February, *Peter Green's Fleetwood Mac* sold an estimated thousand copies per day in the United Kingdom during the first few months, stayed in the Top Ten for fifteen weeks and in the album charts for a year. Commercially, they were marking big time – for a blues band, that is.

Jeremy's wah-dah-dah-ing, Mick's high energy shi-boom and McVie's beefy bass playing, reverential crowds, and a hit album. Who could ask for more? Peter Green, for one. "I had two parts to play because Jeremy wasn't going to make the effort to learn my things – to play properly on the piano. I was told he could play properly but I never saw him do that."

Although these were undoubtedly happy, carefree times for the four-piece band, Peter is still often quick to criticise now, as then, according to Ed Spevock and Andy Silvester. "I remember Pete at his strongest," Ed recalls, "around the 1968 'Need Your Love So Bad' period. Two of Amboy Dukes's brass section, sax player Steve Gregory and Buddy Beadle on baritone sax, were doing some sessions for the *Mr Wonderful* album and we had to pick them up from CBS's New Bond Street studios before a gig. When I got there they were recording 'Need Your Love' and I was sitting on the floor in the middle of the recording studio. I was amazed because they did it live in a single take and I think Pete was singing through two

PA speakers. The only thing that was put on afterwards were the strings. What really impressed me about him, and I only realise it now, is that he just knew what he wanted. I remember him saying to Mick Fleetwood, 'Lay on that beat more!' or something like that. It definitely made me think he'd be hard to work with. I sometimes had run-ins with our sax player about my drumming, but Pete struck me as even more critical."

Mick Fleetwood has already mentioned how he could stand being "beaten up a bit" by Peter, and this is something that Andy Silvester well remembers: "Peter was a perfectionist and wasn't always happy about Mick's drumming. Pete and I used to talk a lot about other musicians and he once asked me to play Mick lots of Jimmy Reed. There was one track I remember in particular, 'My Bitter Seed', which just had this amazing groove to it: the tempo was really slow and yet it shuffled along with a lot of swing...it just flowed. Anyway, I played that to Mick and, simple as it was, he just sat there in disbelief. What he didn't realise was that he himself already had that. Having had bands of my own, you always think the grass is greener on the other side – musicians in other bands are better.

"Pete also sometimes had quite a cruel sense of humour and I think this was under Jeremy's influence. The whole band could be really wicked at times. I had a tape once of Mac recorded live at a club near the Oval cricket ground. Christine was in the wings at the side of the stage watching the show. They did one number during which Peter introduced the band individually. When it came to John, Pete mentioned how his bass player was a really shy person, and John dipped his head as if to lay it on a bit. Pete then said something like, 'You know, it took John six months before he could even summon up the gall to hold Christine Perfect's hand...' Then there was a big silence before Peter said, '...let alone fuck the arse off her!' John was really annoyed by this. He went up to the microphone and shouted, 'You fuckin' Jew!' He managed to control himself but it was close. I'm sure Peter only said that for Jeremy's benefit – it was the kind of thing that he [Jeremy] loved to do."

To describe Peter's relationship with Mick as a marriage of sorts is not at all far-fetched. Mick openly admits that he was basically in love with his leader and more or less worshipped the ground he stood on. But there were also times when Peter's directness rubbed Mick up the wrong way. Another occasion recalled by Andy Silvester was after a gig at the Toby Jug in Tolworth: "Mick was really depressed saying, 'Shuffles...I'm sick to death of fuckin' shuffles!', whacking his hand against the roof so hard he could quite easily have broken some bones." His intensity left Peter obviously quite devastated and he knew he could say nothing to calm him.

It was only Peter out of the band who had a problem with Jeremy Spencer's refusal, or inability, to extend his musical contribution beyond recreating Elmore James and parodies of 1950s American rock 'n' roll teen idols. John McVie still regards Jeremy as the supreme exponent of Chicago blues slide guitar: "In my opinion he was the best around at the time, and nobody has come near him ever since." Mick Fleetwood liked him for his onstage theatricality: "He was a real performer." But Peter now says he found him "quite hard to get on with". Bob Brunning didn't get on with him: "Jeremy was a weak person. He used to do these impersonations of John Mayall and John didn't like it. Mick used to laugh at him but I couldn't see what was funny."

Andy Silvester is convinced that Jeremy's humour influenced the band more than anything else, and not always to good effect. "I remember Fleetwood Mac as a happy band, but one with a bizarre humour. They used to take things too far really and Jeremy seemed to be the instigator. He used to do these really explicit drawings of women's private parts. On their first tour of the United States in the summer of 1968 a lady called Judy Wong had them stay at her place in Los Angeles. Jeremy used to do these horribly explicit drawings of women with their legs wide open, stick them on a shelf in her fridge and close the door so when she went to the fridge to get some milk for a cup of tea, that's the first thing she'd see. I think all of that must have had an effect on Peter, because Jeremy was so perverse."

In early 1971 though, and after nearly four years in the group, Jeremy suddenly left the band midway through the tour, decamping to a Los Angeles religious cult called the Children of God.

The son of an RSPCA officer, Jeremy and his childhood sweetheart Fiona got married when she was fifteen and Jeremy was not long in Fleetwood Mac; they had their first child, Dickon, very soon after. Bob Brunning well remembers congratulating Jeremy on fatherhood: "When his first child was born I expressed great interest, and offered my sincere congratulations to him and his wife Fiona. I was simply amazed when he couldn't remember the name of his brand-new baby!"

Dennis Keen, Fleetwood Mac's road manager in the late 1960s, has some less tasteful memories of Jeremy's weird ways. "His wife used to wank him off on the plane and on coaches and he'd think it was funny. I remember on one tour they were both sitting at the back of the coach. He'd be touching her up, then he'd put his hand under your nose and think it was a joke. His hotel room when we were in the States was thick with dope fumes: for days on end, when they didn't have gig, he'd be holed up in his room all by himself, smoking and reading the Bible!"

During that year Mike Vernon began to share Peter's views about Jeremy: that musically he was very limited and had no intention of being otherwise. "There's no doubt about it, he was amusing but when all's said and done, his talent was to copy Elmore James, and once you'd heard him for half an hour you'd heard it all. He was, though, a great novelty to have when the band first started."

Between 4 and 12 May 1968 the band, plus roadie Huw Pryce, toured Denmark, Sweden, and Norway, appearing on television for the first time on a show made in Copenhagen. Jeremy's mega-swing version of Elmore James's 'Shake Your Money Maker' was released as a single (to promote their debut album in Scandinavia) and actually went to the top of the charts there – a complete anomaly for conservative Nordic tastes in pop music.

Meanwhile, Mick and Jeremy had spotted a new member for the band: Harold, as it came to be called, was a fifteen-inch dildo or "false penis" as Peter now refers to it, that was incorporated into the band's act when they returned to England. As Huw remembers, "Some nights I used to come on stage carrying a tray of drinks for the band and they'd introduce me, lark about and point out Harold lying on the tray. Other times we'd attach Harold to Mick's bass drum head so it could spend the whole gig erect and staring at some very shocked young ladies. Mick Fleetwood loved to shock audiences – he used to wear those wooden balls dangling from his belt – and Jeremy, as I say, could go far too far sometimes by throwing condoms filled with beer or milk out into the crowd. He got his come-uppance once from John Gee, manager at the Marquee, for wearing the dildo sticking out from the flies of his jeans whilst they did their set. It got them banned from one of London's most prestigious venues, but nobody in the band could give a damn. I remember Pete just said, 'There are lots of other good places left to play.'

That's how it was back then – very carefree and very vulgar."

During this, the band's most boisterous phase, Peter was quite renowned for his bad language onstage. "If I use the word 'fuck' in normal speech," he said defiantly at the time, "then I'm gonna use it onstage as well – at least until I get arrested for it." Eventually, though, manager Clifford Davis had to persuade them to tone things down somewhat, because their ribald humour and attitude was upsetting promoters and actually losing them work.

It's ironic that it was Jeremy, the band's least adventurous musician, who gave them their first taste of success in the singles charts that spring when 'Shake Your Money Maker' was a hit in Scandinavia. It was a case of third time lucky: it's no great surprise that the studiously uncommercial and rootsy debut single 'I Believe My Time Ain't Long' bombed out, but the lack of success of 'Black Magic Woman' (released at the end of March, it briefly nudged the bottom reaches of the Top Fifty) must have hurt Peter a bit. Looking back, though, he is characteristically abrupt and matter-of-fact about it all. "Although it was a good song, I guess it wasn't good enough or commercial enough to be a hit. The first really commercial thing we did was 'Albatross'. I knew that would be a hit."

The inspiration for 'Black Magic Woman', subsequently a worldwide million-seller for Carlos Santana, was two-fold: his girlfriend at the time, model Sandra Elsdon, and Otis Rush's classic 'All Your Love'. Peter liked to call Sandra his "magic mama" and, as she now recalls bluntly and with fond amusement, when he wrote the lyrics Peter wasn't getting his oats: "I had decided to be celibate as part of some lofty spiritual quest I was pursuing at the time and so in that second verse when Peter sings 'Don't turn your back on me, baby' his blues are all about frustration!"

The melody line Peter developed from the opening notes of 'All Your Love'. "When I was in The Bluesbreakers," he explains, "John got me started with songwriting, and one of the things he said was that if you really like something, you should take the first lines and make up another song from them. So that's what I did with 'Black Magic Woman'. But then it turned out sounding more like BB King's 'Help The Poor'."

Even with Mick Taylor, now a Bluesbreaker, it was Peter who John Mayall asked back in December 1967 to guest on both sides of his next single – 'Jenny' and 'Picture On The Wall', two country blues featuring

Mayall on piano and vocals, Peter on guitar and Keef Hartley on drums.

In August 1968, Peter would also make one strong contribution to Mayall's *Blues From Laurel Canyon* album on a talking blues by Mayall called 'First Time Alone'. If anything, it was around this time, 1967/8, that Peter's taste and interpretation of all the blues he had listened to over the past five years began to develop into something wholly original: although some of his subsequently best-known work may have strayed from a strict blues structure and form, all of it retained a blues feel. At the time, Peter gave some indication of the more panoramic blues horizon he was looking to when he described The Beatles' 'Eleanor Rigby' and Tim Hardin's 'Hang On To A Dream' as "contemporary blues".

Chicken Shack's Stan Webb emphasises Peter's unique taste: "Peter always acknowledged where he came from, but what happened in the end is that Peter's style came from himself. He's the only white player I've ever heard that has come from himself. He first did everything and everyone, like we all did with Robert Johnson, Mississippi Fred McDowell, Big Mama Thornton, Buddy Guy, BB King and Freddie King; but then Peter developed into the only white player that ended up totally original. That's not praise, it's a fact. Eric Clapton's another matter: back in the early days Eric was far more selfish and self-centred. A few years ago me and Eric bumped into each other at some cricket do and started talking about the old days. He said to me, 'Do you know, I'm really selfish?' I said, 'Yeah, Eric, I know…you never acknowledged Matt Murphy [Memphis Slim's regular guitarist] did you?" And there was nothing Eric could say because he knew I was right. I've got old 1950s records in my collection of Matt Murphy which has stuff that is note for note what Eric played on John Mayall's Bluesbreakers' 'Beano' album."

This point illustrates well the hand-me-down nature of blues. One of Peter's early inspirations for 'Albatross' was "a group of notes from an Eric Clapton solo played slower". So, who knows, perhaps Matt Murphy should get some remote credit for the hit instrumental.

At the end of June 1968 Fleetwood Mac set off for a six-week exploratory tour of America. Everyone, apart from John McVie, approached the trip with some trepidation, mainly because of the many stories of violence and racial tension they'd heard about. When asked by *Melody Maker* on the eve of the tour whether Peter would like to perform his blues for an all-negro audience he replied, "I would like to, but at the moment it's so violent there you have to be known anyway. We will be playing in New York and Detroit and I hope that there, the audiences will be mixed."

In most respects Fleetwood Mac's first American tour was something of a sodden squib; perhaps this was less so on the West Coast where they were only gigging alternate weekends in Los Angeles and San Francisco, which meant they could socialise during the week with musicians like Jerry Garcia of The Grateful Dead and Carlos Santana, and generally soak up the very tail-end of San Francisco's Haight-Ashbury scene before the rip-off merchants moved in and cleaned up.

When they flew across, the single 'Black Magic Woman' and the debut album were out in America on the Epic label, but made no impact at all on the charts. What's more, feeble tour management and promotion meant that attendances were extremely thin for any gigs where they were the main act. Peter still remembers, "On our first visit to New York, we went to play a gig at this club on Broadway called the Space, and there was no one there...no audience at all! So we cancelled the gig and went to another place called the Scene and played there. Then they changed the name to Ungano's and that's where I met Jimi Hendrix. He was just standing onstage playing about with his guitar and he asked me if I would like to get up and play. He was making a lot a wrong notes, sort of slowing them down and nothing was coming out. I liked him as a person though. I remember he let me touch his frizzy hair! But his playing was strange."

Over on the West Coast the band played support gigs, and on alternate weeks stayed at Judy Wong's house in San Francisco. In between weekend gigs Peter and Judy would go to see bands at the Carousel Ballroom, which later became Fillmore West. It was there that they met acid tycoon Owsley, but the significance for self-effacing Peter of that first US visit was that, like it or not, his playing on the *A Hard Road* album had carved out a reputation for him up in rock music's hippest echelons. The Beatles' George Harrison already admired his talent. Peter said at the time, "I really enjoyed seeing Howlin' Wolf, Buddy Guy, Freddie King and white blues man John Hammond. He came as a big surprise to me: I never liked him on record, but he was very good. We also heard Big Brother and The Holding Company and The Grateful Dead. Also, Janis Joplin with The Holding Company. She's incredible. I've never seen anything like that." On the other hand, in terms of Fleetwood Mac establishing their name Stateside, the trip was a disaster. "It wasn't even hard work: you can't work hard when there's no audience," Peter now ruefully explains.

Another setback greeted Peter and the band on their return to England in early August: their latest single 'Need Your Love So Bad' had been in the shops some three weeks and was doing no more than bubbling under the Top Twenty. This soulful blues ballad was Peter Green's version of BB King's version of a 1950s more uptempo R&B hit, written and recorded by Little Willie John. At the start of 1969 Peter told *NME* that his biggest career disappointment to date was that this single didn't make it in England. Evidently he was getting very hungry for a hit.

Though still blues, Mike Vernon's production was the most commercial and accessible of all three Mac singles. Previously, he had collaborated with Mickey "Guitar" Baker (as in Mickey And Sylvia's 'Love Is Strange') and brought him in on this project. Vernon flew Baker over from Paris to write the score for the string arrangement which, along with Peter's vocal phrasing and Christine Perfect's organ playing, turned the single into hooky stuff. But not quite hooky enough.

At the beginning of August, Mac's leader had turned his attention to helping his mate and biggest fan Danny Kirwan – Peter's nickname for him was "Young Eyes" – to audition dozens of potential recruits for a band to be fronted by Danny. The eighteen-year-old had decided to quit his job as an insurance clerk in Fenchurch Street and turn professional. However, Mick soon suggested Danny join Fleetwood Mac. Although, looking back, Peter is rather guilt-ridden about going along with Mick's idea, at the time it had a definite and positive effect on Peter's playing and composing. "I wouldn't have done 'Albatross' without Danny," is his pithy testimonial which speaks volumes.

Danny's debut with the band was at the Blue Horizon club in the Nag's Head pub at Battersea, London, on 14 August 1968. Andy Silvester went along to watch: "Peter announced him by saying something like, 'Now Danny Kirwan is going to do his first number of the night for us, and he's going to blow your minds!' Sitting in the crowd, I thought that an introduction like that just put too much on his shoulders. Poor kid." An ominous observation, as it turned out.

CHAPTER 6

ALBERT ROSS, MAN OF THE WORLD

BBC's Radio Three might have called it a musical *volte-face*, to Radio Two it was probably more welcome easy listening, whilst Radio One gushed forth about a brand new happening sound. Just like Alec Issigonis's 'Mini Minor', launched some ten years earlier, the single's appeal couldn't be categorised – 'Albatross' was classless.

While the instrumental prompted BB King to eulogise about Peter's "sensitive touch", a concert violinist wrote to the BBC enquiring who the composer was and where he might obtain sheet music for the piece. Meanwhile, professional blues purists like DJ Mike Raven shook their heads and walked away muttering "sold out". So while 'Albatross' broke down musical barriers, it also brought out the snob in some.

"Peter Green's Fleetwood Mac," commented Raven soon after the single's release on 22 November, "are already too commercial and have lost their original guts." In the late 1960s Radio One's *Mike Raven's R&B Show* in some ways epitomised the elitist "if it's mainstream it must be crap" attitude at which Peter in effect cocked a snook with 'Albatross'. In its heyday the show was "Auntie" at her best: pukka, exclusive and yet just slightly patronising in its educational tone, something that Mick Jagger parodied brilliantly in an interview with Bob Dawbarn of *Melody Maker* in 1968. "I must apologise for this next record which is so old you can't really hear it, but it was recorded in a barn in 1933 and the music is first class," Jagger laughed. "That radio show is really in the BBC tradition – or perhaps the Alexis Korner tradition – but it's a great programme, really worth listening to." Even droll 1960s libertarian John Peel admitted he couldn't get into 'Albatross' at all, choosing instead to play the B-side, Danny Kirwan's 'Jigsaw Puzzle Blues' on his *Top Gear* show. At gigs Peter nicknamed his instrumental "Albert Ross".

Just one week after Danny joined the band, Blue Horizon released Fleetwood Mac's second album *Mr Wonderful,* recorded in April. As summer drew to a close 'Albatross' was nearing the end of its long incubation in Peter's head and would soon be put down on tape at CBS's New Bond Street studios. "I got the idea for the name 'Albatross'," Peter grins, "from a poem I read at school called 'The Ancient Mariner', and from that young girl's voice in the middle of Traffic's song 'Hole In My shoe' – 'I climbed on the back of a giant Albatross'. That did trigger my mind, as did the Stevie Winwood thing. I wrote parts of it in an aeroplane, but the whole thing took years. I composed in the way musicians do, by feeling it out over time. Then, when Danny came along, we did the second part harmony. Once we got Danny in it was plain sailing."

So, creatively, Peter needed Danny in the band. As Mike Vernon explains, "Danny was outstanding – he had a guitar style that was totally unique. I seem to remember him playing this Watkins beginner's guitar and yet making these wild sounds that reminded me in a way of Lowell Fulson. I'd never heard anybody play like that and I was desperate to record him, but I didn't think his band [Boilerhouse] had what it took. When I found out that Peter had been talking to Danny about maybe joining the band I was one hundred per cent for it and, of course, the results speak for themselves in that the musical direction of what Fleetwood Mac were about changed when Danny Kirwan joined and gradually Jeremy became of secondary importance."

Visually, the addition of Danny Kirwan in the line-up added a kidnapped choirboy dimension to the group's ragged image: an East End Jewish boy playing more Chicago than black Chicagoans is extraordinary; an elfin belting out macho Elmore James riffs is weird vaudeville; but a young lad looking like an early-teens innocent yet playing blues with the tone and authority of Lowell Fulson is surreal.

Danny spurred Peter on to some of his best playing, and this was partly because the leader now had someone to bounce ideas off and spark some creativity. "There was never a lot of creative energy coming from the band," reflects Peter. "When Lindsay Buckingham and Stevie Nicks came in to the group there was creative energy. When Bob Welch and Bob Weston were in the group there was the possibility of creative energy. But before that there was only me and Danny. There wasn't enough creative energy coming from Fleetwood Mac, the two people. It seemed to me that Mick and John weren't so much into playing: they were more into making money. Danny and I tried to bring the band with us, and I suppose sometimes they did move a bit, but it was like budging along the bottom of the ocean."

Not long after its release, Peter would enthuse about their second album even though it lacked the energy and enthusiasm of the first, and certainly didn't sell as many copies: "I like our album *Mr Wonderful*: it was where we were at the time." This is indisputable in that four of the ten tracks featured Jeremy with that same and by now well-worn Elmore James wah-dah-dah-wah-dah-dah riff. The remainder was Peter either in an acoustic Lightnin' Hopkins mood playing with one-man-band Duster Bennett on harmonica, or doing a BB King boogie shuffle. The anguished 'Love That Burns' is most notably a recording where Peter breaks forever the mould of faithful, fanatical reproduction and puts his own stamp on the blues. His understated guitar is often hardly audible and seemingly phrased despite the solid slow beat of the song. Completely original.

Not only did 'Albatross' open doors into the pop world for Fleetwood Mac, almost overnight it transformed Blue Horizon from a specialist independent label into something with a bit more clout. As Mike Vernon explains, "Because it sold a million records and got to Number One, we realised there was money to be made in commercial records. When 'Albatross' was recorded nobody sat down with the specific intent of making a hit record. What happened was that Peter was a fan of Santo And Johnny's earlier hit 'Sleepwalk', and he liked the quality of that Hawaiian guitar sound. He felt he could adapt that and make something with a blue feel. It didn't have to be bluesy: it just had to have a blue feel. The rest of the band were really into it. The slide guitar parts were done by Peter, the bass parts were double-tracked, and Danny and Peter did the bits with the mallets."

'Albatross' was recorded at CBS's New Bond Street studios, originally Oriel Studios. The band spent two days recording and mixing just that track – an exceptionally long time to spend on a single in those days. On listening to the final mix, everyone in the band and the engineer, Mike Ross, agreed that it was a beautiful record.

Without a doubt Peter was ambitious for a hit around that time: he obviously felt he had the talent and believed 'Albatross' could be the one.

For almost a month after the record was released, CBS's initial reservations proved to be correct – absolutely nothing happened. The pluggers at CBS had been trying desperately hard for the *Top Of The Pops* television show to take it, but they refused, saying they didn't think it would be a hit and couldn't find a slot for it, certainly not with the band performing the piece. One week the producers discovered that they had a forty-five to fifty second slot at the very end of one of the programmes when the credits went up and decided to fill the slot with 'Albatross'. The show went out on a Thursday. By Friday CBS had orders in for sixty thousand units and the record went smashing into the charts. The BBC also played it in a documentary programme, which obviously boosted sales still further. Released on 22 November, it entered the charts at Number Twenty-Three three weeks later on 14 December. The following week it rose to Nineteen, then went to Number One over Christmas, at which point the band was holed up in snowbound Detroit, one-third of the way through their second US tour and, for a while, unaware of their new-found status as a pop group.

The astute Clifford Davis wasted no time in securing more "poppy" bookings for his boys: quite soon Alan "Pop Pickers" Freeman would be introducing Fleetwood Mac at Wembley Empire Pool (now Wembley Arena) on the same bill as acts like Barry Ryan and The Paper Dolls. But, of course, a pop group isn't truly a pop group until it has a fan club – or rather an appreciation society.

Jane Honeycombe, then a sixteen-year-old Londoner and British blues fan, plucked up the courage to approach Mick Fleetwood after a gig in the autumn shortly before the band set off for America: "I told them about my idea for a fan club, and Mick said, 'Oh, that sounds like a great idea!' and gave me his telephone number. Although I was just sixteen, I was cynical and didn't for one moment think that that would really be his number – but I was wrong. A couple of days later, I took out the piece of paper, swallowed hard and rang the number and was astonished to find myself talking to Mick Fleetwood, who at that point was sharing a place in Ealing with Andy Silvester. Mick still liked my idea and suggested that I go and see their publicist – a lady called Valerie Bond – and Cliff Davis."

Clifford played Jane the new single, 'Albatross'. Her response was far from positive: "I nearly walked out! That wasn't my band – they'd gone commercial!" Undeterred, Jane started the appreciation society, with Peter as her main link with the band. "My first impressions of Peter? Well, you have to remember I was sixteen and partly in love with him, so naturally he terrified me! Even then he was strange and very different from everybody else. Right from the start what was quite obvious was that Peter was the leader and the nucleus of the band, and everything really revolved around him. Without Peter the band was nothing and they were all to some extent in awe of him – this was particularly the case with Danny when he joined.

"But Peter wasn't ambitious in terms of stardom. When they returned from the States I remember I went to one gig at the Empire Pool, Wembley with Mick, and already there were some changes. Mick was dressed up as a baseball player with a helmet on and we travelled back in this huge limo. There were actually girls on the roof as we were leaving. Suddenly Fleetwood Mac were stars. We all laughed and thought it was very funny, but it didn't interest Peter at all."

If Peter wasn't ambitious in the sense of bigger venues and more money, Clifford, their manager, obviously was. He was naturally very proud of the fact that for much of that year Fleetwood Mac were the highest paid band around: they often went out for a thousand pounds a night, which was a phenomenal amount of money but possible because they were better live than on record, whereas for most other groups in the charts the opposite was true. Clifford was very clever in that sense. Pop fans would go along to their gigs expecting more of 'Albatross' and instead would get rhythm and blues, rock 'n' roll and a great night out.

"But Peter's one weakness," recalls Jane, "was that he was gullible: he could be taken in by people he didn't know very well and yet be very dismissive of people who had his best interests at heart. I don't think the success of 'Albatross' changed him fundamentally, I think it just brought more pressure and he had to learn to deal with lots of new people in new situations. Press interviews for instance. Peter would often speak openly and then think his words had been twisted around. Mick was more articulate – he probably should have done all the interviews, but everybody wanted to speak to the leader. Then, of course, there was the pressure of the next single which couldn't be too commercial, but still had to be a hit.

"If I had to summarise Peter's personality at that time and even now, he is a very critical person, he can be very cruel and he's self-opinionated – and that is said with the greatest amount of love. Although I never heard him criticise the band in a nasty way when there were other people around, he was the kind of person who was never really satisfied with himself or others."

So the autumn of 1968 was at once the start of much bigger things for the band, and also the beginning of Peter Green's fleeting rock superstardom. In only two years' and four hits' time he would be out of the business, up in the backwoods of Maine with musician friends, happily jamming with warbling birds in the trees and, crucially, trying to restore the inner peace that had been lost amongst all the adulation, swollen egos, and crushing workload. But in 1968 the process that he was about to go through – the heavy industry of rock 'n' roll – was pretty much irreversible. Other creative free spirits with whom he was now rubbing shoulders, admiring and being admired by – Joplin, Hendrix – would die careless, solitary deaths in a few years. In that sense Peter was lucky; even so, looking back in the mid 1970s he said, "I tried to remember how it was before the hits, just to be playing for pleasure and I couldn't bring back that feeling – it was terrible, terrible."

Paul Morrison, manager of the Orange Music shop which had opened for business in London's New Compton Street a little earlier in 1968, noticed a change in Peter when the band returned from their second US tour. As well as selling highly desirable second-hand American guitars, Orange designed and manufactured their own range of amplification, which Fleetwood Mac were kitted out with in November and, despite massive air freight bills, took to the States with them in December for their second US tour. In the UK, Paul (himself an accomplished classical guitarist who also played in London blues band, Black Cat Bones) often went to Mac gigs as technical support and in time became good friends with Peter. "When he returned from the second US tour," Paul reflects, "Peter was unhappy about something – the conversations I remember were ones standing in urinals at gigs! It wasn't clear to me why he was unhappy, and it's something I've never quite sorted out in my own mind, but he was beginning to feel detached from the whole Fleetwood Mac process. This may have been due to delusions of grandeur after 'Albatross', or that he genuinely didn't feel part of things anymore. Or it could have been part of health problems which were beginning to take hold around that time. I think a lot of that illness was reactive: he was put in a position that he could not cope with, namely being a very wealthy and successful young musician. But the thing you have to remember is that here was a young man in his twenties with the world at his feet and he's living at home with his mum and dad. Now that's not exactly normal and I think the reason is that he felt very vulnerable out in the big wide world. He was never able to cope with being a star: part of him absolutely loved it and part of him was horrified by the whole idea. Once he'd made it there were expectations of what he should be doing and how he should be living.

"Peter's parents were very proud of their son's achievements but they also kept him down to earth. Yet perhaps with the very best intentions this may have made his confusion worse: to be told on the one hand 'You're just an ordinary Jewish boy. I'm a postman. This is real life and you stay here', and then on the other 'You're a superhuman being and extraordinarily special' which undoubtedly he was, then inevitably there is conflict. Once he was famous I think he was constantly torn between these two states of mind."

None the less, Jane Honeycombe thinks Peter's relationship with his parents and his domestic set-up was always a good thing: "What everybody forgets is that he was very young when he made it, twenty-two. Some people are quite mature at that age but I think he was, in the nicest possible way, pushed by his parents. They'd always been very supportive, but I think in part he was actually doing it for them. Once there was money coming in it was a sensible thing to do to buy a house, and I think he realised it would be best to stay with them because it gave him stability and also meant he was protected. By then everybody wanted to speak to him. His parents were able to shield him a bit."

Paul Morrison smiles as he recalls one incident when Peter took great pleasure in the fact that he was famous, by playing an elaborate game with a couple of girl fans: "Peter was a great people-watcher and loved to observe how fans reacted to him. After a while he came to the conclusion that fame was really all in the mind: if he walked down the street behaving like an ordinary person, he didn't get recognised but when he behaved like a star – posing, looking and feeling self-important – then people would notice him.

"One night we went to a club and chatted up a couple of girls. Peter behaved 'normally'; not once did he mention who he was, but you could tell that they were unsure. We drove the girls back to their parents' home, they invited us in for coffee and the whole time Peter behaved like an ordinary guy. He kept up the act to the very end and the girls had to play along with it. Even though they might have known this was Peter Green, he managed to avoid the star situation for the whole evening and was just this guy Peter. We said goodnight to them, got in the car and drove off and Peter laughed his head off."

Without a doubt, stardom to Peter Green wasn't always simply a case of agonising introspection about his excessive wealth and the world's inbuilt social injustice. Here was a young, good-looking guy who as a performer sometimes craved attention, like all performers do. "I don't have this fan fever thing," he told a journalist around the time 'Man Of The World' had consolidated his pop star status. "Our followers are really very quiet." He then admitted to the reporter that it gives him quite a kick to be recognised and stopped in the street – because it happens too rarely.

'Man Of The World' was mostly recorded in New York during a lull in gigging, on their second US tour. After the commercial success of 'Albatross', the pressure and responsibility of the follow-up smash was squarely on Peter's shoulders. The single turned out to be significant on several counts. Most importantly, it came out on the Immediate label, not Blue Horizon, to Peter's dismay and Mike Vernon's fury. Like the first hit, it was a "sleeper" which required some serious plugging before it rose to Number Two in the charts. Also, it was a classy, crafted pop ballad – all links with blues, even in the broadest sense of the word, appeared to have been severed.

A closer look at circumstances surrounding the split from Blue Horizon makes this the first crucial "what if" juncture in Peter's career. It is perhaps also a revealing insight into the music business in those pre-megacorporation days, which proves, if proof were needed, that big money is invariably accompanied by some conflict of interests. Clifford Davis still remains convinced that "the biggest coup I ever pulled off for Fleetwood Mac was getting them out of their Blue Horizon recording contract". As an ambitious manager he was doing his job by getting his "hot" act out of an independent label and into an appropriate major record company: from Clifford's point of view Fleetwood Mac, with one worldwide Number One to their credit, could hardly be regarded as "beginners" – they were a highly marketable asset. Mike Vernon would naturally disagree, while Peter now re-affirms that "Blue Horizon was sensible for what the group was at that time – we were all beginners, apart from John McVie". On the other hand there was the songwriter, the artist. Peter had established a good professional and personal rapport with producer Mike Vernon and once out of Blue Horizon, he felt exposed and at something of a loss.

The band (minus Jeremy Spencer) would spend the middle part of 1969 recording their third album *Then Play On* with Peter ostensibly in the producer's chair, as well as being songwriter and star musician. He now reflects on his role as a producer: "We should have had a producer on *Then Play On* then it might have sold better. We tried to produce it ourselves, thinking that might be more fun. We did have a lot of fun but then it's all very well to say, 'Yeah, let's produce our own records from now on we don't need anyone,' but we weren't completely aware of what the producer's job was. We should have kept Mike Vernon – I didn't want to leave Blue Horizon but Clifford Davis was going for bigger money."

Twenty-five years on, Mike Vernon still smarts at the memory of losing Fleetwood Mac, albeit from Blue Horizon's burgeoning roster (by then this included Chicken Shack, Eddie Boyd, Champion Jack Dupree, Duster Bennett and Gordon Smith): "Losing Fleetwood Mac was a battle and I would like it to go on record that it was not a direct battle between Blue Horizon and the band, but between Blue Horizon and the band's management who created, I think, totally unnecessary barriers between the band and us. All right, Blue Horizon had grown up as a blues label but it was never the idea that it should just stay a blues label. Nor for that matter, did I think that Fleetwood Mac should stay a blues band. They wanted to develop and to me 'Albatross' and 'Man Of

The World' are examples of that. I spent time with them in New York on their second tour doing 'Man Of The World' and then came back to London and finished it off with engineer Martin Birch at Kingsway Studios in Holborn. Martin ended up finishing the record without me because there was a certain feeling that maybe I was not into what they were doing – but that was not the case. What was happening was that I was being railroaded by the management who had realised that the contract had run out and promptly thought, 'We can get a bucket-load of money elsewhere.'"

To Clifford Davis the deal that Peter had struck with Mike Vernon prior to Clifford's arrival on the scene as the band's manager was simple: one year's recording contract, followed by two one-year options on Blue Horizon's side, to be taken up only if they still wanted the band. "I just sat praying that Richard Vernon wouldn't notice the renewal date for the contract coming up. And he didn't! I notified Blue Horizon the following day that they had failed to take up the option and therefore Fleetwood Mac were free of any further contractual obligations to Mike and Richard Vernon." To make the Vernon brothers' oversight even more painful, all this actually happened while 'Albatross' was high in the charts.

Mike continues, "I can understand Clifford trying to get a bucket-load of money, but he didn't actually come to us and say, 'We've just had a massive offer – two-hundred-and-fifty thousand pounds – from Immediate, can you match or better their offer?' There is no question that CBS [Blue Horizon's distributors] would have matched or funded any deal to keep Fleetwood Mac, but we were never really approached, we were just told. Okay we made an error and we admitted it, but we said, 'Let's renegotiate with CBS and make this band the international success we can make it.'"

Mike further recalls how Clifford had promised that, even though it was outside the contract, 'Man Of The World' would still come out on Blue Horizon: Fleetwood Mac had made it with Blue Horizon and would honour that. But it came out on Immediate and the band never saw a penny of that quarter of a million pounds that Immediate had promised. Clifford ended up doing a deal with Warner Brothers. The Warner-Reprise deal was reportedly to have been good, but not as good as the two-hundred-and-fifty thousand CBS would, according to Mike

Vernon, willingly have come up with.

When told of Peter's views about the producer's role, Mike now wryly observes, "It's the same old story – musicians only see their music from their own point of view. They see their performance, their song, their sound and their arrangement. But what does Joe Blow think about it? The producer is the guy between the man in the street, and the band. When I heard their next album *Then Play On* I was disappointed. I really felt I could have made it sound more tangible and given it more of a groove. As it was I think it sounded a little synthetic and I know that we tried desperately hard with their other albums not to have that: their first dog and dustbin album has got so much feel to it and the second one was deliberately given an old sound. Funnily enough a similar thing happened with John Mayall: his early records, the *Blues Breakers* and *A Hard Road* albums, had a strong feel; but gradually as John started to take over control in the production of things like *Bare Wires* he began to lose a bit of that – thankfully he's got it back now."

From Clifford Davis's point of view, Mac's manager undoubtedly kept his cool during the split with Blue Horizon, especially when the brinkmanship with Immediate (at that point already a sinking ship which went under later that year) began to go against him. Clifford gave them the 'Man Of The World' tapes for two good reasons, both in Peter Green's and Fleetwood Mac's long-term interests: first, a couple of years earlier Peter had signed away his copyrights in a so-so publishing deal with Malcolm Forrester; second, it was crucial to get an 'Albatross' follow-up out without further delay. Peter had been introduced to Forrester in his Mayall days, and the publisher was now connected with Immediate. Davis and Forrester are thought to have cut a deal where Clifford would get back Fleetwood Mac's songs and copyrights and Immediate would match CBS's offer for a three-year recording contract. As things turned out, he got the single in the shops and retrieved old copyrights, but that was about it. Even though no money actually came his way from the negotiation and Immediate stitched him, Clifford then promptly put himself even more out of pocket once again looking after Fleetwood Mac's and his own long-term interests.

'Man Of The World' was released on 4 April 1969. At first sales were slow – the single needed a "leg-up". Today's plethora of twenty-four hour satellite television channels and music shows often means that, it's the media who have to court record companies by seeking exclusive "firsts" in screening new videos. But in those pre-video, pre-satellite days of television the very opposite was true: there was *Top Of The Pops*, BBC2's *Disco 2*, Radio One and Radio Luxembourg. That was it. So, opportunities for nationwide on-air promotion were absurdly restricted and – to put it politely – some television and radio show producers and DJs exploited the situation to supplement their frugal BBC salaries. Ever since the Alan Freed case in the 1950s, "payola" (an American euphemism for this sort of bribery) was endemic to the music business: at the end of the 1960s and in the early 1970s certain BBC DJs were caught in sex-for-airplay barter deals. Clifford Davis knew that 'Man Of The World' had to be a hit and acted accordingly: "It was a big hit. I made sure of that. I spent a lot of money making sure it was played on the right programmes. And you can read into that whatever you like!"

Mike Vernon remembers "considerable input" from Danny Kirwan in the making of 'Man Of The World', as gradually his presence was taking the band out of mainstream twelve-bar blues, into blues rock and rock ballads. Peter and Danny's harmonised guitars, for a while at least, seemed to keep Peter amused. Today he's still amused by memories of Danny's eccentric, eclectic musical taste, taking in a wide range of influences from Django Reinhardt and Louis Armstrong, to George Harrison and even Peter Green: "We used to call Danny 'Ragtime Cowboy Joe'! He was into all that roaring twenties big band stuff as well as country and western."

While they were over in America on that second US tour Fleetwood Mac continued to forge a new, rockier style. Even so, during that visit some out-and-out blues sessions took place, most notably Otis Spann's *The Biggest Thing Since Colossus* – an album which features "Peter Green, Original Blues Man", approaching a peak. According to Mike Vernon, Otis (former pianist with The Muddy Waters Band, and the Clarksdale legend's half-brother) loved Peter's playing almost as much as he loved Bourbon. That this was the case can perhaps be best heard on the piano guitar drums rave 'Walkin'', a simultaneously intoxicated and intoxicating piece of Chicago blues-rock (Mike Vernon: "Otis's head sometimes touched the ivories as often as did his fingers"). *Colossus*, Spann's penultimate album, was recorded in New York shortly after the *Blues Jam At Chess* sessions in January. A victim of cancer, Spann died in April the following year, 1970, aged just forty.

Mike Vernon still regards the Chess sessions as "a very good piece of product" but looking back Peter and John McVie are not so sure. "Those black guys," Peter stresses, "knew that you can't get the hang of it – they knew that whatever a white guy tries to do is not gonna be the blues of coloured people. It's a pose all along. In Chicago that time, I played too forcefully – too much and too loud – because my experience in life didn't match up to theirs. Perhaps white folks should've left those coloured tunes alone and stuck to singing hymns! At those Chess sessions my voice sounds like I've been drinking ginger beer, or am singing down the toilet!"

As far as John McVie was concerned, those Chess sessions dented his professional pride: "From the moment we arrived in the studio those guys made it quite clear that they didn't give a shit about who we were – we were just a bunch of white kids and they had a 'whitey plays the blues' attitude. I also got the feeling right from the start that Willie Dixon didn't care for me!" So 4 January 1969 was a long day for John in which it was his turn to have the blues about the blues.

Country blues master John Hammond now thinks that Chicago in the 1960s was an exception and that skin colour has never held back determined blues talent: "In Chicago there were too many blues men and not enough work. Every working musician – regardless of skin colour – was looking over his shoulder in those days."

Certainly today, as third- and fourth-generation black and white blues men tell it like it is, the question of skin colour is irrelevant: Robert Cray in some ways has been influenced by Eric Clapton, who in formative years looked to Freddie King, who influenced Albert Collins, who gave Cray the idea to start a band in the first place. During the second half of the twentieth century it's taken for granted that the music is a melting pot of styles, coming from blue souls wrapped in all shades of skin. Danny Kirwan, though, still seems locked in a 1960s time-warp: when he talks about blues, his demeanour is suddenly transformed. In serious and heavy tones he reflects, "Peter Green and me, we stole the black man's music. What we did was wrong. The feel of blues music..." mid-sentence Danny adopts a French accent, perhaps finding himself in Django mode, "belong to ze black man. It's ze way he feel when he wake up, go to work and go out on a Saturday night. Now a white man can never know or feel zat feeling – he can only imagine it." Several people who have seen Danny recently have formed a similar impression: here is a musician in self-destruct mode and seemingly driven by remorse at having once dug his heels in too deep on strange and sacred ground – black man's blues.

Of course it would be fatuous, fanciful and in this context rather sick to talk about dark, diabolic forces at work against Danny and to a lesser extent Peter as well. But it's also impossible not to hold some niggling doubts. Their massive blues guitar-playing talent, in both cases so precocious it was unreal, certainly turned out to be Danny's making and breaking. Blues – at the intensity with which Peter and Danny explored and lived the music back then – thrives on danger. To spend a couple of hours in Danny's company at some seedy Soho pub now, is to discover another aspect to this mighty, cathartic music. It's horribly sad, but seemingly inevitable that the next headline about Danny Kirwan will be one announcing a destitute, alcohol-related and premature passing in a London hostel or side street.

Back in Chicago's Chess Studios in January 1969, though, the white boys did themselves proud. Perhaps the most poignant and historic moment came when Jeremy Spencer got up to belt out Elmore James's 'Madison Blues' accompanied by none other than James's original sax player from the 1950s, JT Brown. Peter's high points during the sessions include Chester Arthur 'Howlin' Wolf' Burnett's 'Sugar Mama' and the Perkins/Day classic, 'Homework', which Peter would go on to produce for manager Clifford Davis as a solo single. Other local musicians on the Chess sessions included Buddy Guy (who for contractual reasons was transparently disguised as "Guitar Buddy"), Willie Dixon, Otis Spann, Honeyboy Edwards, harp player Walter "Shakey" Horton and Spann's drummer SP Leary.

Blue Horizon waited almost a year before releasing the sessions as a double album, *Blues Jam At Chess, Volumes 1 And 2* on 5 December 1969. The release irritated Peter: "On some tracks there is only one of us playing and, as we didn't record enough for a double album, there must be numbers by other people. So it can't be a Fleetwood Mac album. It is a bit annoying that Blue Horizon can't wait until *Then Play On* is out of the charts, and they are not going to be able to release anything near comparison to that." Clifford Davis, ever the diplomat, was more forgiving: "Of course we're not falling over backwards to promote this LP, but we're not ashamed of it. It should make quite a good collector's item."

The fact that these and other business hassles cropped up with monotonous regularity during 1969 made Peter yearn for the life before the hits had begun to come. Then it was all about the joy of the music: no two nights being the same. Now gradually Fleetwood Mac was also becoming a money-machine. In July, shortly after the chart success of 'Man Of The World', Blue Horizon re-released a re-mixed version of 'Need Your Love So Bad' just a year after the original had come out. The strings were more prominent on the re-mixed version and Clifford Davis refused to have anything to do with it while Peter, who never liked the idea of re-releases thought that if the record was going to make it, it would have made it last time.

Business matters also prompted the band to cancel its third US tour, scheduled to start in mid July, as Fleetwood Mac found themselves in the middle of a litigious bun-fight between the Columbia and Atlantic recording companies in America. Columbia had placed a restriction order on Atlantic which in effect prevented 'Man Of The World' and the imminent release *Then Play On* from reaching the shops in the States. For Peter this was all very boring and a far cry from no-contract-necessary, gentlemen's agreement gigs at the Fishmongers Arms and the Toby Jug, Tolworth.

He was already getting jaded, admitting at the time that he was not that keen to work: "The others are in a big hurry, but I don't want the band to work too much, it's a complete waste of time." Peter disliked the routine, the same thing every night. He believed they should have used the time to make albums: "If there's a good album everyone can hear it. If you play in one place you can only be heard in one area of the country. I don't like big concerts and all that bit, I've always liked the small, packed club."

Peter was becoming increasingly keen on doing free concerts around this time, mid 1969, but even here some downers lay in store. When Fleetwood Mac agreed to do the Camden Fringe Festival at the end of May, organised by Blackhill Enterprises and also featuring Rory Gallagher's Taste, Edgar Broughton and Duster Bennett, crowd violence brought proceedings to a halt. Before an estimated crowd of twenty-five thousand gathered at Parliament Hill Fields, Fleetwood Mac went on stage around midnight only to be greeted by a squad of skinhead "bovverboys" whose chanting and bottle-throwing forced the band back off again. Whilst Peter shrugged the incident off as yet another bit of showbiz blues, it made his father Joe's blood boil enough to write in to *Melody Maker.*

In a letter headed "Sterner Measures For These Hoodlums", J Green of London W14 wrote: "My son travels all over the country playing to different audiences practically every night, and last Friday was one of his nights off. But instead of taking advantage and resting, he offered his services with the rest of his group, to play a free open-air concert along with other artists. Everything would have gone off fine, when along came a small band of hoodlums – not may I add, long-haired freaks, as is their usual description, but a gang of crew-cut young thugs who seemed to delight in spoiling a night out for the vast majority of people who were there to enjoy themselves.

"After many nasty incidents the concert had to be abandoned, much to the disgust of the organisers who went to a great deal of trouble to arrange it. It is time sterner measures were taken by the law and stiffer sentences imposed on these so-called citizens of the future."

Charlie Watkins (of "Watkins Copicat" and WEM Public Address systems) was sound engineer that night at Camden: "Before they went on I'd had some aggravation backstage about the sound from a woman who was with the Fleetwood Mac party and I was being all apologetic. Then I remember Peter Green just staring at me, or more like staring through me, and he didn't say a word. I felt very uneasy. Then he just walked straight past me – all bad vibes – and never said a single thing. I'd been told by people in the business about what a nice guy this Peter Green was, so when he was like that to me it came as a bit of a shock."

During 1969 what was becoming quite clear was that Peter was beginning to actively despise the success that previously he had courted, almost with a vengeance. Spiritually, a void was looming. On his return from the second US tour in mid February he told both Jane Honeycombe and Paul Morrison that he had experimented further with LSD and mescaline. He told Jane that, contrary to what he had expected, drugs had made him far more, not less, introspective. He told Paul of one time on mescaline where afterwards he couldn't remember a single thing he'd said or done for over half a day. Such drug-induced trauma, together with the pressures and hassles of leading a band virtually single-handed, on to full-tilt big time in this country and America were all starting to take their toll. Increasingly, he was living out the angst and *ennui* he had fantasised about when he wrote the lyrics to 'Man Of The World' about a year earlier. Growing up into a rock star, for Peter, meant living in a cossetted world of empty dreams.

Even the BB King Blues Band/Fleetwood Mac UK tour in April was in one sense a disappointment for him: here he was, playing in some of Britain's finest concert halls with a living legend – Riley "The Beale Street Blues Boy" King – who had probably inspired him most of all and who was a cousin of Bukka White, another of Peter's all-time favourites. At the Royal Albert Hall, London, opening night on 22 April, some "Mac have sold out" purists gave the band a hard time during their set, only to see Joe Green rise from his seat in the front stalls, defy them and proudly stick up for his son pronouncing him as "the best". Later on in the evening, headliner BB King articulated similar sentiments as a part of his act.

At one point BB broke a string and put it down to nerves explaining to the audience, "Man, you'd be nervous if you could see who I can see right now." He was referring to George Harrison and Eric Clapton sitting in a private box, enjoying the show. But then BB declared, "But I've got to say that, I'm sorry, Peter Green is the best." Then a couple of nights later, live at the Regal, Cambridge, mentor and protégé exchanged musical ideas, figures, and history backstage. Peter would play a rhythm, saying, "This is something John Mayall brought back from America." BB would take it up, hammer it for a while, play various other riffs and finally announce, "Robert Nighthawk is the one who really made it. That's the cat. Earl Hooker did it too." Just a year earlier Peter would have been knocked out by this kind of thing, but now the thrill was going. Instead, after the eight-concert tour ended, the band let it be known that they were dissatisfied with the half-hour slot given to them during each of their two sets per night and were therefore planning a concert hall tour of their own.

Today Peter recalls one incident during the 1969 tour where, perhaps encouraged by the generous words of praise BB publicly had heaped on him at the Albert Hall, he then tried, to get closer to the man. "One time on the tour coach," he reflects, "I got up and went over to sit next to him. Around then I was spending a lot of time thinking about religion and faith and I kind of hoped he might have something to tell me – things that we might talk over. But I guess he wasn't comfortable doing that. One thing he did say was that playing guitar I had a sensitive touch." A couple of years later, Peter took part in BB's rather star-studded *In London* album, along with Alexis Korner, Ringo Starr, Steve Marriott, Klaus Voorman and many other Names. BB now remembers noticing a big change in Peter's personality: "In the studio he was quiet and I got the impression that he was very disillusioned with the whole music business. He played great on 'Caledonia', but the way I remember him is sitting around. I was just pleased to share his company, and he seemed to get some comfort from mine."

Conga player Nigel Watson, who collaborated on early 1970s singles like 'Beasts Of Burden', points out that Peter didn't really approve of BB King's musical direction at the time: "In the early 1970s Peter even became disillusioned with what BB King was playing: he called it showbiz and thought BB hadn't really taken the music any further."

In fact, 'Showbiz Blues', with country slide inspired by Bukka White, was one of the tracks recorded during the spring and early summer months of 1969, in Kingsway Studios, Holborn, as the band finally finished off their third album. Rudely entitled *Bread And Kunny*, that is until their new label Reprise stepped in as arbiters of non-scatological taste – *Then Play On* once again put the pressure on Peter to come up with something new. Danny's input, seven of the album's fourteen tracks, drew from material he had written over the previous two years, whereas Peter's stuff had to be of the moment or, to use a cliché of the day, "progressive". It was really getting to Peter that the band were not always pulling their weight creatively – a criticism that John McVie is now quick to contest: "Peter was the spearhead – the leader who we followed. I didn't write the songs so all I could do was follow."

According to Paul Morrison, when it came to recording his own new batch of songs for the album Peter deliberately froze the rest of the band out: "I remember when they were making *Then Play On* Peter wouldn't let the band in the studio. He wanted to do all the parts himself; bass and drums as well as guitar. It was around the time he was heavily into classical music and Vaughan Williams in particular. I had a classical guitar that he really liked and I was flattered because a lot of times he would let me in the studio but not the band. I remember once going to John's flat. There was a guitar lying around, so I picked it up and started playing. John said, 'That's nice – what is it?' and I told him, 'It's on your new album!' He hadn't even heard it. So to Peter at that point the band was becoming something very peripheral. I think he even felt he could play drums better than Micky Fleetwood and saw flaws in everything they did."

Road manager Dennis Keen could see all this too – Peter's isolation – but felt powerless to do anything so bold as gee the others up and give them the spur which he says was due: "We were in Kingsway, all five of us [Jeremy didn't participate on *Then Play On*]. If Peter didn't get his guitar out there wouldn't be a sound made. If Peter was late, they'd just spend the time sitting about, drinking coffee or whatever. Instead of Danny saying, 'Oh I've got a number, let's work it out and when Pete comes we'll see what he thinks,' they'd do nothing. It was like that! Pete would have welcomed any input, but that was never the case around that time, although it was better a bit earlier around 'Man Of The World'. I could see Pete really enjoyed doing those two studio jams – 'Searching For Madge' and 'Fighting For Madge'. He used play back the tapes, take them home listen again, come in the next day and engineer Martin Birch would play around with the mix. The rest of the band never contributed one iota to that. Peter did all the editing and cutting."

Obviously, Paul Morrison and Dennis Keen have different interpretations of what was really going on during the making of that third album. While Paul saw Peter drawing away from the band, Dennis felt at the time that the leader was looking to them for creative energy, but then always seemed to hit a brick wall. "Part of the problem," Dennis surmises, "was communication. Peter was the leader, but he wasn't one to start flashing the sergeant's stripes – he did towards the end, you know, tell John what part to play, but only because he had to. I can only remember one rehearsal in the whole time Peter was with them, and that was at the Lyceum one afternoon when they tried out a big new PA system. So it had to be during gigs that Peter tried to get them to 'join' him in some way. Thinking about it now, perhaps he wasn't able to get this across."

What can't have helped matters much was that the backdrop to all this – the mood of summer 1969 – was rather crazed anyway. While children were starving in Biafra, Neil Armstrong became the first man to pogo on the moon's surface (at vast expense), and on the day of the moon landing, counter-culture psychiatrist RD Laing stood somewhere in north Africa and drunkenly ranted up at the astronaut for "trespassing". (Laing was the definitive 1960s shrink who declared that psychosis was an entirely reasonable reaction to the mad ways of the world – and for some time the world of psychiatry listened. In the mid 1970s, as it happens, Peter might have done a lot worse than have a few sessions with him – but no one thought of that then.) It was also during that summer that Brian Jones was murdered, one-conspiracy theorist now alleges, as revellers partied on by the side of his swimming pool, too out of it to notice or to care that their host was being rubbed out before their eyes. And violence broke out in Ulster. For anyone with Peter's spirit – one that naturally tapped into a more collective consciousness – these were without a doubt crazy-making times.

Chris Welch, recalls a fittingly weird scene around this time involving Peter in his office in London's Fleet Street: "I remember one time, it must have been 1969, he suddenly burst into the *Melody Maker* offices, unannounced. It wasn't very grand – one room on the third floor, full of desks and filing cabinets stuffed with cuttings and photographs. Peter burst in and said, 'I want all my pictures back. I don't like any of the pictures of me that are appearing in newspapers.' He went straight to the cabinet, which you're not supposed to do, opened a file and started throwing pictures around, trying to find photos of himself. I think the idea was to tear them up or throw them away. He didn't speak to me, that was the other strange thing, although we'd got on well that time before in the Red Lion. Eventually, the librarian persuaded him to put everything back. But something had obviously upset him a great deal."

Evidently, Peter's mindset now really was that line of prototype rap he'd recently written: "Don't ask me what I think of you, I might not give the answer that you want me to."

The rock legend emerges – Peter Green from the *Then Play On* era

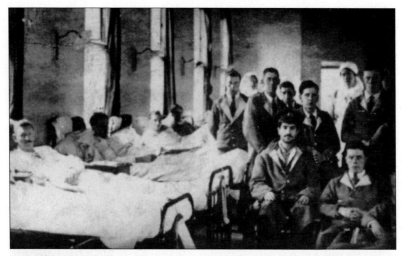

Grandfather Greenbaum (seated on left) in wartime hospital shortly before post-war repatriation to Poland, circa 1918

Anne and her younger sister, Goldie Green, at Antenna House, Bethnal Green circa 1950

Joseph Greenbaum – thirties dude

Peter aged five

Peter aged twelve with the hand-me-down acoustic guitar

Michael, Linda and Peter, Clacton-On-Sea, circa 1950

Michael Green in Buddy Holly glasses with plain lenses for onstage posing only, circa 1960

"Rollin' Man" – Peter with that rugby shirt and that 1959 Les Paul in his Blues Club days, early 1968

Joe, Anne and Peter – proud parents with their gifted son – in the garden of "Albatross", New Malden, Summer 1969

Mayall with his replacement for "God" during the *Hard Road* sessions at Decca's West Hampstead studios, Autumn 1996

Music press ad for Peter's debut forty-five, early 1966

Programme for Fleetwood Mac's Windsor debut

FLEETWOOD MAC
FINDING THE TRUE BLUE HORIZON

Musical fathers and sons, Danny "Young Eyes" Kirwan and Peter, Holland 1968

John McVie with Peter and without inhibitions. Promo poster from late 1968

Laddish pose in Hampstead announces Mac's new five-man line-up with Danny Kirwan, August 1968

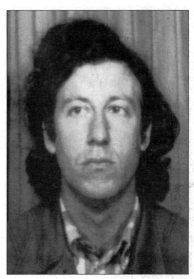

Guitarist with attitude at the New
Malden family home, late 1960s

Early 1970s passport picture

Sandra "Sandy Mary" Elsdon-Vigon and
Peter in meditative mood, 1969

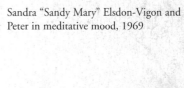

Four-piece Fleetwood Mac's two
guitarists, early 1968

Studio shot, 1969   Peter in hippy stage attire, Putney 1967

Duelling Les Pauls: Kirwan and Green at the *Then Play On* sessions, Kingsway Studios, Holborn, London 1969

CHAPTER 7

WEIRD SCENES, ACID QUEENS, JESUS FREAKS AND GURUS

During the last part of their second US tour in early 1969, Peter began a spiritual journey which was probably set in motion by LSD. "When I took LSD," he reflects, "it was like breathing underwater. When you come down off it, you're back to the same thing again: you can't breathe underwater. Ever since then I've been trying to work out what it was, to see if that feeling, that ridiculous high, is attainable to us in any other way without taking the drug, to rediscover it without someone blowing your mind. And I can't work out what it was with acid that made you feel so free and so happy. But the thing about all the trips I took (about eight in all) was that the only time I ever had it was when it was given to me: I never bought it."

What Peter couldn't have known was that by then the original Haight-Ashbury peace and love movement had changed into a tacky perversion of the original credo: already many hippies' preoccupations were moving away from ideals and prophets to ideal profit. Increasingly, Peter was surrounded by guru hustlers and street-wise chameleons who changed hats lots of times each day according to whether it was enlightenment, or highly lucrative drugs, or both these things, that they were peddling at that particular moment. Four or five years earlier Peter's honesty would have been in its element in San Francisco, but in the late 1960s they must have seen him coming. He was spiked the first few times and after that his own curiosity got the upper hand.

Stan Webb, of Chicken Shack, has trenchant views about spiking, the drug dealer's speculative and free introductory offer, based on some horrific personal experiences: "When Peter first came across acid, he wasn't at all that way inclined. Later on, when he got into it, it became a challenge for him like it did for Eric Clapton – Saint Eric as I call him – who somehow went there yet got back.

"Peter was a very strong character, but he got into taking those weird things. When I first knew him, before 'Albatross', he'd have the occasional smoke and that was his lot. What happened to him might well have been exactly the same as with me, because I got spiked once on LSD which gave me a nervous breakdown and just about screwed me up for three years: for ages after I would sit watching television and suddenly burst out crying. When it was done to me I ended up on a tube train going to Kilburn Art College for a gig. Someone said hello to me and I tried to stab them. I didn't know what the hell I was doing. I ended up in this ambulance with the old blue light going, and a nurse giving me glass after glass of orange juice, as well as three great spoonfuls of Marmite for the riboflavin in it which calms you down. We had a Swiss road manager once who became deaf in one ear after he got spiked."

Peter was, some still insist, first spiked with acid in San Francisco in 1968 and then a couple of years later more insidiously in a hippy hang-out just outside Munich. Munich has since been seen as the most convenient explanation of how such a clean-living and focused musician, whose extreme simplicity was also his genius, could then appear to disintegrate into an acid casualty fazed by life's complexities.

In 1968 when Fleetwood Mac, the four-piece nothing-but-the-blues combo, flew out to the United States for its first tour each of them tried LSD for the first time, although Peter was least keen. Peter and Jeremy stayed with Judy Wong, now a no-nonsense music biz trouper who's seen it all. Back then though she was a demure and rather shy oriental woman who, in her own words, "hadn't heard the f-word or the c-word, never mind used them". With Peter, and especially Jeremy, *in situ* all that was going to change. "Peter sometimes swore, but Jeremy was literally two people," Judy reflects. "I didn't expect some lunatic Englishman to open my windows at four in the morning and shout obscenities for the sole purpose of waking up the neighbours." Jeremy said in a 1974 interview with Steve Clarke of *NME* that Peter did not drop acid on this first US tour. Yet many know otherwise, and some even suspect that Jeremy may have had a hand in first "turning on" the uninterested guitarist.

Jeremy can only have been a part of it because, to all intents and purposes, Peter's fate was sealed the moment he arrived. He was already a cult celebrity over there and, as such, a highly desirable prospect for the drugs underworld. His reputation as Eric Clapton's successor in The Bluesbreakers had gone ahead of him and this meant that when he started hanging out with Judy at music haunts in San Francisco's bohemian sleaze quarter – Haight-Ashbury – there were some heavy names on the scene eager to shake hands. The Grateful Dead's Jerry Garcia was one of them. The Dead were looked after by the electronics genius who had conceived of (and paid for) their huge public address system, which they would use at musical "freak-outs" where the audience was tripped out on acid. The acid was, reputedly, supplied by the same electronics genius, one Owsley, Tycoon of Trips. It made for great business.

Augustus Owsley Stanley III was the grandson of a Kentucky senator and twice a drop-out. Here was a bohemian scientist with a calculating business brain quick to realise the market potential of the 1960s peace and so-called "underground" movement. He may not have made money out of Peter Green directly, but Owsley's cachet allegedly came from rubbing shoulders with famous rock stars. It was his purest-of-all acid that reportedly fuelled The Beatles as they dreamt up the psychedelic vistas of their *Sergeant Pepper's...* concept album.

Profit margins to be found in LSD manufacture when he set up his Baer Research Company in the mid 1960s were as mind-blowing as the stuff itself: twenty thousand dollars' worth of basic chemicals would gross maybe two-three million dollars on the streets. Although in 1966 he was ahead of the game, by 1968, when Fleetwood Mac were in town, the police were after him. As soon as he heard Peter was around Owsley was very, very interested in meeting him, as Judy Wong remembers: "Peter and I went to dinner with him somewhere on Broadway. He was a very intelligent person who impressed Peter by being knowledgeable on a wide range of subjects. Owsley only ate meat – no potatoes or vegetables. The three of us would hang round together and although I knew that he passed round acid, I think he was just genuinely interested in getting to know Peter. One time we went over to Owsley's house in Berkeley, which is just across the Bay from San Francisco. His house was just off the campus of the University of California, completely out of the way, which suited him just fine. When we got there Peter and I were amazed to discover that the whole place was decorated with owls – not stuffed owls, but owl salt and pepper shakers, owl figurines, owls everywhere! And his fridge contained only one thing – meat. We're not talking chops, we're talking legs and huge joints. To this day I've never seen anything like that and, of course, to Peter it was a weird bit of *déjà vu* going straight back to his butchering days."

Owsley always stressed that he wasn't an acid missionary like Dr Timothy "turn on, tune in and drop out" Leary. Owsley assured Judy that he would only supply if that was what was wanted and she was quite comfortable about the whole situation. However, one night, backstage at Fillmore West's – then called the Carousel Ballroom – Owsley offered Judy what she thought was Coca-Cola. "Then in a mad scientist, ghoulish voice," Judy recalls, "Owsley inquired, 'And I wonder how Mr Green and Mr Fleetwood, and the others are doing?!' I dashed off into the hall where the boys were listening to the band. When I found them I remember Mick saying he felt strange but all right."

Later on, when they got back home to Judy's place, Jeremy experienced problems coming down off it and, he has since said, was scared witless, thinking about death and his own mortality for the first time in his life. Mick and John enjoyed the experience sufficiently to trip again soon after on the mountain near Sausalito. And Peter? Well, at that point he could take or leave it – only instead he was given it.

After that first tour none of the band continued with the acid experimentation back in England, but when they went back to America in December for a three-month stretch, Owsley eventually hooked up with them in New Orleans. "In New Orleans," Mick Fleetwood remembers, "when we were playing with The Grateful Dead, we had taken some acid and we knew that the whole audience had been spiked from the water fountains at the Warehouse club. After the show one kid went home and announced to his parents that he was Jesus – Mom and Dad got scared and complained to the police, who went straight after Owsley." Mick's ex-wife Jenny Boyd remembers this rather heavy night and also recalls a somewhat paranoid Peter, perhaps freaked at having being spiked to the point where he couldn't even play guitar: "That was the thing I couldn't really understand about him [Peter] and drugs. That time in New Orleans at the Warehouse gig where we all got spiked, I remember being back in our hotel room with Mick. Peter was with us and we were all still on Owsley's acid. I remember looking at Peter and thinking that this wasn't natural to him because he had his own energy and didn't need anything. There was one incident with Peter at that concert: they were all so high they couldn't play their instruments and were having a mass panic. Danny rushed up to me and said, 'Jenny, I don't know what to do – I can't play anything!' At one point Peter couldn't play anything either, and only Mick was able to perform a bit but to me he looked like a skeleton on stage...complete madness! Afterwards we were all still out of it and I remember walking towards Peter and suddenly he said, 'Oh no! Stay away from me. I don't want to get caught in your world!'"

While Mick cannot condone Owsley's questionable legacy, he still has fond memories of the man: "He was the wicked pixie, and I always told him that. I still keep in touch with him: he makes exotic jewellery and lives in a tent on the Gold Coast near Cairns in Oz. He lives in the right vortex at the right time – when the end of the world comes he'll be on the right axis and won't get sprung off the earth. He was responsible for turning half the planet on and a lot of heartache has come out of it. But on the other hand, he has turned a lot of people's lives around to the positive by a once in a lifetime experience. The fact remains that he made millions out of acid – this chap was on the front page of *Time* magazine."

Owsley and his wife (a chemistry student) met at the California college in Berkeley, dropped out and went into the acid business. They had a production plant in Berkeley, then in Los Angeles and first produced the stuff when it was still legal. For years he stayed out of jail because he had so much money, but then it ran out and the FBI clamped down. They caught him the night he spiked Peter and Mac in New Orleans, as Mick remembers with mixed emotions: "It was purely by coincidence that we escaped the police that time. Pete couldn't play because he was too high. I was so high that I literally drove us back to our hotel with my feet: I was sitting on the back seat of a Mercury station wagon absolutely out of it on acid and turning the steering wheel with my feet while somebody else worked the pedals from front passenger seat. We tried to follow Owsley and the Dead's car along the cobbled streets but got lost. Thank God! They got busted down on Bourbon Street. The police were really wanting to bust Owsley and he'd only managed to elude them because he had the finances. He was on some vague probationary thing. But that time they got him and put him away for five years."

When the band returned from that second US tour people close to Peter started to notice a change in his attitude and demeanour. Ex-girlfriend Sandra Elsdon-Vigon feels that it was drugs that eventually undermined their deep friendship, a process which started around then. Sandra, now a psychotherapist living in Los Angeles, was very anti-drugs. She still recalls her anger at people like Owsley and Jeremy who led Peter in that direction: "I remember Owsley coming to visit one day at Peter's house in New Malden when he was over with The Grateful Dead. He brought with him a huge vial of acid that he left with Peter. It was something that we would really argue about."

By all accounts Owsley truly believed he was doing Peter a favour. Carlos Santana, who Sandra remembers as a very sweet man, at that time was into everything and Peter kind of got drawn in. "There was an outdoor festival at Shepton Mallett with Fleetwood Mac and Led Zeppelin – Peter and I had a big fight because Carlos was plying him with cocaine and acid and whatever else. It was awful for me because I could see that Peter was someone who just shouldn't touch anything like that. But to Peter it was all very exciting: he really admired Carlos and his band, and all the San Francisco lot. He just got swept up in it."

Peter had met Carlos on Mac's first US tour a couple of years before Santana made a monster hit out of Peter's 'Black Magic Woman', recording a version that fused Latin and African rhythms.

Fan club secretary Jane Honeycombe only got to know Peter a little before that second tour but, like Sandra, noticed a difference when they returned in February 1969: "Shortly after they returned John held a small party at his place and Mick was there with Jenny, Danny was on his own and I ostensibly was with Peter. The conversations were all to do with drugs: we were all smoking. Suddenly I didn't feel terribly well and went to the loo. Mick and Peter came to the door after a while to see if I was all right and to my surprise Peter sort of told me off for smoking dope. Rather foolishly I told him later that I'd really like to try acid. Peter got very angry. He said, 'If anybody ever gives you any of that stuff I'll kill them.'"

This instance of "Do as I say, not as I do" was typical of the "old" Peter Green at his most forceful and opinionated. But it wasn't to last: trip by trip, line by line and toke by toke the drugs – by his own admission – "turned me into a softy".

CHAPTER 8

CLOSING MY EYES TO
HEAR THE PEOPLE LAUGH

That same summer of 1969, Peter was searching intensely for an answer and was quite desperate for relief and respite from all the new-found traumas and stresses of showbiz. Drugs provided at least some temporary escape from business hassles and the trappings of fame. Yet the musical ideas kept coming through thick and fast, often to disappear before he had time to capture them on tape. Here was a musician in the mainstream of life who, whilst drawing from a seemingly bottomless well of creativity, was also teetering close to the edge and at some considerable risk of falling in.

Experiments with drugs had left Peter more disillusioned, than traumatised or agitated and whereas he had expected it all to liberate him and make him more carefree, it had actually made him more introverted. The constant question was: "Is there more? There has to be more to life than this." This was when the religious thing started.

Peter engaged in long conversations about faith with Jane Honeycombe, who had been brought up a strict Roman Catholic. "When I first knew him that wasn't at all the kind of conversation he was into," she recalls. "I think that gradually developed into his worries about money. Peter, always looking into things and typically taking them to their extreme, would want to do or become the things that he believed. This apparently frightened Mick and John because Peter was, they believed, the kind of person who, if he felt strongly about something, needed everybody to agree with him."

Also around this time Jenny Boyd – younger sister of Pattie

Harrison/Clapton, inspiration of Donovan's 1960's hit 'Jennifer Juniper', future wife (twice over) of Mick Fleetwood and now a writer and psychologist – shared a London taxi with Peter that summer. "Just after Mick and I had got together again in 1969," Jenny recalls, "Peter rang me up. I hadn't seen him in years and the very fact he called me was quite unusual because at that time there was this unwritten rule that you don't talk to your friends' girlfriends because...they're your friends' girlfriends! Anyway he called me and said, 'Do you mind if we meet?' It so happened that I had to go up to Oxford Street for an appointment, so I said, 'Let's share a cab.' So we met up and once in a taxi he said, 'I know you've been to India and you've been on this search for years, Mick's always told me about it. What is it you've found?' It was like he'd just discovered this great spiritual awareness, and he knew that I'd been on that path for quite a few years. And so, in the cab ride from Kensington Church Street to Oxford Street he wanted me to give him the answer: to tell him what it's all about. But he did it in such a beautiful, open way. Of course, I felt totally inadequate because something like that obviously needed so much longer to talk through.

"All I could do was reassure him that yes, he was right, it is there. He was always very curious, always asking himself questions. Now while that's an admirable quality, it is such powerful stuff that it can drive you crazy: you have to make a real conscious attempt to keep your feet on the ground, otherwise you can get taken away."

Sometimes she would accompany Mick on tour and towards the end of 1969 she began to notice changes taking place in Peter's personality: "It worried me when I saw him on the road with the band because I wondered how much of his ego was also starting to play a part. The thing is that with the other thing – the spiritual part – ego doesn't play any role at all. Yet he was almost starting to believe that he was some kind of Messiah. If you believe that everything has a light and a dark side, then that taking over was the dark side of it. With someone as intense as Peter, it's as bright as it is dark – the brighter the light, the darker the dark."

Peter then radically changed his appearance – donning religious robes, growing long hair and a beard – as if to advertise his radical new attitudes and beliefs. Girlfriend Sandra soon grew concerned: "That summer Peter was really excited by all the possibilities that were presenting themselves. This correlated with a spiritually exciting period. We were both for quite some time very spiritually connected and searching. I was into Eastern philosophy and belonged to the Buddhist Society, so we'd go to Watkins bookstore and get all these esoteric books. We went to a Tibetan Buddhist retreat in Scotland. Then I made the robes – one white and one red velvet. For Peter they were nothing to do with any Christian faith. I think psychologically it was definitely a move into psychosis, or perhaps a precursor of it: he was getting stuck into identification with God! Because of all the adoration people were giving him, he was finding it very hard to differentiate between that exalted state and mere mortality – albeit with a God-given talent. And at that point he was acutely aware that he had a gift which then became a power. As I see it, he wasn't strong enough then to contain that power and it soon led to lofty identifications."

"Now when I talk to God I know he understands; he said stick by me and I'll be your guiding hand. But don't ask me what I think of you; I might not give the answer that you want me to." With such self-aggrandisement, this, the second verse of 'Oh Well', is in sharp contrast to verse one's "I can't sing; I ain't pretty" sentiments. Elevation follows self-deprecation, all set to music which, on the A-side, is aggression tastefully running riot, whilst the classical stuff on part two runs the gamut from repose to melodrama.

Peter Green's *magnum opus* was perceived as exactly that at the time by everybody but his own group and so its release served to set him apart from the band for good. Perplexed Jesus freak or no, the single's sheer creativity must have been daunting for those around him. Mick and John even bet him that it wouldn't chart. "Mick and I," John now wryly concedes, "each bet Peter five pounds that the single wouldn't chart. We just didn't have Peter's vision about the parts one and two idea." They disagreed so much that at one point the leader was seriously contemplating releasing it as a solo effort.

Peter won the bet and collected almost immediately as the single went to Number Two. After that the situation within Fleetwood Mac became more and more fraught. The leader privately told manager Clifford Davis that he wanted to leave, but was persuaded to stay on for the sake of the others. If evidence of dissension were needed, there's a video recording of 'Oh Well' played live that captures the band's very obvious lack of *esprit de corps* around this period. In it Mick screws up the rata-ta-tat cowbell bit and right on camera a biblical-looking Peter then laughs goadingly at his hapless drummer's efforts. Meanwhile Danny characteristically is oblivious to all around him and instead is bending notes to insane effect, whilst Jeremy, playing maracas, looks bored and out of a job. It's almost as though the wacky leader is berating his play-safe colleagues for ever having had doubts about his abilities and offbeat beliefs.

Peter now explains away that phase as an identification with Jesus; but he's quick to emphasise that the way he saw and felt the transformation in himself was not as some "drug-induced delusion of grandeur" which is how others saw it. Identifying with Jesus, he says, was more a gesture of humility. Mich Reynolds, then married to manager Clifford Davis, remembers an instance of this shortly after Peter left Fleetwood Mac: "Star-struck young girls were still coming around to his house in New Malden. Sometimes he would come out and chat to them. After one such occasion an overprotective father got to hear about this, went round and just hit Peter in the face when he answered the door. He told me about this and I asked him what his reaction was. 'I just smiled at him, turned the other cheek and stood there in the doorway.'" At this point the assailant apparently sloped off looking very confused.

"There was a time," Peter admits, "when I did start reading about Jesus and thinking along the lines of 'He has returned, and I am Him'. Then I started reading the Bible and coming up against riddles: why did He have red hair, supposedly, and I didn't? Then I'd remember that I did have auburn hair as a child. These thoughts though were before the acid: once I took LSD that got rid of all that – all that vanity."

'Closing My Eyes' from the *Then Play On* album, was written when he was in this frame of mind and captures the intensity of his spiritual awakening – the feeling of being compelled to search, but not knowing what it is he is searching for. It also describes the inevitable deflation that followed when Peter tried to externalise such a deeply personal experience, and explain it to friends like Jenny Boyd. Inevitably, he found himself lost for words. "This song," Peter said at the time, "was written around the time I had such a great faith in Jesus that I felt I was walking and talking with God. I wanted to tell people about it, but they turned it round and tried to shatter my dreams. This was written after they had broken my faith."

The fact is that nobody in his circle of friends at the time remembers anything remotely like this spirit-breaking malevolence being directed at Peter: so the "they" who broke his faith, more probably came from within and, as such, were an early sign of a deep depression that was looming as, tour by tour, hit by hit, nervous exhaustion began to set in.

As Jenny Boyd sees it, the acid experience disturbed – though for a while it did boost – his already massive energy levels, his sensitivity and the need to search. "That taxi ride," she points out, "was Peter in his curiosity stage. He was almost continually breaking down inner walls within himself. Like the classical music he explored with 'Oh Well'. As a rock guitarist from London's East End, for him to even attempt something as beautiful as that says a lot. He was just breaking down these walls of restriction, and realising that there was a big, big world out there – and a big world inside too. Music became his god and, especially after the acid, he found a lot of spirituality there. I remember after that New Orleans trip we all started having far more philosophical discussions about the band's performance and we started to see it as a spiritual thing: the group were giving their unity to the audience. It may sound obscure and very 1960s now, but I was likening it to the fishes and loaves, nowadays the fishes and loaves being like the music. The audience has an energy from its togetherness, so there's an exchange."

Peter in a way still echoes Jenny's thinking today: "I don't quite understand performance. I think a lot of it is luck, and a lot of it is happiness; you have to be happy with yourself and pleased with your efforts. It's a magical thing." Obviously, this kind of performance magic is volatile in the extreme and the downside is that the musician or performer easily can become a victim.

Zoot Money, Peter's musical companion from purple-heart all-nighters at the Flamingo, emphasises how the dangers inherent in the performer/audience situation night after night, were ones which may not always have been good for Peter's mental health: "You have to understand the dilemma of the structured set-up in the late 1960s, in the aftermath of the Vietnam War and all that stuff. Put simply, freedom was rife amongst young people and so, perhaps forgetting Bob Dylan's advice, they did need to follow leaders and somehow contain or control that freedom. Young people looked to somebody. But fame, from the performer's point of view, is a bit like being caught up in a tide: you start off with good intentions and good feelings, and you want to spread them through playing music. That becomes a spiritual thing, or whatever it is when it makes contact with other people who then enjoy it. Anyway, it becomes ritualistic involving many, many people.

"At that point it takes on a power of its own which is then no longer something entirely controllable by you, and so you have to find ways of making it work for you. You can either let that power subside naturally, or smash hotel televisions and set fire to things! But for any musician the most difficult task is to keep that power working over time: once someone like Peter gets so much fame in a short space of time, then you have a lot of mental balls to juggle at once. Initially it's simple enough to control a crowd of two hundred, or even two thousand people, but things get far more difficult and stressful when you get up to twenty thousand or sixty thousand. None the less the process is the same: it starts off with you and then extends along the stage and makes contact with a lot of people out there who have brought their own energy as well.

"Merely making that work in a good way, night after night is impossible. As audiences get bigger, so does the risk of technical hitches that can turn you off. So suddenly from every night being a good night and spiritually uplifting, you're now lucky if it's one in ten. That's the best average I've ever had and that's really lucky! So just holding on to that positive spirituality that strengthened you in the first place and drew you in, becomes a major problem. At the tail end of the 1960s and the start of the 1970s that was where Peter and many other musicians found themselves. So those people, myself included, naturally started looking to mystical books and the Tarot in the hope of finding something that might help. And then there were drugs. You hoped all these things might lead you to a spiritual revelation in some form."

Without a doubt, Peter's 'Closing My Eyes' was inspired by some form of revelation: feeling a higher presence around him day after day.

What this perhaps served to do was send him on a quest; a quest in which his spirituality was almost completely linked to his music and as Jenny Boyd says, his god was his music. Zoot Money light-heartedly alludes to this serious matter, remembering the unique mood of the 1960s when it seemed as though certainly everybody under the age of thirty – from astronauts to pot-holers – was on some kind of inner as well as outer search. "The thing about my generation during the 1960s is that we had to go out and artificially create the traumas for ourselves: we didn't have to fight a world war in the trenches which was the kind of trauma where many who did that get an incredible, blinding revelation. My generation did get something like that when they had taken too much acid, when, even in familiar surroundings, you are in fact subjected to the same kind of mental stress or trauma. It is a totally mental thing – if you're blind in the middle of a battlefield and you don't actually see the carnage all around you then of course you'll be at peace with yourself. That's a wicked analogy. What I mean is that in a way you do become lighter in death, and within the sea of trouble when you actually give yourself over to a higher spirit."

So for Peter in 1969, with music as his higher spirit, creatively he was soaring: "Peter at his happiest," Jenny Boyd points out, "was an inspired person who placed complete faith in his inspirations, wherever they took him. There was 'Albatross', the classical music, then the improvising and jamming and then in a similar way there was his idea about Fleetwood Mac being like a band of gypsies enjoying themselves by roaming the world and giving their money away to ease suffering. That idea he regarded as an inspiration that came to him and he believed in it just as he did the music for 'Albatross'. But sadly, what I then saw in Peter was that same energy and flow of creativity turn inwards, and turn into something much darker when the rest of the band, Mick especially, didn't agree with him. Peter and Mick up until that point were very close – they loved each other – and I don't think either really ever got over what happened. Neither of them understood why."

So in the context of that defiantly idealistic era, the 1960s, Peter's desire to help feed the world should not, in theory, have been construed as insane. But it was, and he was locked away because of it. In effect, his was a low-key Live Aid but without the egos, knighthoods, and instantaneous global music-business career launches.

In March 1970, just a couple of months before he left Fleetwood Mac, Peter's charity band ideas were reported in the music press. In an article entitled "Giving Away The Green Stuff", the 14 March edition of *Melody Maker* said: "Peter Green surprised the pop world this week by announcing intentions to 'give away' a large proportion of his income as a guitarist with Fleetwood Mac. A spokesman for the group said on Monday: 'All the group agrees with Peter's aims and they will probably give several charity performances. Peter plans to give up his own money as well, although we don't know exactly what he intends to do with it.'"

This deft bit of music business PR did its best to mask the reality of the situation, which was of course that, with the infamous Munich showdown only a couple of weeks away, the band in effect was re-arranging deckchairs on the Titanic. Peter was intent on one thing, and the rest of the band would soon be forced to declare their hand and trash his philanthropy.

In another interview, this time with Nick Logan of *NME*, the group leader explained his thinking further: "I'm not going into poverty with people on the other side of the world who are starving, although I did think of doing that. It would have made me feel better. This way the more money I earn, the more I can give away." During the interview he was anxious that Nick Logan did not regard his secondhand seven-hundred-pound Jaguar XK150 (seven hundred would be nearer seven thousand today) as an extravagance: "I would love to go yachting. I love cars. I would love to buy an AC Cobra, but the thing is that before I do that I would like to know that everybody is getting their bowlful of rice every day."

However, Sandra Elsdon-Vigon now has a very different view of Peter's motives, seeing the charity notion as not really about charity or being altruistic. She now believes that Peter thought that if he got rid of those things – all that "unclean" money – then he would somehow also get rid of some of the power and get back to where he was before: a gifted guitarist who didn't find himself identifying with God. Ironically this move to regain his freedom backfired on him: news spread like wildfire and after he declared in the music press that he wanted to give his money away, he was inundated by begging letters – "My grandmother's dying...", "My mother needs an operation...". Of course Peter soon realised that he couldn't answer all their pleas and that scared him too.

So, to describe Peter at that point as anxious about the question of money is an understatement: it had become a painful obsession and a neurosis. This is confirmed by Paul Morrison, his friend from the Orange Music shop, who remembers well a car journey with Peter around this time: "We were driving along and he was describing to me in great detail the inner turmoil he felt about whether to buy a particular car. He really wanted an AC Cobra, which was the fastest car around then, but he couldn't bring himself to spend the money – I think they cost about five thousand pounds at the time – so instead he bought the old Jag XK150 for seven hundred. For him this was a really unhappy compromise. The pop star wanted the fast car but the ordinary Jewish boy wouldn't let him. He was never able to resolve that conflict and I think it was that that brought on the illness."

In the few months before the split in May 1970, Jenny for the first time ever, sensed negativity coming from Peter and how he began to lose interest in the band after it was decided that Fleetwood Mac were not going to do the charity thing. It was a major disappointment for him and was also the turning point. When Peter went to Mick and Jenny's wedding in June 1970, shortly after he'd left the band, Jenny noticed a cynicism she'd never seen before. Mick had asked Peter to be best man, but Peter just didn't turn up in time for the wedding ceremony. "Mick was incredibly hurt," recalls Jenny. "Peter and Sandra eventually arrived hours later but I think it was a kind of 'Fuck you!' – he didn't believe in marriage as an institution and felt we were giving in and becoming the conventional middle-class mortgage and kids thing, while he was a free spirit. The fact that he did that to Mick I think shows just how much Peter felt he had been let down."

But Peter's relationship with the band remained one of love and hate right to the end, as revealed in an interview given shortly before leaving for the European tour in March: "I'd say that like the last time we came back from America, the band is closer than it has ever been and Danny and I are now working and playing together, which we haven't done before." He then went on to disclose that he and Danny were planning an album based around their two guitars and that he was going to record a solo album for release at Christmas. "We've got about twenty new numbers as well and we should really be recording now. But we've got so much touring to do."

It is quite possible that more than anything else it was the pressure of touring that caused Peter to leave Fleetwood Mac. After the three-month American tour at the end of 1969 and beginning of 1970 there were already plans to return to America in the autumn: 1970 was going to be the year that they'd conquer America. Whereas previously they were main support for headlining acts like Jethro Tull and The Joe Cocker Grease Band, it was decided that next time round there would be no more supports – their leader's talent would get them headlining every time. Dennis Keen, Mac's road manager then, recalls the group's bullish attitude: "They'd been playing second or third on the bill up until that point, but promoters were beginning to notice how they were packing out places like the Whiskey-A-Go-Go in Los Angeles as the sole act. So in autumn 1970 we were going to break out and be as big as Jethro Tull." There was just one snag: when could they record the new album if the year already was completely taken up with tours?

Peter's mother, Anne Green, now remembers just how gruelling her son found those tours: "When Pete came back from America towards the end of his time with Fleetwood Mac he would go upstairs to his bedroom and virtually sleep for a whole week. He would come down for the occasional meal or cup of tea, but most of the time he just wanted to sleep."

Still drained by the recent American tour, anxious about the band not spending enough time in the studio, receiving begging letters daily in the post and with the engineer overworked and overpaid, as he saw it, Peter was on the brink of nervous exhaustion. The train gathered speed through Europe on a gig itinerary that took in Paris, Basle, Amsterdam, Rotterdam, Londerzeel, Copenhagen, Odense, Gothenburg, Stockholm, Hanover, Berlin, Hamburg and Dusseldorf. Then on the last weekend in March, Fleetwood Mac had an afternoon gig in Munich. Backstage a classy, bohemian German rock chick had Peter marked out. Swathed in a mink mini-coat, she was raunchy, irresistible, into acid and full of anti-capitalist attitude. Peter's resistance was particularly low.

CHAPTER 9

TRAUMA CITY:
THE MUNICH TRIP

John McVie described Munich and its aftermath as "Trauma City". Although at the time it was just another gig on one more gruelling tour schedule, many say something happened there that has moulded the rest of Peter Green's life, something malevolently in-keeping with the political climate that targeted rock music on the world stage and particularly in west Germany at that time. Another conspiracy theory, no less.

Anarchism and alienated youth often seem to court each other, but in 1970 Europe's live music circuit became youth's unlikely target. Well, not really that unlikely, when you consider how the face of rock in the early 1970s was changing. Forget all that rubbish about free concerts and happenings in the 1960s. Rock by its very nature was starting to grow up into the big capital-intensive business it is today. Do you want to hear loud, quality music and see a good show? Well, that costs money: bigger PAs, road crews, lighting rigs, juggernauts and so on.

In just a couple of years, ticket prices soared to cover costs and create, it must be said, realistic profit margins for an industry set on long-term growth. The Germans particularly resented this and proceeded to riot outside pop concerts, demanding to get in for free. The Rolling Stones' autumn 1970 European tour was littered with nasty incidents: forged tickets, arson and violence. And it all came from street fighting men and women who refused to pay. As a result, Fleetwood Mac's manager pulled them out of a planned European tour at the end of that year that Peter left. But in Munich that March weekend, all these things were still in ferment. Looking back, John McVie describes that anarchic mindset: "'I'm not bothered what the action does, it's the action itself that is important.' That's what we were up against. Those people who lured Peter away and spiked him. They were sure they were doing right."

Fleetwood Mac were in Munich for three days, and on day one played an afternoon gig. Road manager Dennis Keen takes up the story: "We were in the dressing room after the gig and a group of people came in – this always happened over there as we were more popular in Europe than anywhere else. Amongst them was this gorgeous, really gorgeous girl. Pete was a sucker for nice chicks, and she just asked him if he wanted to come to a party. Pete said yes but the rest of the group weren't in the mood, so only Pete and me went. Eventually we got to this big house with a huge grand drive. When we went inside there was a party of about twenty people sat around, we were offered a glass of wine, and the next thing I knew all hell broke loose in my head – we'd been drugged. Nobody had offered us any tablets, they just went and spiked us.

"I was wandering round this house, talking to people in English and surprise, surprise not getting any response. I didn't have a clue where I was, or what was going on. I was twenty-five and a strong man in mind and body and was I high! Nowadays I'd have freaked.

"I only have one memory of Pete in the whole twenty-four hours that we were there. I was going round the house trying to talk to these people and I went downstairs to the basement. They had a studio there and I could hear all this sound coming out, so I opened the door and there's Pete playing this guitar with all these other guys. But the sound they were making was awful: this kind of freaky electronic droning noise. It wasn't music as I knew it.

"After what must have been about eight or ten hours I was wearing off and I couldn't have liked what was going on because I was thinking about ringing the hotel in Munich. I always used to carry a book of matches with the name and telephone number of the hotel on it which I would show to taxi drivers in order to get back. I didn't ring Clifford Davis until the morning but then asked him to come down and get us out of there. By then it was all going a bit weird. I don't know what it was that wasn't right, but I just knew we had to get out. So Clifford,

Mick and Dinky our road manager drove down and they got us out.

"For all I know during the time that I was out of it they may have been drumming something into Peter. They might have been saying, 'You've got all this money. You should be giving it all away.' But it wasn't like it was with Jeremy Spencer a year later, who everyone could see had been totally brainwashed and in my opinion brainwashed for the better. Jeremy looked a lot worse before he went and then looked alive afterwards: you could see he'd found what he'd been looking for. In Peter's case he started to go down after Munich. As the tour bus travelled on from Munich the next day, he told the band of his decision to leave."

Twenty-five years on Peter's own memories of what happened in Munich differ somewhat from those of Dennis Keen: "We were met at the airport by this girl and boy, both of them wearing fur coats. I found myself walking with them instead of our group – it was nice for me to walk with them. They came back to the hotel with us and there they told us that they had this commune in a big old house. To my knowledge only Dennis and myself out of the English lot went there.

"While I was at the house I remember playing lead guitar: there was a kit of drums and an electric piano. Some of it got recorded and I kept the tape – it was different and good, one of my favourites, this LSD tape, which many years later I gave to my wife in Los Angeles.

"I was put to bed by this girl – I don't know where Dennis was at the time. I was just lying there on my own on just a mattress, and thinking I was made up of crystals. Some people might be frightened to sleep if they felt like that, but I was so tired I just went straight off to sleep so that I'd be ready for the next gig and I could play well. On the next gig we played I felt marvellous – fresh and not grubby."

During an interview with Mark Ellen of *Mojo* in early 1994, Peter recalled, "They had a mansion, a great big place it was. I went back with one of the road managers. He gave me some LSD, I ate it and as I'd got my guitar we played with some music for a while. Then I just sat around thinking and thought about everything. I was thinking so fast, I couldn't believe how fast I was thinking! And I ran out of thoughts. I must have been thinking solid for about an hour. Just sitting down on my mattress."

Curiously, Jeremy Spencer has implied that he also went to the

115

Munich houseparty. In a 1974 *NME* interview he told Steve Clarke, "I don't know why Pete left the group exactly. It looked like it was coming up. He met some of these people in Germany – I didn't in fact have anything to do with it – but we took some acid and played some music. It was pretty weird. I didn't like what he was playing. He was just jamming. But there was no point in trying to stop him leaving."

There's also little point in trying somehow to extrapolate the truth about what really took place in Munich that time. Bearing in mind that it happened so long ago and that during those twenty-four hours in question the key players in the drama were both on acid; in these circumstances, lofty notions of truth fly out the window. Perhaps Munich's real significance in the 1990s is all the mythology that has been attached to it ever since. It is possible that the German hippies were part of some extreme cult, or that they were political activists. It is possible that attempts at brainwashing – sadly, so fashionable in those days – did take place whilst Peter was downstairs in that basement studio. But no one can ever know for sure.

Similarly, no one can ever prove that Munich was the trauma that set off some or all of Peter's subsequent health problems and erratic behaviour. Given this eternal uncertainty it is perhaps better to stick to what few known facts there are, even though these might demystify the legend somewhat and replace it with something more mundane yet credible. Legend by definition cannot be mundane, but life – even on the road – often is.

Given Peter's sensitivity, not to mention his fazed and confused state of mind around that time, it was courting disaster to drop acid just when he did. Perhaps he was simply desperate to bring things to a head with the band. It was Dr Timothy Leary who preached the importance of "the set and the setting" to would-be space cadets by emphasising how they should only drop acid at the right time and place, and in the right company, conditions hardly applicable to Peter on that day. Peter knew a split from Mac was looming and, what's more, he knew that they knew that he knew – that was his mindset. As for the setting, there may well have been some heavy mind games lurking behind the Munich commune's camaraderie, but exactly what these might have been is not known.

What is known is that he enjoyed the music that was going down.

At the end of the day in question Peter did not freak out, he went to sleep exhausted, feeling as if he were made up of crystals. So if it was bad, impure acid that was handed out there, it wasn't bad enough to permanently wipe out millions of brain cells in Dennis Keen's cranium. He's as sparky and sharp today as he was back then.

The facts that are available suggest that Peter and Dennis spent just one night at the commune. It was not the three-day acid binge which is now part of rock legend: in purely practical terms the band's tight tour schedule rules out that possibility out – after Munich on that last weekend in March, they had three more gigs in Germany before the tour drew to a close in Helsinki on Friday, 3 April.

Munich's real legacy for Peter Green was that it consolidated ideas he was already forming about an eccentric change in musical direction. The music coming up out of the basement that sounded so awful to Dennis was a glimpse of the guitarist's new vision – more Stravinsky than Vaughan Williams (Peter studied both these modern composers and had, in John McVie's view, woven Williams's *Lark Ascending* into 'Oh Well, Part Two'). His new music may have been dark, unstructured and scary. It was certainly uncommercial.

The band's reaction was understandable: this was the leader whose inspiration in the shape of 'Albatross' eighteen months previously had dragged them out of the blues clubs (just in time, as the late 1960s boom began to implode) and on to *Top Of The Pops* and the concert halls. And he was now seriously suggesting that they give part of their earnings away and play music that was commercially unsound.

Conga player Nigel Watson collaborated with Peter in the early 1970s on tracks like 'Heavy Heart' and 'Beasts Of Burden', both defiantly uncommercial singles. He now recalls how even two years later in 1972 Peter was keen to play him the Munich "LSD tape": "We were a bit spaced out and sat listening to music at my place in Woldingham. I remember Peter played the single 'Green Manalishi' at thirty-three rpm by accident: the power coming out of those opening chords was mindblowing! Then he put on a tape he'd recorded in Munich while he was on acid. I found the playing weird, even scary at times, but it was still there: free form in one sense, but spot on in another. He was obviously really pleased with it.'

This does suggest that not everything going on at the Munich mansion amounted to a sinister assault on Peter's psyche. Even so, anarchy was very cool in Germany at that point, and because Peter was so exhausted, his hosts were in a good position to coax him out of the tacky capitalism of big-time rock 'n' roll for good. After all, as John McVie says, they knew their actions were right.

CHAPTER 10

MANALISHI

The Green Manalishi defies analysis really. In fact, the word derives from "greenbacks", American slang for dollars. A song about money as the devil incarnate, in a way marks the start of Peter Green's slow retreat from a crazy world to a place and time of his own.

Between 1970 and 1977 attempts to go back and regain the simple inner peace that he had taken for granted as a butcher, gradually became more desperate. More than anything else, it was the trauma of fame that had hived him off from everything and everybody, and in 'Green Manalishi' – like Bowie's 'Space Oddity' a couple of years later – he sketches out rock star alienation. Whereas Bowie would describe it as "floating in a 'mowstapeculiar' way", Peter Green, when he wrote 'Manalishi' in 1969, was still resisting, trying to hang on, and "trying to keep from following you".

The song augured feelings that eventually overwhelmed him, and writing and recording it, he now says, sapped all his strength: "It took me at least two years to recover from that song. When I listened to it afterwards there was so much power there – it exhausted me." Yet the experience remains one of his happiest musical memories from the Fleetwood Mac days, as he explained to Mark Ellen of *Mojo*: "Making 'Green Manalishi' was one of the best memories. Mixing it down in the studio and listening back to it, I thought it would make Number One: lots of drums, bass guitars, all kinds of things, double-up on bass guitars, six-string basses, tracking on it. Danny Kirwan and me playing those shrieking guitars together." The track was recorded at Warner-Reprise's studios in Hollywood on their third US tour, and then mixed back in London about a month before Peter left the band on 28 May 1970.

All kinds of inspiration made Peter's songwriting prolific throughout 1969: listening to Vaughan Williams and Stravinsky, learning the cello, perfecting his use of the wah-wah pedal. And then there was the acid and mescaline. 'Green Manalishi' was the product of a mescaline-induced dream Peter had had in which he was seemingly dead. It was not, he now stresses, a wake-up-screaming nightmare, it was far more insidious than that, like a new reality, full stop. Death's siren, in his case, was a green dog barking at him from over the other side, and the fact that it was green to Peter meant money – greenbacks: "This little dog jumped up and barked at me while I was lying in bed dreaming. It scared me because I knew the dog had been dead a long time. It was a stray and I was looking after it. But I was dead and had to fight to get back into my body, which I eventually did. When I woke up, the room was really black and I found myself writing the song. Next day I went to Richmond Park and did the lyrics – the words were coming through thick and fast. Then I went back home and worked out parts for all the instruments on my Ferrograph tape recorder."

'Green Manalishi (With The Two Prong Crown)' was released on 15 May, some six months after Peter had written it and just two weeks before he left Fleetwood Mac. When the group went to promote the single on *Top Of The Pops* they had a bust-up with the BBC, who wouldn't let them use the eerie vocal effects. Peter refused to do the song live on television without them and so the single was promoted with stills of the band instead. It got to Number Ten in the chart, whereas his three previous hits had notched either the runner-up or the Number One slot.

The eight or so weeks between Peter announcing his intention to quit in Munich and playing his final gig with the band on 28 May were extremely busy and a sign of the times. With help from his older brother, Len, he organised a charity gig at London's Lyceum in aid of the Jewish Welfare Board. Fleetwood Mac were supported by "friends" – two groups, Idle Race and Masterpiece. This concert was a blueprint for live rock music as Peter Green thought it should be: loosely arranged jam sessions between slicker "official" sets by each of the three acts. A variety show.

Peter put in three appearances during that spring Sunday evening. The first was with electric fiddler Nick Pickett in the quartet Masterpiece, then with Fleetwood Mac for a long set, after which he assembled an impromptu band comprising himself, Mick Fleetwood, Danny Kirwan, Pickett and Jethro Tull's bassist and drummer Glen Cornick and Clive Bunker. Green was on stage for a total of four hours.

What was intended to be his last London gig was at the Roundhouse Pop Proms on Friday, 24 April. At twelve-fifteen am, as the crowd yelled for more, Peter stayed on stage after the rest of the band had gone off, quite ready to play more. A week or so later up in the north-east at the Redcar Jazz Club they played a three-hour set which included a taste of Peter's new interest in African drumming. At one point during a Danny Kirwan song 'Coming Your Way', some three-man drum rhythms were laid down: Peter played an African talking drum, Danny used a single stick and cowbell and Mick pounded away on his full kit. Real showtime, and ironic that just three weeks before their leader's departure, Fleetwood Mac were getting their act together in a more dramatic, brash American style. They'd always played superstars, but now they looked as though they played like superstars as well.

A touch of B-movie melodrama brought to an end what was scheduled to be Peter Green's last gig with Mac at Bath City Football ground on Saturday, 23 May. With the all-day festival running way behind schedule, the band came on stage at ten-forty-five pm and at midnight, when they were only halfway through their set, the organisers turned off the floodlights and power supply to the stage. Mick Fleetwood provided a lengthy and defiant drum solo as a farewell to his leader whilst the crowd lit bonfires around the ground. The band were not able to play another single electric note that night; it could have been such a legendary ending to Peter's time with Mac – instead all was darkness and muted confusion.

The following Thursday, back in London, the group had arranged an extra concert back at London's Lyceum along with The Grateful Dead. As it turned out, the Musicians Union barred Dead's appearance so Mac did this final, final gig on their own. There were reports after the show of Peter backstage, blitzed by Owsley's acid and trying to set the amps on fire.

Peter's last television appearance with Fleetwood Mac was

broadcast on BBC Two's *Disco 2,* on 30 May, which had been recorded eight days earlier. Less than a year later in America he would fill in for Jeremy Spencer, who had left the music business to join the Children of God. What happened to Peter and his former colleagues in the intervening time serves to illustrate how one year can be an eternity in rock music.

CHAPTER 11

FREE FORM

O n 20 June 1970, Mick Fleetwood was quoted in *NME* as saying, "I think if we could have done a month ago what we are doing now Peter might never have left, I really do." The months following were not going to be easy and, as John McVie just about remembers, "much hash" was brought in to help the four musicians re-frame their hapless plight. Then in the late autumn, Mac (now with Christine McVie on board) bought Benifold, a house near Haslemere, where they lived and recorded: a rock band with a country seat.

Peter now explains how, originally, that had been his idea too, but the suggestion, he says, fell on deaf ears at the time: "We were due to get some royalties from Warner Brothers and my idea was to live in a commune: a house somewhere in England where we could all live, do our practising and make our records. But any overflow of money we had, we could give away to help the starving in countries like Biafra. When I spoke to them about this in a hotel somewhere John McVie and Jeremy Spencer agreed with me at first, but Mick Fleetwood didn't. Danny wasn't around at that time, he might have been in another room, and Clifford Davis didn't know what to say. Mick said that he would rather give up the group than give away his money. So I said I was going to break up the group and re-form it with people who wanted to do this idea. Mick still wouldn't do it so I told them I was only bluffing. And instead I left for my freedom."

Freedom for Peter, in those first few weeks after leaving the band, amounted to being busier than ever, which is ironic given that he was the most exhausted of them all in the original Fleetwood Mac's final months. But the big difference now was that this new life was free from business pressures and responsibilities.

When the charity band notion was being thrashed out through long nights in grand European hotel rooms thick with dope fumes and misunderstandings, Mick Fleetwood was under the distinct impression that Peter's designs were far more radical than "overflow" or 1960s "getting it together in the country band commune scenario". "When this whole charity thing started," Mick explains, "it was a case of, 'We can't make any money. We've got to give it all away and play for nothing.' I didn't want to give my money away and I suppose Peter didn't like that. John was supportive of Peter's position and I remember asking John at a gig why we couldn't use the money to finance an orphanage or something like that. I mean, this was all such naive commentary which was so typical of the time we were living in. The bottom line according to Peter was that we would be like monks in a monastery; able to survive, feed and clothe ourselves, and everything else would go to the cause. Well, I just didn't want to do that. I remember thinking, 'I've got a girlfriend, I've got a flat to pay for, what do I have to do, give it all up?' and that was the thing that freaked me out.

"Looking back now, what we were actually seeing were the beginnings of him changing – a major metamorphosis – but at the time we didn't see it like that. We just saw him pulling away from us, and somewhere in there we were lost. We were hurt and we were devastated when he left. Were there bad vibes? Specifically no, but...we were like lost sheep." Mick still shudders at the memory.

Over the next year or so Peter would work on his music more intensely than at any point before or since. It didn't seem like work because financial considerations never came into it. After four years as a pro, the reluctant entertainer, bound and gagged by contracts, had broken free and was able to be an artist. The metamorphosis went on apace.

"When you play for money it crowds in on you: when you're not playing for money you're free to walk off any time you like and the audience can see you're not playing for money. If I hadn't gone professional," Peter still maintains, "I might have played more

Shadows, even The Beatles. I changed back to lead from playing bass because I thought that by doing that I could go professional during the blues boom. I had to go that way to accomplish something I wanted to do."

Manager Clifford Davis sympathised with Peter's changing attitudes at the time: "He's always had a big thing about about going on stage knowing that the audience has paid a pound to see him [roughly ten pounds today] and feeling that sometimes he's had to put on a big act to give them the best he could for their money. I think he often felt that he was letting them down."

Peter's departure from the mainstream music business, then, reflected his disillusionment with business, not music. Playing music remained his lifeblood, a fact illustrated by his schedule in the wake of his decision to leave. In between farewell gigs during his last weeks with the band he played all the instruments and produced on a single called 'Come Down And Follow Me' recorded by his manager Clifford Davis. Then he spent the first week in June helping Memphis "Every Day I Have The Blues" Slim out with his *Blue Memphis* album in London.

Among others at the sessions were John Paul Jones, Chris Spedding, Duster Bennett and Conrad Isadore. The *Blue Memphis* project echoed Muddy Waters' *Electric Mud* psychedelic blues album recorded a year earlier, in that it melded traditional blues with modern effects: Slim's piano with Peter's wah-wah guitar. Peter felt it was an honour to be playing alongside Memphis Slim, whose one-time guitarist, Matt Murphy, was a guiding influence for him back in his Putney days.

Blue Memphis was too modern for some. In fact, much of Peter's work over the next couple of years would be met with a similar response by music critics.

Whilst guesting on *Blue Memphis* Peter was also tentatively organising his own solo project *End Of The Game* (see Chapter 12). With only one week until the sessions were due to start, the musicians he had in mind were Nick Buck, the American keyboardist and session man, Zoot Money, Alex Dmochowski and John Morshead (both ex-Aynsley Dunbar Retaliation) on bass and guitar and Godfrey Maclean on drums. On Sunday, 14 June, Peter made his live post-Mac debut at the Salisbury Hotel, Barnet, for free, although his bold idea of putting on good music and charging only five shillings admission no matter who was playing – whether it was Ten Years After or inspired local three-chord tricksters – lost the promoters a lot of money; approximately a hundred-and-twenty pounds on the day.

Peter did the gig, one of seven acts on the bill, as a duo with American keyboardist Nick Buck. It was all improvisation. Nick Logan from *NME*, who was in the audience later wrote: "Playing from the heart and quite brilliantly at times, he was well received by an attuned audience, although it remains to be seen how long this formless format, carrying with it the threat of self-indulgence, can be sustained." At least another two years, as it turned out.

Other similar low-profile and impromptu pub gigs followed, and even one high profile, big event when, two weeks later he went to the Bath Festival Of Blues And Progressive Music to re-join his old boss John Mayall on stage in a one-off line-up including Aynsley Dunbar on drums, and Ric Grech on bass.

It seemed as though everybody now wanted the chance to play with freewheeling Peter Green. After the midnight Mayall gig at Bath he stayed at the festival site ready to jam on Sunday. "Electric-Afro" percussionists Noir borrowed ten pounds to buy the petrol to get them from London to Bath in a hurry that day because they'd heard that Peter was looking for them. Sadly, when the four-piece black group arrived and were setting up their gear, rain stopped play, but the following weekend Peter said he'd join them on stage at the Afro-Rock Carnival at London's Roundhouse. However, just one month or so into his new way of life Peter, the altruistic hippy found himself once more surrounded by somewhat less altruistic hippies hoping to rip off a teeny weeny bit of the man's reputation for their own good.

Peter had first spotted Noir (a name carefully chosen for its Black Power connotations) when they stole the show at an Eric Clapton concert at London's Lyceum, no less. That led to the Bath Festival hook-up and then all manner of Peter Green/Noir rumours. Noir's place in rock 'n' roll history has to be that of a band who spoke of "light" groups, such as Led Zeppelin. By "light" they meant heavy on guitar, but light on percussion. According to this definition, the heavy percussion bands of the time were Chicago and Peter's favourites, Santana.

Noir – three Jamaicans and a Ghanaian – were black Londoners with attitude. Prototype rappers, they were hoping to spend time in the Congo playing with local drummers, rather like Mick Fleetwood would some ten years later with his *The Visitor* project, and they wrote songs attacking "the system". The system, they maintained, was a music business which only allows one black group to get through every ten years or so. Noir were determined to be the next Big Black Thing, and could well have been that until their manager tried to do it on the back of Peter Green.

The day after the Roundhouse gig, when Peter was reported to have joined Noir for a jam, their manager promptly told music weekly *Disc* that Noir was to be his permanent backing group, that they were currently rehearsing together and that their debut gig would be that Wednesday at London's Marquee. It was textbook Tin Pan Alley hustler stuff – tell the press something's already happened and, who knows, it might just come to be.

Peter wasn't having any of it. "I'm not playing the Marquee date," he told *Disc* from his New Malden home. "I've not spoken to their manager. I've only met two of Noir. There is a possibility that I may play with them some day but nothing has been fixed." Peter gave hot and happening Noir the freeze.

Around the same time two other characters met with more success in exploiting Peter's trusting nature. Both were musicians with name bands on the British blues scene which, by 1970, was well on the way out. Times being hard, they fastened onto the idea of starting up a small factory making African-style talking drums. The partners knew of Peter's interest in African drumming and persuaded him to stump up the capital. Not a single drum was ever produced by the company, and the backer never saw a penny of his investment again. "Some friends wanted to do this musical experiment, and they asked me if I had any money they could borrow," he sighs. "All I had in my bank account was six hundred pounds, so I lent them that. They never gave it back to me." This was but the first of many such incidents. During the course of the 1970s and 1980s a succession of till-dippers – friends, drinking partners, even lovers – came and then seemed to go when the money ran out.

This aside, June was an exhilarating month for the ex-leader, and pretty much as he had intended life after Fleetwood Mac to be. He absorbed and expended large amounts of creative energy on an extremely varied musical diet. Having spent the last three years motivating the same four musicians (with, he now says, varying degrees of success), in just one month he must have exchanged musical ideas with a couple of dozen fresh faces.

CHAPTER 12

NO WAY OUT

June 1970 was the month Peter had to complete his debut solo album *End Of The Game*. Zoot Money remembers a phone call one night: "It was Peter saying, 'Do you fancy coming down to the studio tonight? I have to complete an album for Warner-Reprise.' I answered with a very definite yes. At that point he had a deal, but I don't think he actually wanted to do any more records and had to be pilloried. I'd known Peter since the all-night jams at the Flamingo and when he called I felt very much the same way musically – that it should be a free expression of ideas. So, I arrived at the studio at ten in the evening and just played for three or four hours. There was no structure, just an exchange of ideas, and when we finished I put on my coat and said, 'See you on vinyl,' and left."

While Zoot got the impression that the album was something Peter was forced to do, guitarist John Morshead (not long out of The Aynsley Dunbar Retaliation and also taking part in the sessions) remembers that he cut a rather isolated figure in the studio: "He was in a corner by himself, very much in his own world. There was hardly any talking, just jamming. Some of it was really good and other bits were not. When I heard the actual album I remember thinking that some of the good stuff had been left off."

Bassist Alex Dmochowski, another Dunbar exile, made an altogether darker contribution to those sessions according to conga player Nigel Watson, who would collaborate with Peter on some of his early 1970s projects like the singles 'Heavy Heart' and 'Beasts Of Burden'. "That album was a battle, made under some heavy pressure from Alex," he says. "They were all totally stoned all of the time. It was like a competition with Peter and Alex each trying to play what they were tripping. Peter had been on medication, but Alex had got him off it and they did other drugs. All the time around then he was looking for musicians who could join him to create a new feel. The feel in *End Of The Game* was very introspective: Peter was trying to find out what was making him scream, musically."

The pushy musicians around Peter can't have helped his state of mind. Alex had high hopes around that time of persuading Peter to form a "supergroup" with him called Horsepower, but after much vacillating Peter knocked the idea on the head after someone blabbed to the music press and the rumour became front-page news.

From the moment Peter left Fleetwood Mac everybody wanted a piece of him: all he wanted was a bit of peace. Sick and very tired of the big time, he was content to play low-profile gigs with Nick Buck (formerly of Hot Tuna), whereas when many who Peter had regarded as friends saw him, they saw dollar signs on the horizon. This made him cynical, suspicious and eventually paranoid. Sadly, the transformation from a sparky, trusting and pure person, to a disillusioned shell of his former self happened in no time at all. The change is brought into focus by the optimism clearly heard in his voice during one of his last BBC shows with Mac, as he told DJ Brian Matthews, excitedly, about his plans for the future: "The main reason [I'm leaving Mac] – there are many little reasons – is that I feel it's time for a change and there are a lot of things that I want to do. I'm not sure if I'll form another band: if I found a perfect situation I might do that. But if anyone's planning any free festivals, non-profit making, or if anybody's got any ideas for charity work I'd be interested to know more about them."

Up to this point in the interview Brian Matthews sounds just a touch patronising, however his tone is definitely perplexed as he asks, "You don't want to really earn a living from music?" to which Peter, polite as ever, replies, "That is necessary so I can keep alive and have instruments and amplifiers – so I'll earn money from records, which is the main thing, to make lots of LPs. I've got lots of ideas for that and the first thing I'm going to do as soon as I've finished with Fleetwood Mac is make my own LP." Peter then introduces his song 'Sandy Mary' as one of the numbers he may include on that debut album: he didn't, but Cliff Bennett did subsequently release it as a single.

As Zoot Money sees it, "*End Of The Game* was some kind of last statement that music should always be that way. That way to Peter was after drugs, much religious searching and some revelation. The positive side of what happened to Peter then, and I think he was a great example, is John McLaughlin. John had some kind of revelation as to what he should be doing with music instead of adopting and assimilating other people's styles. He's gone along a path which embodies the way he lives, his beliefs, and also the way he plays."

The title of the album was a pun inspired by Alex Dmochowski, which refers more to the hapless plight of near extinct species of animals or jungle mammals, than to the world-weary *ennui* of a guitar hero. In Peter's eyes the open-ended project failed. "There wasn't enough there," he admits. "When I was editing it, I found out that there wasn't enough to make up a record: it was only free form. The jungle idea wasn't mine – I'd already written about that with 'Before The Beginning'. My idea of a jungle is the Indian jungle where the elephants quietly work – in the African jungle they run around screaming."

Although the term *avant-garde* is often used by critics to talk up what they feel is incomprehensible rubbish, *End Of The Game* really was ahead of its time. Today bits of the album could be edited down to make a good acid-house dance single, while other bits would now be called ambient, or new age. But in 1970 the best that *Melody Maker* could say was that it was "certainly the most disturbing album release this year".

Following a summer spent gigging with Nick Buck, Peter agreed to visit the keyboardist in New Orleans in the autumn, after he had checked out a Free College he'd been told about in Vermont and hooked up with some musician friends in Boston. Andrew Kastner, now a guitarist with LA soul-funk band Jack Mack And The Heart Attack, then had a local band called The Act. He had first met Peter when Peter was with Fleetwood Mac playing at the Boston Tea Party. Kastner remembers jamming with him, following him all over the place and how, one morning after a night's playing, he found Peter outside on the steps of the house happily jamming with the birds as they sang their dawn chorus: "That knocked me out to see this awesome guitar player trading licks with the birds!"

What was less invigorating for Andrew, however, was to see how the whole rock star experience had left Peter so deeply disillusioned about the music business: "We had one conversation where he told me that if he had known what working in this line would be like he wouldn't have done it.

Either he was talking about the business side, or being in a band, I don't know, but it was during the time they were making *Live In Boston*. My dream then was to do what he was doing and I found what he said pretty heavy because I was a young, naive person. Even so, having thought about what he said I decided to give it a try anyway!"

Around the time of his stay with Andrew Kastner and friends, Peter also spent some time at the Godard Free College in Vermont. The term "free" is a little ironic, as Stan Webb wryly points out "because it was full of extremely rich kids – doctors' sons and daughters". Chicken Shack on tour in the States at that time bumped into Peter there: "We landed on this strip of tarmac which they called an airport and there was this reception party standing around a big table with champagne on it waiting for us. When we got to the college the first person we see, lo and behold, is Peter – and what's more he's dressed in a kaftan. I thought, 'What's happened to him?' because at one point he was so much like me, you know, a laugh with the lads and screw anything in a skirt. But now he's wearing a kaftan, holding court out on the lawn and being all philosophical, with young students hanging on his every word and looking up in admiration."

Chicken Shack bassist, Andy Silvester, also remembers a philosophical Peter at Vermont. "The morning after our gig some students were sitting out on the grass, playing some talking drums or something like that and Peter joined in with them on another drum. I can remember him giving me this long talk about the planets, the moon and 'Why are we here?' and all I could tell him was that the best thing to do is enjoy life while it lasts. Funnily enough, at the time he agreed with me about that. Before this it was me who went to him with questions: I always found him very helpful and able to give me good advice. He was always so positive, and powerful. But what seemed to be happening was that, while he was very coherent, he was becoming negative."

Peter enjoyed his stay at Godard. "You could do whatever you liked there," he says. "You could spend your time doing whatever you liked. Some people were making candles, while others were just wandering around. I was one of those who were just wandering around. They had a music room where I used to play my guitar nearly every day. They had a stage and touring groups came and played – Rod Stewart, Savoy Brown, The Faces and Duster Bennett – and the kids who were there could play their instruments with the groups for a while."

When he left the college, he flew down to New Orleans to stay with Nick Buck and it was during what should have been a pleasant social visit that something sinister happened to Peter totally by chance and totally in-keeping with the cultist early 1970s, when brainwashing was regarded as kind of hip. At that particular stage, Peter needed it like a hole in the head. It's something that he will still bring up out of the blue in conversation, using phrases like "the night someone stole my soul". "I was with Nick in New Orleans," he recalls, sounding bewildered, "and we went round to this guy's flat. He was rolling weed and we were happily smoking. Eventually Nick decided to go, and I should have left with him, but the guy said I should stay. I did – I don't know why. I was captured by this bloke. He said he was a warlock – a male witch – and although I was tired, I still couldn't get away from him. He just kept on asking me questions. I couldn't find an answer to any of them. He was staring right at me, asking me more questions and I stayed until we saw the sunrise. I don't think I ever saw Nick Buck again." Nine years later in an interview with Steve Clarke of *NME*, around the time Peter's comeback album *In The Skies* came out on PVK, Peter brought up this same incident. As he remembered it then, the warlock – who previously had been a professional guitarist – wasn't asking the questions, he was giving all the answers and the gist of his message was that Peter should give up the selfish life of being a musician to concentrate on mending fences with his long-neglected friends.

Back in England in the late autumn, Peter seemed unaffected by the New Orleans brainwasher. One of the first things he did was to get in touch with Andy Silvester, with his mind set on forming a new band. Andy recalls, "After Pete had left, the rest of Fleetwood Mac moved into their communal country house, Benifold. Pete invited me and Dave Bidwell [The Muskrats and Chicken Shack's original drummer, sadly deceased] down for a jam, apparently with a view to forming a band. It was really embarrassing for me and Dave because Mick and Jenny Fleetwood, and John and Christine were there at the time. We went into this music room to play together: it didn't lead anywhere and I think it was then that he realised he couldn't really improve on the rhythm section he'd already had with Mick and John. I don't know what he was trying to achieve really. It was like he was trying for something that didn't exist, or perhaps that did exist but was above everyone else's heads. After a while he gave up and turned it into a joke – he put one of his favourite jokey voices, which was like an old cowboy, saying, 'Heh, heh, dis whirl ain't big 'nuff fer you an' me boy, heh, heh!' And so he went on in that voice until it got on your nerves a bit."

Peter also remembers this awkward social situation he masterminded – not for its awkwardness, mind you, but as one big laugh with Dave Bidwell: "Dave and me just couldn't stop laughing – don't know what it was but we just kept looking at each other and laughing." Sour grapes and pique must have figured to some extent in Peter's strange sortie to Mac's house of all places, although the event must have left him in rather a depressing quandary: one by one, the perfect scenarios he had conjured up in his imagination, to parry the blow when Mac wouldn't go along with his charity band notions, were turning into pipedreams. So what next?

Well, he returned a favour to drummer Godfrey Maclean who played on the *End Of The Game* sessions by helping out on a couple of tracks on Godfrey's soul-jazz band album, *Juju*. As 1970 drew to a close he teamed up with Alex Dmochowski, jazz sax session man Ray Warleigh, former Graham Bond Initiation, Brian Auger and Warm Dust drummer Keith Bailey, for a few London pub gigs. This band didn't work out as Peter had hoped and in 1971 he was reported to be looking for musicians to play on a second solo album scheduled for March, which would feature vocal tracks like 'Sandy Mary'.

The hand of fate, however, was soon to intervene. Out of the blue, Peter got a phone call from Clifford Davis in Los Angeles, who was on tour with the Kiln House line-up of Fleetwood Mac. Mid tour Jeremy Spencer had debunked to join the Children of God and Clifford was calling to ask whether Peter would come over and save his old band from financial ruin by playing for the last six weeks of contracted gigs. Peter agreed, but on two conditions: first, that conga player Nigel Watson would accompany him and second that there would be no Fleetwood Mac's greatest hits nonsense on stage, they would jam from start to finish. Though this thought horrified the band they acquiesced: as they say, when you're up to your neck in alligators, it's easy to forget about getting stuck in the swamp.

Nigel Watson remembers the scene in mid February after Peter got the SOS: "We took a flight from Heathrow at two in the afternoon and got to Los Angeles fourteen hours later. Clifford [at that point also Nigel's brother-in-law] met us and drove us straight to the Swing Stadium at San Bernadino for the gig. They rehearsed in the dressing room for half an hour, then went out and did the gig. Afterwards we all got absolutely pissed. Peter could have played all the old Fleetwood Mac numbers but he just didn't want to do that. His attitude was 'If they want Peter Green, they'll do the music I now want to do'. Once they got into the tour, Peter began to take the leading role for the whole gig, which annoyed Danny Kirwan who felt overshadowed."

Nigel remembers one occasion in the dressing room, after a gig where Mac were headliners on a bill including Van Morrison, when Danny threw a bottle of beer over Peter because he was so jealous. Peter just laughed it off. "It wasn't that Peter was out to put Danny down on stage," he says. "He just played around him trying to egg him on. But Danny didn't have the fire, or the skills of improvisation and so he got very frustrated."

Danny, by then twenty-one years old, was already pretty lost in a drink and drugs wasteland. Jenny Boyd noticed a big change in him after Peter left, when a lot of pressure fell squarely on his, always rather paranoiacally hunched, shoulders: "At first, Danny was like a son: he used to come and have supper with Mick and me a lot in our flat at Benifold. He was like a little Peter Pan. Once Peter had left and they were all rehearsing at Kiln House, it was pretty stressful because they didn't know if they could make it as Fleetwood Mac on their own. Danny suddenly started having these total outbursts and tantrums that had no grounding to them at all – a side of him would just kick in and be totally inappropriate to the situation. I think drugs and alcohol got Danny totally nuts in the end. He was just too sensitive a soul."

Peter's six-weeks as a "ringer" came to a climax at the Fillmore East in New York when he took the place by storm with a four-hour improvised version of 'Black Magic Woman'. Until then he'd kept a low profile on stage, occasionally indulging in a bit of irreverence (like calling the audience "Yankee bastards"). That night at the Fillmore he was more upfront and promoter Bill Graham almost had a riot when he tried to end the gig at midnight. The guitarist finally ran out of ideas, or rather the stamina to play them, at four am. Although John McVie now remembers that kind of jamming as "invigorating", at the time he confessed, "We were scared stiff. We'd go onstage every night, look at the audience and didn't have a clue what we were going to play."

Mick Fleetwood has since spoken of the band being "bored out of our minds" playing the music that Peter wanted to play, so there was never really any question that the tour was just a stopgap. "After the US tour," Nigel Watson continues, "when Jeremy Spencer disappeared, Mac all went home and we stayed on for a month to visit San Francisco, Nevada and Denver, Colorado. In San Francisco we stayed at Mike Shreeves's [Santana's drummer] house in Mill Valley and one day we got chatting to a half Indian guy called Hank from Nevada who made moccasins for a living. He invited us up to stay at his cabin in the woods past Sacramento, where he taught us a lot about survival out in the wild. It was this visit to Nevada that inspired the song 'Beasts Of Burden' [recorded and released in mid 1972]. Peter had always loved animals and, especially after his experiences in the music business, had reach the conclusion that he much preferred them to humans. At least animals sniff you out before making friends. People smile in your face and tear your bollocks off with the other hand. That's how Peter saw it."

On his return from America, Peter spent time applying for jobs at London Zoo and Chessington, but was turned down because of his lack of qualifications. Then, during 1971 he stayed with two friends – Adrian and Lynn Boot – at their house near Surbiton. Adrian, now a photographer, was then a chemistry student at Surrey University. He, Peter and others were not averse to the occasional highly-controlled experiment with lysergic acid diethylamide: "I met Peter through a circle of friends and for some time I didn't know who he was. He was looking for somewhere to stay, so we let him stay at our maisonette in Lovelace Lane. He was with us for nearly a year – he taught me to drive in the time. I was a student and did odd jobs during the holidays. One summer I worked as a gardener at Mortlake cemetery, which was how I got Peter the job there. He didn't play very much then, but was still very interested in listening to music, although his taste in music then was *totally* uncommercial: African music, Etta James, Donny Hathaway."

It was no surprise that Peter admired Donny Hathaway, the young black American, whose material melded Beethoven and gospel. In Hathaway he saw qualities he felt were lacking in himself: a highly trained musician and accomplished pianist who, although he came from the classical school, became a session musician at Chess Studios. Donny's musical vision in summer 1971, was to take the musical colours he'd glimpsed in Ravel, Debussy and Bach, and make use of them in both an acid-rock and country and western format. Attitude like this blew Peter's mind.

"It was clear," Adrian reflects, "that he was disillusioned about so many things. The fact that he couldn't get a job as a zoo-keeper depressed him, but then being in a position where he couldn't do things was all part of the game. He really enjoyed working at the cemetery, because the people we were with were very eccentric people often with long and complex stories to tell. I remember a couple of Second World War casualties there. One had been a doctor before he joined up, went away to fight and had lost touch with his family for a couple of years. When he arrived back after time in a prison camp he went to where he used to live in the East End of London and all he found was bomb crater where his home used to be. He went to the pub on the corner to discover that his whole family had been wiped out, and no one had bothered to tell him. He cracked up and had been working at Mortlake ever since. Peter really identified with this guy: a professional who could, if he wanted to, do other things but found sanctuary in pushing a lawnmower round a cemetery.

"Working there was fun. We weren't hassled because there were no taskmasters and you soon got used to the grief surrounding you. It was very easy to insulate yourself from all that so one didn't feel morbid at all – it could just as well have been a park. I left at the end of the summer to return to my studies but Peter stayed on and was still working there when I returned mid term. He obviously enjoyed it: it certainly had an immensely therapeutic effect. I'm saying that now with the benefit of hindsight, because at the time I wouldn't have thought any therapy was necessary – there didn't seem to be *anything* unusual about the guy other than the fact he used to be a pop star. Okay, many people had been dropping acid, and some of them had been affected quite severely and gone completely off the rails but they were few and far between. Then there was a band of people who I guess were temporarily fazed by it all. But I wouldn't even put Peter in that category. It's quite plain to me that both musically and politically he was just too radical for his time: he wanted to use his money constructively, he wanted to get involved with running a zoo, he was interested in all sorts of causes in Africa and Third World development. It was a Live Aid syndrome, but ahead of its time and as thinking like that wasn't at all fashionable then, everybody thought he was a lunatic."

Adrian recalls their experiments with drugs as always being under very controlled conditions. "We were all science students and terribly cautious as to what we took. I think what Peter wasn't able to get when he needed it most was somebody he could respect and talk to. At that point he didn't like any formal religion – he was spiritual but not really religious. Also, I never regarded his decision to quit the music business as at all odd; having worked in the business I could see it was really *only* about money. So I thought it was far more important for him to do what made him happy."

It was while Peter was staying with the Boots in Surbiton that he got the call to replace Jeremy temporarily. Before going out to America he'd been in the De Lane Lea studios, Holborn, along with Nigel, Snowy White and others for a week of jamming from which his first solo single was taken – a sombre instrumental called 'Heavy Heart' b/w 'No Way Out'. It was released in June, and the critics had a field-day rubbishing this seven-inch paradox – a cavalierly uncommercial single.

Peter himself recalls vividly the night before he joined Adrian as a gardener at Mortlake: "With things like acid and mescaline it's so easy to go on a trip and it should be easy enough to come back afterwards. But after one trip I took on some stuff called Sunshine, I had such a ridiculously good time all night long. When the morning came, I came down off it a bit hard. I'd decided the night before that I was always going to feel this good. I would get a motorbike and go round visiting friends and roll joints and smoke ganja weed and grass. I bought the motorbike, but I didn't really go round and see anybody much. That made me realise that it was going to be harder than I thought staying on the trip."

Madge Jones – the Madge of 'Searching' and 'Fighting For' on the *Then Play On* album – was staying with a girlfriend in London at this time. One afternoon Peter knocked on the door, paying them a social call. "We were both really surprised," Madge recalls, "to see him after all this time. He was wearing a biker's jacket and looking far more macho than I remembered him in the early blues band days. He had really changed as a person as well. He sat down, started to roll a joint and began talking about politics, world problems and things like that. Very soon I could see that the things he was saying really rubbed my friend up the wrong way. I couldn't believe how he'd changed from a shy, polite person into this arrogant, opinionated sort of guy. In the end my friend virtually had to ask him to leave."

Bob Brunning, who didn't know Peter as a drug-taker, also received a visit from him during his biker stage: "After Peter and I had done the Dave Kelly solo album, I was really disturbed by what I saw. I rang him to tell him the album was out and invited him round to our house. He came in saying, 'I don't want to hear the record – let's go down the pub instead.' I just couldn't believe it. He'd come across on his motorbike, all macho, but it just didn't sit right. We went down the pub and talked, but he clearly didn't want to talk about music. He said he'd given away all his guitars, didn't want to play music, and didn't want to talk about it. Peter was always a very sensitive guy and you could see that it was all going wrong."

The Dave Kelly sessions that Bob Brunning is referring to took place only a year earlier and Dave himself remembers a very affable Peter at the Philips studios in Marble Arch: "It was just after he'd done his *End Of The Game* album which I always thought was absolutely brilliant. I remember he arrived at the studio in his white Jaguar XK150, with his girlfriend Sandra who proceeded to get on with her needlework as we played – a real hippy scene! Peter asked me what I wanted him to do and I explained. He was very helpful, very constructive in the studio and a charming man. We recorded two tracks, one of which we didn't in fact use in the end, because of, let's call them 'external pressures'. Philips must still have that one in their vaults."

In June 1971, just before the summer and autumn he spent working at Mortlake, Peter recorded one track for the all-star BB King *Live In London* sessions, 'Caledonia'. BB now remembers "a disillusioned and very quiet Peter in the studio who didn't say much at all; but I got the feeling that he just seemed to find it a comfort sitting near to me for a while." Following that, Peter found time to record 'Beasts Of Burden' b/w 'Uganda Woman' with Nigel Watson, although it would be almost a year before the record was released as a single. 'Beasts Of Burden' is obviously written by a very angry young man: angry at the contradictions and hypocrisies of the developed western world, and drawn to the simplicity and harshness of primitive life in other continents. The first verse read: "Creatures dying, vultures flying, songbirds singing, hyenas laughing, ageing horses who gave all they had to give, beasts of burden who worked for the right to live." 'Uganda Woman' is a musical reference to the basic beauty found in an image of a black woman walking along, carrying a pot of water on her head.

Peter encouraged Nigel to join him in his pursuit of primitivism: "We once spent a few days sleeping rough in the New Forest. I'd come back early from the Fleetwood Mac 'Bare Tree' autumn 1972 US tour. Danny had been fired by then and I was blown out by all the weird scenes going on in the group. Peter and I spent three days in the woods living off our wits. We killed a rabbit for something to eat, gutted it, ate it and were promptly sick. We communicated to each other by whistling and tried to be as one with nature: we swam in the river and had tick-checks. It was all a bit of a game really because when we got *really* hungry we nipped off to the nearest shop!"

Soon afterwards, Nigel hospitalised himself, having developed the muscle trembles symptomatic of Parkinson's disease. Eventually this was proven to be psychosomatic, something which he regards as the after-effects of life on the road: "I spent three months in hospital, blown and trying to recover from my music business experiences. For me, as for several others, Fleetwood Mac was too much, too quickly: one minute I was laying down carpets for a job, and next thing I know I'm in Los Angeles playing in front of thousands in a football stadium. A bit mindblowing really."

For Peter 1972 saw a continuation of his gradual retreat from the music business and the insidious approach of depression and nervous exhaustion – a condition which would be exacerbated over the following two years by Draconian medical treatment. At one point, in the summer of that year, he looked set to replace the late Les Harvey as guitarist in Maggie Bell's Stone The Crows (Harvey had been electrocuted on stage in Swansea the year before). Maggie described what happened, to *Mojo* magazine in May 1994: "We picked him up at the station. He had a rucksack and his hair cut really short. He looked very healthy. We were supposed to do the Lincoln festival in May and we spent six weeks rehearsing at keyboard player Ronnie Leahy's house. Peter played so well right through rehearsals, and then two days before the festival we got a phone call to say he couldn't make it."

Peter's departure from the business for what turned out to be six years came in January 1973 when, uncredited, he helped Fleetwood Mac on one track of the *Penguin* album. The song in question was a Bob Welch composition 'Night Watch' (Californian Welch had replaced Jeremy Spencer in spring 1971). Welch made an interesting observation about Peter around the time of that session. "Bob called me a chicken-killer," Peter points out obviously amused. "I guess what he meant by that was that I never played with musicians who were as good as me. I always played with chickens that I could kill!"

CHAPTER 13

LADY'S MAN: A JEWISH HIPPY'S LOVE STORY

Peter's all-or-nothing intensity, a quality believers would describe as typically Scorpionic, fired several of his love affairs in every sense. In the Peter B's, the earnest nineteen-year-old popped the question to Beryl Marsden at a stage in the relationship when she was quite happy just kissing on the back seat driving to and from gigs. Once he was a rock star, too many temptations and distractions presented themselves on the road for his long-standing relationship with Sandra Elsdon-Vigon to survive. As his health vacillated in the early 1970s he needed an angel. Luckily he met one in 1971.

A nice Jewish girl whose middle-class parents had emigrated from Iraq to live in a suburb of London, she was there when hospitalisation – and it's debilitating medication – put the man everyone once knew as Peter Green in limbo. She was there when Peter returned from his first blitz of ECT (electro-convulsive therapy) which left him in a state of distraction: he would mutter the start of a sentence, pause, and then perhaps finish it forty-five minutes later. Yet having gone through all this with him, she called the whole thing off two days before their wedding late in September 1975, and with Peter's tacit agreement walked out. For the first time in their four-year on-off relationship, the instinct for self-survival got the better of her. The lady in question would prefer not to be named, so let's call her just that – Lady.

Back in the late 1960s, one Saturday in summer she was walking through Hyde Park to the sounds of Pink Floyd billowing in the distance as they performed a free concert. It was a fateful moment: "When I saw what was going on I thought it was fantastic and the following Monday I rang *The Daily Telegraph* information office to find out who'd organised it. I was told Blackhill Enterprises. I went along to see them and offered my services for free for the first six months. One of the first events I organised for them – Andrew King and Peter Jenner – was 'Stones In The Park'. We'd put Blind Faith on the month before and Mick Jagger came backstage to suss it all out. A few days later his agent phoned and gave us about three or four weeks to organise it, which was plenty."

Lady helped to organise the free festival at Parliament Hill, where Peter and Fleetwood Mac had tried to play, before crowd violence brought proceedings to a halt: "I didn't even stay for their performance because at that point we were a bit anti-bluesy at Blackhill. My band was Edgar Broughton and although I'd listened to a lot of blues at college we were more into underground. The Third Ear Band were on that bill: it was pouring with rain until they came on and then suddenly it stopped, so of course as spaced-out hippies we all took that as a sign from God, and all that rubbish!"

Not one to be in awe of famous rock stars, Lady's first meeting with Peter at Blackhill's offices in 1971 was just an everyday kind of thing: "He was living at Lynn and Adrian's [Boot] and he came along to the office perhaps to see Lynn. I think we needed a light bulb replacing in the loo and we weren't brave enough to go up there, so I asked him to do it for us. I knew who he was, but while he was fitting the light I yelled up, 'We'll have some tea while you're up there!' Perhaps he wasn't used to being treated like that, without any reverence at all. I was going out with somebody else at the time and wasn't the least bit interested in Peter; but then I wasn't going out with anybody else and suddenly I was!"

The first time Lady and Peter went out together was on a trip to Bournemouth with Lynn and Adrian. They travelled in Adrian's Mini-Moke beach buggy. It was raining and they got soaked. Peter invited Lady to stay with them at his parents' house. Peter took Lady for a walk along the seafront and proposed to her. "At that point I'd known him for about six hours, so it was incredibly strange but I thought he was really quite cute. Up until that point he knew I was Iraqi but he didn't know I was Jewish – he proposed to me when I told him I was Jewish. I think it meant quite a lot to him.

"My first impression of him that time at the office was that he was quite strange and far away and at that point I rather liked people who were strange and off-the-wall. But in conversation he was obviously all there and it's something that I've always thought about him, that he is *incredibly* intelligent but never had the education to express it."

Peter's family was totally alien to anything Lady had ever known. She was from an Iraqi Sephardic (Middle East/Spanish/Portuguese Jews) Jewish family, which she describes as the lower of the two types of Judaism. "Because I was brought up in north-west London in a predominantly Jewish area I rebelled against it and very rarely admitted I was Jewish," she says. "I didn't like the typical north-west London Jewishness and wanted to be as far away from that as possible. But I'd gone to a direct grant school and had a very nice family who gave me everything, financially and emotionally. So I found it very strange that a boy should be subsidising his parents – not necessarily wrong, but completely alien. He told me that his father had given up work the moment that Peter had made his first large sum of money: he went off sick with a bad back or something!"

Though intense, Peter was witty with a dry sense of humour which appealed to Lady and she was soon drawn to him. "At the time I think he took to me because I was quite a sort of down person: quite boring, mundane and ordinary. Although I'd worked in the music business we *never* spoke about that, or about his experiences. What he wanted from me was my ordinariness."

The only time Lady can remember Peter's past catching up with him was during a visit to Hale, Cornwall. The couple were having a drink in a pub when someone came up to Peter and said, "You're Peter Green aren't you?" Peter grabbed him by the lapels and said, "What of it?" Then Peter and Lady left.

So, Peter had at last found a supportive Jewish non-Princess, as she describes herself. Between 1971 and 1975 theirs would be a stormy relationship with several final partings followed by as many impassioned reconciliations. Very early in the relationship she twigged that the Green household was zany in the extreme: "Compared to my parents, it was like a mad family. His father looked like Alf Garnett, sounded like Alf Garnett and said the same sort of things as Alf Garnett. At midday he'd come down in his pyjamas and dressing-gown, take the cover off the green parrot's cage, and start dancing around the lounge with the parrot which squawked in a way that terrified me. Meanwhile their dog, a Border collie, would get in on the act by humping Joe's leg as he waltzed round the room. I honestly used to think it was all quite insane."

Peter and Lady bought a house together in Ham, although they didn't stay together long after that. For most of their relationship they would rent places or stay at Peter's house with other members of his family.

Within weeks of them coming together she witnessed the selfless philanthropy that eventually got him locked up: "He wrote out a cheque to War On Want for eighty thousand pounds. I couldn't believe it. Perhaps he was testing me to see if I was after him for his money. Before he sent the cheque he asked me to ring round all the charities asking them how much they spent on administration and what percentage actually went to the needy. So, when I first knew him he didn't have any money left. Occasionally, when the pair of us were really broke, we'd actually go and do something. Sometimes a letter would arrive with a royalty cheque for a thousand pounds and we'd breathe a huge sigh of relief because we could eat properly!"

Manager Clifford Davis obtained films from people like War On Want so that Peter could see how his money would be used. "Clifford showed me some films," Peter reflects, "showing where a lot of the money was spent on teaching people in starving countries new methods of agriculture so that they could grow their own crops. But I didn't think that was the best thing for me to give my money to: I thought I should give them food supplies." The size of the sum was apparently decided when Peter went to WOW's offices. He would point to an area on the globe and ask how much it would cost to put things right there.

Peter's trip to Israel to work on a kibbutz also came quite early on in his relationship with Lady. "How it came about was so typical of him," she remembers. "He literally woke up one morning and told me he had to go to Israel to be with his people. After I'd recovered from the shock, I understood completely. So, off he went. After a few weeks a postcard arrived from him with two lovebirds on it – which the dog almost chewed up on the mat – and on it he'd written that I was the only 'real person' he'd ever met, but that he had to stay on and be with his race. He ended the note saying he was thinking of joining the PLO. When he got back I discovered why: he'd gone to work on a kibbutz and they hadn't let him drive the tractor! He also said he'd really enjoyed sitting on the edge of the desert watching the nomadic Arabs and felt more akin to them. He actually ended up really hating the Israelis." What Peter enjoyed most about his time on the kibbutz was the work routine: starting work at first light and finishing at dusk.

During this time, 1972/3, when Peter's illness really started to take hold, Lynn and Adrian Boot were spending a year in Jamaica. When they returned in 1974, Lynn especially was astounded by the deterioration in his condition: "He had put on so much weight because of the medication and just walked around like a zombie all the time. Whatever they did to him it was appalling."

Mich Reynolds also spent time with him during this period: "It wasn't a nervous breakdown – it was a slow decline. I spent many evenings with him and sometimes he wouldn't talk at all – just observe people or observe me talking to people. He'd sit in silence, hair all over the place, and a lot of the time I thought he was taking the piss out of people. It was difficult to know when he was doing it for effect and when he couldn't actually help it. For example, I took him out shopping one day because his mother said he needed some new clothes – he'd put on weight by then. I took him to Wimbledon and we went into a café to get something to eat. When we came out he started to imitate an ape as we were crossing the road: he stood in the middle of the road just laughing at everybody looking at him. It was obvious he was doing it for effect, but then later when I lived at Longmeade he couldn't always control his thoughts and actions. He once swore that he saw a spaceship at the bottom of the garden coming towards him before disappearing. Much, much later he said he kept seeing things crawling up the walls."

Peter and Lady never tried to make out to each other that everything was all right and that it would all miraculously somehow come right in the end. They tried to confront his illness whenever possible, but in time this became very distressing for Lady to have to deal with: "There was something wrong with him – we both knew that. There would be long loaded silences and a change of mood from the start of a sentence to the end of it, not all the time but at pretty regular intervals. One moment he'd be talking and loving me with every word that he spoke, but before he got to the end of the sentence he hated me. And I had no idea why. I hadn't physically moved or thought of anything or done anything to be loved or hated. But to get all those emotions within a period of fifteen seconds was really hard. Another time we'd had this great reunion where everything was wonderful and we'd gone out for a meal. Peter decided to have a really hot curry, so hot that the waiters were advising him against it. He seemed to change after he had this curry. We went back to the house and were looking at some books about Red Indians – Peter was very interested in Red Indians and how they lived so close to nature. We were sharing a chair and both looking at this book when he suddenly got up and said, 'I hate your sort of person,' went up to the bedroom and moved the wardrobe in front of the door in case I tried to get in. This was in one of the houses he shared with his parents. I put up with all of this because I really, really loved him and we both hoped that it wouldn't be like that forever."

But comic relief also sometimes sprang out of Peter's erratic mood swings: "We rented a cottage in Cornwall for a few months and spent one hilarious Christmas there. That Christmas eve he went out and left me on my own, then at two or three in the morning he came back and said, 'I've got your Christmas present.' I got all excited. Then he brought in this cauliflower he'd nicked from the fields nearby!

"The day before we'd gone into Penzance to buy a turkey. I'd never cooked a Christmas dinner before but I struggled on as best I could. I got up really early in the morning to cook it – you know, with all the trimmings. I put it all on the table and proudly announced, 'Christmas lunch is ready, Peter!' He just looked at me and said, 'I think we should be vegetarian.' So I picked the turkey up, opened the front door and threw it out into the garden."

When Peter was first hospitalised at West Park, Epsom, in 1974, daily phone calls to his partner were just about his only brush with sanity: "I was staying at a friend's house while they were away. I'd just moved in and Peter was going to come over that night. He didn't turn up and I had no idea what was wrong. The next day was my birthday. Peter phoned me and said he was in a mental hospital in Epsom. After that he phoned me every evening. I wanted to go and see him, but he categorically would not let me. I later found out that he'd been committed by a Dr Tintner who his mother had worked for."

Peter recalls the events that led to him being hospitalised: "They tricked me into agreeing to go to a nice place where Jewish boys and girls would be and then took me to the hospital in Epsom – the madhouse. Dr

Tintner was in my house and, I don't remember the exact words he said, but it was something like, 'I've got this place I'd like to take you to tomorrow. I'll pick you up.' I said, 'What sort of place?' and he said, 'Oh, you know, young boys and girls there.' Anyway I went down with him and next thing I knew I was stuck there and eventually they gave me ECT. They gave me injections and tranquillisers. I could hardly walk, or keep my eyes open. I felt terrible there."

Even so, his indefatigable and dry sense of humour didn't fail him, as Nigel Watson recalls: "When I went to see him at West Park the first thing he said when he saw me was, 'Christ, you ain't in here as well are you?' Then, still thinking I was also a patient, he said we could have fun and he started singing that pop song 'Knock Three Times (On The Ceiling If You Want Me)'. You could see he was well out of it on the medication they were pumping into him – like in a trance."

"I don't think he had shock treatment initially," Lady continues, "because Peter told me that at West Park they laced the puddings and syrup with a drug to keep everybody quiet. I'd be talking to him on the phone and suddenly he'd go quiet then say somebody had come up and stared right into his face. It really scared him. I knew that if he was really scared by this then he shouldn't be in there: it's a place for those who are too far gone to feel fear. I just knew that there was no way that Peter was insane. Around then we went through quite a lot of break-ups: he'd go away or go abroad, then come back. My brother had just bought a chemist's shop and I went in to help. Peter must have been an out-patient by then because he was having ECT at St Thomas's in London, which was like a couple of hundred yards away from the shop. Very often he'd come to the shop after he'd had the treatment and I couldn't believe it: he just stood there, like, for hours with his arms slightly in front and in a trance, telling me how very frightened of it he was."

Lady and Peter continued their relationship while all this was going on, but slowly she realised, ironically, that she was fighting a losing battle with the doctors. He was responding – if that's the right word – to the treatment by becoming more and more docile. The loaded silences between the couple grew longer and more intense, and things felt more and more strained.

Increasingly fazed by events, the couple none the less decided to throw in their lot together and buy a house in Ham near Richmond, a place where they might be able to get on with their own lives. Even better news was the fact that they'd decided to get married in September 1975: "I remember the day we had decided we were going to get married. We went downstairs and Peter said, 'Mum, I've got something to tell you. We've decided we're going to get married.' Because she had at least pretended that she liked me I thought she would have given a nice response. I'll never forget what she said: 'Dad and I will have to cut down on the phone and the other bills then.' The implication was obviously that I was out to cop the readies and Peter would stop the payments to them once we were married. I was so hurt. When Peter's parents met mine, though, she must have seen that my family were not exactly strapped for cash."

A date was set – 6 September 1975 – and plans for the wedding went ahead with the Rabbi of the bride's synagogue, who at one point took her to one side and advised her against taking the big step. Of course, outwardly this only strengthened her resolve, or so she thought: "Then, two days before the wedding, we were sitting in our lounge, watching the yachts sailing past on the Thames. Suddenly there was a loaded silence for nothing that I was aware of having done and looking out of the window again, I saw a stupid gold aura thing that came out of the river and into our lounge window. Written on it was, 'Go home to your parents.' I wasn't in the least bit astounded when I saw this: it was a message from God. I very quietly went upstairs, packed a few things, came down and told Peter I was leaving him. I asked him if he'd mind driving me back to my parents' house and he very calmly said, 'Not at all.' He didn't try to fight it and we didn't argue. He must have seen it too. My father was so calm about it and accepted everything, but my mother went hysterical, probably at the thought of the wedding having to be called off with two days to go."

To this day Peter remains the Iraqi lady's great love, even if the relationship was virtually doomed from the start. Watching her go about her work at Blackhill's offices, Peter had handed her a note. It read: "The depression you try to escape from/Is your lonely soul's broken heart/Realising its mistake, and crying/You are torn between the tragic truth of a lost soul/And the falseness you have been led to believe is your way of life/I choose the first to be my *self*/If you look hard and deep you will see it in all man/If you don't see it – you will see madness."

CHAPTER 14

WHAT AM I DOING HERE?

When the so-called shotgun incident story broke, the national press made a meal of it. Fleet Street could not have wished for an easier target at whom they could direct that day's fickle finger of scorn: "Pop Star: Free Me From My Cash" read the headline on an inside page of *The Daily Express* on 27 January 1977. The article, which was as accurate as it was understated, used a formula of journalese that would repeat itself when even nastier men of the press began to stalk Peter in the late 1980s. The *Express* piece read: "Peter Greenbaum, who was lead guitarist with Fleetwood Mac, has been arrested following a row over thirty thousand pounds that he did not want...He was so desperate to stop the payments that he had to be arrested at the office of accountant Clifford Adams in Paddington last month...Green admitted having a pump-action .22 rifle without a firearms certificate at the accountant's address. He denied threatening to damage Mr Adams' office and no evidence was offered...The guitarist's father said at his home in Canvey Island: 'The magistrate made the right decision. Peter definitely needs help. He must have given away tens of thousands. He would help the whole world if he could. He lives in an Alice-in-Wonderland world of his own.'"

This piece in the *Express* prompted more press reaction, which was a pity because it contained some crucial inaccuracies. There was no confrontation at the accountant's office – whose correct name was David Simmons (Clifford Adams being a pseudonym for Clifford Davis, Peter's manager). It is also debatable whether the crux of the story – the thirty thousand pounds that Peter was supposedly desperate to return – is a fair representation of what actually was going on at the time.

John Junor – subsequently knighted for his brand of hard-hitting and responsible journalism – took the story in *The Daily Express* at face value and went on to add injury to insult in his *Sunday Express* column that weekend. Aptly entitled "Careless Talk", Junor wrote: "The Fleetwood Mac pop group was never exactly a household name, and it has been nearly six years since Peter Greenbaum stopped being the group's lead guitarist. Yet a court is told that even today Greenbaum is receiving thirty thousand pounds a year in royalties for past recordings. Greenbaum seems to be an eccentric. He didn't want any money from his past. He tried to have it stopped. He had a row with his accountant and brandished a gun, which was why he appeared in court. The court's decision was that he should be admitted for treatment to a mental hospital. But when the economy of our country is so balanced that a minor pop guitarist can earn thirty thousand pounds a year for recordings he did six years ago, isn't it the rest of us who should be in a nuthouse?"

However, the damage had been done. The tale was now a news story and in the normal run of things, would eventually mature into legend. Chris Salewicz of the *NME* wrote a more informative and considered piece a week later (5 February 1977): "Appearing under his real name of Peter Greenbaum, former Fleetwood Mac guitarist Peter Green (thirty) was last Wednesday, at Marylebone Court, committed for treatment at a mental hospital. This followed an incident last month when Green was arrested following a row with accountant Clifford Adams at his Westbourne Park address over Green's demands that royalty payments from his hit records be stopped. Amounts involved are in the region of thirty thousand pounds a year. Green admitted having a pump-action rifle without a firearms certificate, but denied threatening to damage windows at Adams' West End offices. In his defence David Bray told the court that since his client left the group in 1971, 'It appears there have been some difficulties and his attitude is that he wishes to make his own way through life rather than make use of any royalties from his past records.' Making the hospital order, Sir Ivor Rigby told Green, 'I hope you understand that I am really only interested in trying to help you.' Since Green decided to quit in 1970 this was not the first time that he spent time in a hospital. The stories that have filtered out in the media about Green's existence since he left Mac have been appropriately colourful: Green going to work as a gravedigger, Green playing in a pub band in Southend, Green flying out to Los Angeles with only a one-way ticket, getting sent back, buying another ticket (return this time) in London and going back again. The reality, as might be expected, is less romantic. As old associates of Green's who have still remained in touch with him tell it, a picture of him emerges that is considerably different from the legend. Apart from the odd days when he'd return to stay at the home near Southend, which he bought his former postman father, his life has been one of dossing around London sleeping on music business acquaintances' floors.

"Always penniless, he apparently considers his royalty money to be 'unclean', he is apparently well into passing off demands that he should pay large phone bills, and asking friends to buy larger houses so that he may live there as part of his 'hippy' philosophy. Of late, in addition to having declared that the coalman's life was the one for him, Green has become even more obsessed with his 'Jewishness' than he was in the years immediately after leaving the band. It was then that he changed his name back to Greenbaum and visited Israel. Lately, as well as being more insistent than ever that his money should go to Jewish charities, Green has apparently been engaged on something of a desperate search for the perfect Jewish wife. He has also been particularly anxious to maintain links with other Jewish musicians. For a while he stayed with Marc Bolan. Bolan, presumably in an attempt to help Peter get himself back together, gave him a guitar. Green left it in the boot of Peter Bardens's car. At the time he was arrested at his accountant's, a warrant was also out for his arrest on various petty motoring offences. Only the other week he was so impecunious that a journalist from *Sounds* lent him ten pounds. 'People,' comments one person with whom he's being staying recently, 'say that Peter's just suffering from San Franciscoitis – that he just did too much dope – but that's not true. He doesn't smoke or do dope at all.'"

What actually happened, say Peter and his brother Len, was rather different to the headline news. Peter now has detailed recollections of events leading up to the incident, and of the telephone conversation between himself and his manager, Clifford Davis, that somehow ended up being reported as a confrontation with Peter in person at Clifford's offices "brandishing a gun".

"I'd just come back from a holiday in Canada," Peter points out, "staying with a girl I knew out there. Before I came back to England I had some money left over – about eighty dollars – and I didn't know what to spend it on. Anyway, when I was going to collect my plane ticket I passed this really good gun shop and went in. I told the guy that I had eighty dollars to spend and he said, 'You can't have a handgun because you need a licence for that, but what I have got is a pump-action .22 fairground rifle.' So I bought that and a couple of boxes of cartridges and I was on my way. It broke down into two pieces and I carried it in a cardboard box. So when I got back to England I just strolled through Customs and didn't declare it." Peter left the gun at his parents' house in Canvey Island.

"Then," Peter continues, "when I was talking to Clifford Davis on the phone, I wondered if he had any money for me because I didn't have any after the holiday. He told me he didn't, but that David Simmons had it. David Simmons was an accountant's boy – you know made coffee and things like that – and eventually he did all right and became my accountant. I remember I made the phone call from Our Price records. On the telephone to Clifford, I forget how it came out, but I said, 'I'll shoot you.' And when Clifford told me David Simmons had my money I said, 'Well, I'll shoot his windows down too,' because he had a place on a posh street in London. Clifford might have thought it was the gun I already had, which was a rather rare single-barrel twelve-bore shotgun. I never used it because there was nowhere to shoot unless you belonged to a gun club, which I didn't. But when I made the call I didn't have either gun in my possession; my mother and father were looking after them at Canvey Island. So it was an idle threat. But when Clifford asked if I was threatening him I don't remember exactly what I said – it might have been yes... it probably was.

"The next thing I know I was round a girl called Betty's house and the police knocked on the door. They said they had a warrant for my arrest for using threatening behaviour towards Mr Davis and Mr Simmons and asked me to go with them. First of all I spent a night in

Marylebone police station and then next day they took me to a jail somewhere – it could have been Wandsworth, but I'm not sure because they moved me about a bit."

In Peter's opinion though it was an idle threat: the gun was fifty miles away, still in that cardboard box, in fact he never took it out of that box. He had however smuggled the gun in and had in this respect broken the law.

While he was in prison Peter was held under observation. He subsequently failed a psychiatric test and was sent back to a hospital in Epsom. "I'd been there already," he recalls. "The thing is you're not *held* there by anything – you're *stuck* there. After the injections you haven't got the strength to walk to the toilet, never mind go home. So I stayed at the hospital until I was able to actually walk away."

Mich Reynolds, Clifford Davis's ex-wife, who now runs the Fleetwood mobile studio (still a successful enterprise some twenty years after it began operating), has remained a good friend of the Green family. In the early 1970s she tried to help Peter through his bleakest times. Mich remembers a call out of the blue at the start of 1977: "His mother phoned me to say Peter was due to appear in court and had nobody to represent him. I went to Marylebone Road and sat in the gallery. When they called his case, Peter came up looking for all the world like a tramp. They started to read the charge and I could see he honestly didn't have a clue where he was. He looked round, saw me and said, 'Mich! What are you doing here? You shouldn't be here with all this: this is crazy, insane. Go home!' I wanted to see him afterwards, but they wouldn't let me. I went to see him at Brixton – I used to take stuff and took an acoustic guitar in for him."

Mich has few doubts as to why Peter was charged in the first place. She maintains that the court case was blown up out of all proportion, probably due to Clifford and David, who knew that if Peter kept giving his money away, then they too would lose money. So they took seriously something Peter said in jest. "I had many conversations with Peter during that time, and it still upsets me that people considered him insane just because he wanted to give his money away. Peter knew he had a God-given gift and he told me on several occasions how he thought the best thing he could do with that gift was help people who were less fortunate than himself."

It is tempting to view this incident in terms of the idealistic artist on the one hand, and the profit-orientated big bad manager on the other. It's an old cliché: nobility versus base instincts, and money as the root of all evil. Yet something says it can't have been quite as simple as that.

That Peter went through hellish turmoil as he tried to break away from the business of rock stardom is beyond doubt. But it should also be remembered that at one point right at the start of his career, he and manager Davis were coming from exactly the same place: East Enders out to prove that barrow boys can make it in the big wide world, just like anyone else. And though their paths diverged, Peter today still acknowledges Clifford's role in building up his career.

Seeing Peter's charity notion from Clifford's more sceptical point of view is to understand that Clifford had made a big investment in Fleetwood Mac and Peter Green, both financially and emotionally. Of course, he was in it for the money, that's why groups appoint managers in the first place. But for Clifford's talent, it's conceivable that the original Fleetwood Mac could have been one-hit-wonders. He was astute enough to realise that 'Man Of The World' had to be a hit, whatever the short-term personal cost to himself.

It's not the case that Davis stalked Peter throughout his career; for instance, when Peter left Mac, Clifford assumed that it would also mark the end of their partnership. He told *Disc* at the time, "He won't stay with me for management because we've always had a verbal agreement that any time he wanted to leave he could. Peter hates responsibility and I think I've been his shield in the past. The only way he can feel free is if I'm not around any more. He doesn't want people to depend on him."

Yet Peter elected to stay with Clifford who, from what Peter now says, did at first try to understand his ideas about giving money away, if not agree with them.

"The main reason they put me into hospital," reflects Peter, "was for giving my money away: they wanted me to realise that I was on drugs when I tried to persuade the rest of the boys to give away our overflow of money to Biafra. I was on a drug at the time, mescaline. I took it at first to see if I was strong enough to resist all these things, but I wasn't. I was taking it, and yet in the distance I could see someone – the strong person – who thought he could get through it."

Clifford seems to have tried to understand the urgency of Peter's compassion: at one point approaching the charity War On Want to obtain some films for Peter about Third World development. So, Peter's "idle threat" could well have been the final straw for Clifford, a financially-motivated man who was watching someone he knew well apparently squander his money for reasons that were not always entirely clear to anybody – Peter included, it must be said. What's more, his family also figure in the equation.

In the nicest possible sense, they had grown to depend upon their talented son to help them out financially when times were hard. Peter himself was happy to do this and had bought "Albatross", the house in Coombe Gardens, New Malden for them. It was a close-knit family, and continues to be so to this day: without a second thought, Len and especially his wife Gloria are quite selfless in the way they now look after Peter. But as Len Green is the first to point out, when his youngest brother became famous he also became the "family purse": "I remember one time – I think he'd just come back from touring the continent with Fleetwood Mac – Pete phoned me up from his accountant David Simmons's office. He said, 'I've just had a cheque arrive here for seven-and-a-half thousand pounds. How much do you want?' He was used to carrying a wad of notes around with him all the time – about a thousand or fifteen hundred pounds. Anything more than that he thought he didn't need."

Len had struggled all his life to make ends meet, and by this time, having been out of work quite a few years, he owed water rates, house rates and several months' mortgage payments. So Peter's question was like an answer to all his prayers. "Send me five grand and it'll get me out of trouble," Len replied. The following morning the postman delivered a cheque – no accompanying note – for five thousand pounds.

The significance of the so-called shotgun incident is perhaps three-fold: first, it shows that by 1976 an understandable conflict of interests had arisen regarding Peter's estate, and because he was still subject to erratic mood swings, no one was willing to take his altruism at face value, except the grateful charities on the receiving end of his donations. Second, the national press ridiculed and made a scapegoat of someone in no position to answer back and all for the sake of a good, though essentially inaccurate, story. (In today's climate, where showbiz personalities are quick to sue the press for hints of slander, Peter might well have been awarded substantial damages for what was unquestionably some sloppy and misleading reporting.) Third, and perhaps most disturbing of all, is the thought that a highly sensitive individual with a recent history of mental problems should be put through the trauma of police cells, court appearances and imprisonment in this way without any effective representation to shield him. The image of one of the country's most naturally-talented musicians answering questions in court, clueless as to why he's there in the first place, reflects rather sadly on the nature of community care in Britain.

CHAPTER 15

LOS ANGELES SMOG
IN THE SKIES

The outcome of the court case was that magistrate Sir Ivor Rigby sectioned Peter for further treatment in hospital. The venue this time was Horton Hospital, next to Long Park in Epsom. Horton's eight-feet-high concrete perimeter wall obscures hospital annexes in which the ground-floor windows have been bricked up, presumably to keep inmates in, and not trespassers out. Phil McDonnell, former roadie for Fleetwood Mac, was appalled when he heard about Peter being there, and took immediate action to have him moved to the Priory. This was the five hundred pounds-a-week private clinic where on a previous stay he'd bumped into Lionel Bart, the brilliant writer of hit musicals during the 1960s who was there, alas, trying to dry out.

Peter responded well to treatment at the Priory, and during this period of recovery his brother Michael made a career move which would pave the way for Peter's return to the music scene some two years later in 1979. "I joined PVK," Michael explains, "through meeting a guy called Peter Vernon-Kell. He had a record company and asked if I would be interested in joining as a plugger. He explained how he'd got together with this financial wizard called Peter Cormack who'd never even heard of Peter [Green] – his background was in plastics – but he had this knack of making companies profitable."

Peter Vernon-Kell was a businessman, producer and musician, roughly in that order. In the early 1960s he'd flitted in and out of

the London music scene (playing guitar with a band that eventually became The Who) and his early failures made him determined to succeed second-time round. "I decided that I would only return to the music business when I had the money and capital to make a real go of it," he explains.

Before PVK Records got a cash injection from Peter Cormack, they'd had a taste of success with Freddie Starr. In mid 1977 the company put out feelers with Michael to get Peter onto his roster. "I told Peter VK that I'd already thought of asking Peter," Michael adds, "but he seemed happy in his retirement now that he'd got over the court case and other things. Still, I had a word with him and to my surprise he seemed quite interested."

Peter VK decided on a gentle approach in order to get Peter playing once more: "I used to have these sessions in my studio with friends and Peter started coming along but not playing. Nobody shoved a guitar into his hands and I think he found it unusual that we didn't appear to care if he should come or go. Eventually he asked to play bass, although I think he was more interested in my collection of cars, especially an E-Type Jag that I had at the time and which he subsequently pranged. His mood was very in and out. I had a brother who suffered from epilepsy and Peter had the same kind of drugged-up look about him. Every now and then there was a flash of who he really was when he would laugh or smile. He literally hadn't played a note in five years, but then picked up this battered old Fender Jaguar and went straight into working out an intricate instrumental called 'Proud Pinto' – it was hard to believe. Apart from his fingers getting sore quite quickly, it was as if no time had elapsed whatsoever."

Peter VK soon discovered that the best thing to do was surround Peter with good musicians and then just let him doodle, even though this could be a frustrating experience for a producer: "He would often come up with an unbelievably good riff or phrase when the machine was switched off and when I asked him to repeat what he'd played when the tape was rolling we nearly always drew a blank."

So as 1977 unfolded it was a promising time for Michael and all three Peters: the guitarist was off the medication, began to lose weight and was becoming more positive, and it looked like a good album was starting to take shape. Around this time Peter broached the subject of him and Peter VK going out to Los Angeles. Ever since meeting Californian Jane Samuels at bass player Steve Thompson's (formerly with John Mayall) house soon after leaving Fleetwood Mac, the two wrote to each other, something that fired the jealousy of Peter's girlfriend at the time: "These letters would arrive from this girl who played the fiddle and I'd get furious – they were quite obviously love letters." The notepad passion grew when Jane returned to Los Angeles, and in one letter that Peter wrote her whilst recuperating at the Priory earlier in the year, he had proposed marriage.

Jane was at Los Angeles airport to meet the two Peters when they arrived and they went to stay at her small house in the hills. She immediately took them out onto the verandah and insisted on playing her violin. Peter VK remembers her playing: "She was terrible! But obviously for Peter love was deaf. He even wanted her to play on the album, which is what she was very obviously angling for. I told him if he wanted a violinist I would get him one, but that she was no violinist."

Peter's family had met Jane when she went over to stay with them. "She was a quiet girl," Peter's mother recalls, "but very fond of money I felt." Jane brought out twinges of xenophobia in brother Len: "One afternoon Gloria made us all a really nice tea – cakes, sandwiches, scones and jam – and Jane kept on asking me for the jelly. I said, 'Sorry, we've got everything else but we ain't made any jelly.' Of course she meant the jam!"

Amongst Peter's friends, the general consensus about the woman he now wanted to marry was less lighthearted and cosy: Peter VK didn't take to her born-again evangelism, which Judy Wong now remembers as possibly having something to do with "Jews For Jesus" Messianic Christianity (Jane being Jewish). "She converted Peter," Peter VK points out, "while we were staying at her house, and Peter tried to persuade me to do the same. I wasn't having any of it. At first he seemed inspired by his new faith – Jane wrote the words to that song 'Seven Stars' [from *In The Skies*] during a bible-reading session they both had. But in the long-run I think it confused Peter and did him some real harm."

Their wedding took place at Mick and Jenny Fleetwood's Bel Air house on 4 January 1978. The night before, back in England, brother Michael had had a panic attack about Peter tying the knot and only stopped himself from ringing Peter to tell him it was wrong for fear of further confusing him. Jenny couldn't really understand Peter's decision: "We didn't know why he was doing it, but we sort of went along with him and supported him as friends."

Jane became pregnant, but by the time their daughter Rosebud was born in the late summer, the marriage was floundering. Mick Fleetwood remembers how Peter shared some troubles with his bosom-pal: "I thought from the beginning that Jane was a little strange, a little austere and heavy. She was a born-again Christian and of course there's nothing wrong with that, but suddenly Peter was surrounded by it. However she was pretty, which Peter loved.

"But later he told me how he was starting to feel that she was on the dark side of things: he felt that she was attacking him from within. It was very heavy. I remember when Fleetwood Mac were rehearsing the *Tusk* album he came along a couple of times [Peter's guitar is featured at the end of 'Brown Eyes' on *Tusk*]. He made it quite clear to me that he now saw this woman as a threat and that basically he felt that she had made a covenant with the devil. Now that may well have been Peter's paranoia, and I have to say that it would be unfair to blame her for what happened to him afterwards. But she *was* like one of those people who get caught up in cults and that was worrying."

What also can't have helped much was a fair amount of substance-abuse throughout this time: happily off the prescribed medication he so loathed, Peter was by all accounts tooting endless lines as "well-wishers" fell over each other to see him right. Meanwhile, any of the beneficial time-release effects of the stabilising medication he'd stopped taking almost a year earlier were wearing off. In this frame of mind any decision-making that went on mostly did not take place in – to quote John McVie – the full light of day.

When both Peters first arrived in Los Angeles there was no

L-r: Peter, Jeff Whittaker (in background playing congas), Gus Isadore, Reg Isadore and Greg Brown, live in Bournemouth in the early 1980s

Early 1980s promo shot

PVK-era album cover shot with replacement 1959 Les Paul

Jeff Whittaker and Kolors on the road, early 1980s

Rasta image Peter Greenbaum stage shot, early 1980s

The caring touch – eldest brother
Len and Gloria Green, 1994

Man of the world, Peter
Greenbaum, 1944

Rosebud Samuel-Green,
mid 1980s

Eric Clapton, Arthur Brown and Peter in The Splinter Group's marquee backstage at the Guildford Folk And Blues Festival, August 1996

The legend returns: Peter in 1996 with his BMI award for 'Black Magic Woman' notching up two million radio airplays world-wide

Peter's long overdue return to the stage, Buxton Opera House, 5 May 1996

Peter plays Ronnie Scott's, Birmingham, Autumn 1996

Hitting the high notes of 'Black Magic Woman' backed by Cozy Powell, Edinburgh 1996

Above: The Splinter Group Mark III
backstage at Birmingham's NIA on the
final night of the BB King tour,
November 1997. L-R: Roger Cotton,
Peter, Nigel Watson, Neil Murray and
Larry Tolfree

Right: The Splinter Group Mark II relaxing at
Culdaff during the Irish tour, May 1997. L-R:
Spike Edney, Neil Murray and Cozy Powell

Peter shows off his burgeoning guitar
collection at home in Surrey, January 1997

Checking out another
guitar shop, summer 1996

Back on stage together after almost thirty years: Peter and BB King jam, joined by Nigel Watson, Croydon Fairfield Hall, November 1997

Old friends relax together. Gary Moore joins BB and Peter in the artists' bar shortly before showtime, Croydon Fairfield Hall, November 1997

Behind every great man there's a strong woman. Studio shot of old friends Mich
Reynolds and Peter, Summer 1996

doubt that the guitarist was "falling back into music again" as he himself put it at the time: Messrs Fleetwood and McVie had by then formed their own management company, Seedy Management, run by Judy Wong, and Peter, they all agreed, was to be their blue-chip client. Getting him a major deal with Warner Brothers would be no problem, after all *Rumours* was making the company a fortune at that point, which meant Mick had corporate *schtick*, as they say in Burbank-speak.

Mick went with Peter to buy him a replacement guitar – exactly the same kind of 1959 sunburst Les Paul that he had played in Fleetwood Mac, bought from a collector for five thousand pounds. Peter was overjoyed to have it, yet shortly afterwards he gave it away to a stranger he met in the hotel lift who said he liked music. Peter VK, not unreasonably, freaked when he found out. Mercifully the beautiful 1959 Gibson was soon traced to the local pawnbrokers where its extremely temporary new owner – a hustler and space cadet – had promptly taken it to get two hundred dollars more with which to score that day.

As for securing a record deal for Peter, Mick had a meeting with Mo Ostin, head of Warner Brothers: "The first thing Mo asked me was, 'Is he together?' and in my view he was together so I said, 'This guy is fine. I'm with him all the time. He's not going to jig out on you.'" Mick got Peter a very good deal, going on for a million dollars for three albums to be made in his own time. Then, the day came for signing. "I said, 'Pete this it – if you wanna start making music, you gotta get the money and sign on the bottom line.' Then right there and then in the office he suddenly turned and said, 'I can't do this. It's the work of the devil. This is not what music should be.' Jane came down later that day and tried to persuade him to do it without any success. So I went in to see Mo Ostin, apologised and said, 'You can have your four-hundred thousand dollars back.'"

Peter VK describes that bizarre business meeting as like "a scene out of *Dallas*". But he could see that Peter knew his signature would lead to pressure from the record company executives and that that was the very opposite of what he wanted. Peter wanted instead to go back to England and go into the studio, which eventually was precisely what he did do.

When Peter's brother Michael went to pick him up at a hotel near Heathrow, he wasn't at all prepared for the shock that was in store: "When I first saw my brother I had to go downstairs and have a drink, because it just wasn't the same person. His voice sounded very weird, muffled, and the first thing he managed to say to me was, 'I look like Barry White.' It broke my heart. I don't know what had happened to him over in the States but he'd just gone backwards: he had absolutely let himself go."

Soon after that, in the spring of 1979, Peter VK released *In The Skies* which charted at Number Thirty-Two in Britain, but went on to sell a massive eight-hundred thousand copies in Germany where it was welcomed as the return of a triumphant hero. The reality was somewhat less amazing: Peter's health was extremely fragile, too fragile to run the media gauntlet of press interviews to promote the album. Rock writer Steve Clarke did meet him in the Montcalm Hotel, London, for what was a very disjointed interview subsequently published in *NME* along with a rather disturbing photograph of the guitarist, taken against his will as he smiled uncomfortably on odd occasions during the talk.

In The Skies featured Snowy White who, according to Peter VK, was badgered by Peter throughout the sessions to play all of the lead guitar. In deference, Snowy (formerly with Pink Floyd, Thin Lizzy and Linda Lewis) did his best not to, although he does solo on the title track, and later secretly confessed to Michael Green, "I'm not even fit to play rhythm guitar with him." So reluctantly Peter was sometimes pushed to the front.

Peter Bardens joined him once more on keyboards, Kuma Harada (sessionman with Mick Taylor and Polly Styrene) on bass and Reg Isadore (of Robin Trower Band) or Godfrey Maclean on drums. The album alternates blues, rock ballads, funk and classical guitar. 'Fool No More' is heartache blues played at a slower tempo than on the original version recorded during sessions for the dog and dustbin debut LP and eventually released in 1971 on *The Original Fleetwood Mac* out-takes album. His playing in the late 1970s is less explosive with few anguished outbursts and flurries of notes, but such restraint only heightens the emotion. The track is a showcase for Peter Green's canon: namely, that less in fact is more.

Around the time most of the album was recorded, in autumn 1977, Peter Bardens was persuaded to put on a few London pub venues with Peter and Snowy, by Greg Brown (later in The White Sky Band): "I thought Peter sang very well on *In The Skies* and it was a promising album. My friend Greg Brown, who'd always been a great fan, built a band around Pete about then. I played with them on maybe two or three gigs and then resigned because it was just such a shambles. You'd have to gaffer tape a guitar onto Peter to get him to play, he was in no condition to go out and perform. Also Pete wasn't really playing lead guitar – he'd leave it all to Snowy like he did in the studio, and that was a bit of a shame because audiences would come along only to hear him."

In Germany the album stayed in the Top Ten for months during 1979 without any promotion. The pressure was soon back on to produce a follow-up.

Before *In The Skies* came out, Peter had suggested to Michael that they should form a publishing company. This he duly did, called it Tashman Music, and landed a three-album deal with Chappel. Peter put the deal Michael's way partly to boost his brother's finances. However, eighteen months later his generosity in a sense backfired by putting Peter under pressure to deliver at a time when his tank was running on empty. It was left to Michael somehow to sort it: "We had a meeting – Peter, Peter VK, Peter's lawyer, and myself – and Peter VK said to Peter, 'We're going in the studio next week,' and Peter said, 'There's no point, I've got no songs. Mickey's got some so we'll have to use his.' That's how *Little Dreamer* came about: with me burning a lot of midnight oil. Some of the tracks were written the night before we went in the studio – 'Loser Two Times', 'Walkin' The Road' – and then when we got into the studio I'd be worrying about whether Peter would be able to perform them. In the end he was all right which was some achievement considering his health at the time."

The album's title track, 'Little Dreamer', is Peter in his element, improvising: "'Little Dreamer' was an instrumental he made up on the spot. He didn't really want to do one but I managed to talk him into it: he'd mentioned a couple of days earlier that he had a tune in his head so I suggested he went into the studio and played what was in his head."

Guitarist Ronnie Johnson joined Peter on this and the following two albums *Whatcha Gonna Do?* and *White Sky*. In an interview with *Mojo* magazine, Ronnie gave some insight into Peter's wacky ways in the studio and also his continual experimentation with the colours of sound: "The sessions were interesting and a lot of fun. Peter arrived at the studio for the early sessions with these incredibly long fingernails and the producer was frantically trying to cut them so Peter could play. Another time we were really going well and suddenly Peter stops and looks across at John [Edwards, now bass player with Status Quo] and says, 'No, no, no. You're taking me to Brighton and I want to go to Shepherd's Bush.' We just collapsed laughing. That may sound a bit bizarre, but in terms of the music, there was an element of truth in what he said. Peter grew in confidence as time went on and the last sessions I did for him were for an album called *White Sky* [May 1981]. He bought himself a Marshall amp with a Leslie hooked up to it and was trying out different sounds. On the days when he was all right he was very together and playing extremely well."

This pattern of good and bad days, introverted days and eccentric days, was and still is Peter's normality. As Peter was still prone to impulsive gestures of generosity, Peter VK and Peter's lawyer thought it wise to invest his money in property lest he give it all away on a whim and in the couple of months that the conveyancing was going through for a small property in Richmond, Peter stayed in Beckenham, Kent, with a guitarist that he'd recently befriended called Kris Gray. At this point *Little Dreamer* was out and *Whatcha Gonna Do?*, Peter VK's last production for Peter, was in the can. What's more, Peter had done sessions with early 1960s blues-daddy Brian Knight, for his new album, *Dark Horse*.

This period, as Kris remembers it, was one of rest and recuperation for Peter as he had time to try and make sense of the rather frenetic pace of life that began just two years earlier when he met Peter VK and then moved to Los Angeles. "I had a band called Hard Road," explains Kris, "named after the Mayall album, and I'd sent Peter and his brother a demo we'd done of 'The Same Way'. After a few telephone conversations he asked me to pop by his brother's house where he was staying. When he opened the door he said, 'Hello, are you Jewish? You look Jewish to me.' I told him I wasn't but he still thought there was some Jewish blood somewhere going back. Anyway, after we'd gone out for a pint a few times I said that if he wanted a change he could come and stay in our spare room until it was time for him to move into his place at Richmond. It was obvious that he was a bit exhausted because when he moved in he spent a lot of time during the day in bed. He spent most of his time in pyjamas, he'd get up and I'd cook him something which he'd eat then sit around for a while and then go back to bed. When he was up he'd chain-smoked and listened to *Little Dreamer* or Thin Lizzy's album *Chinatown,* featuring Snowy White, again and again. Funnily enough it didn't get on my nerves because he was kind of tranquil – not all agitated and restless."

During his stay with Kris, Peter did talk about recent events. He told Kris about one incident with Jane in Los Angeles, when he was dreaming that he was attacking her and had only realised that he *was* attacking her when he felt the police put a gun to his head. He described a lot of that period, from the mid 1970s onwards, as a dream and how since that time he had had trouble putting together what was real and what was fantasy. He very much felt that the ECT was the root of all his problems, making his condition worse and not better. One good thing had come out of Peter and Jane's marriage, though, his daughter Rosebud and Kris remembers how Peter phoned Los Angeles every week (always paying for the calls), to find out how his daughter was.

Peter's house purchase soon went through and he moved out of Kris's place. Kris visited Peter soon after: "I couldn't believe how small and claustrophobic it was, like a telephone box with a bed in it. I went round a few times and the same guys were always there [some of them later formed Kolors]. They seemed to have taken over. There was a lot of smoking going on and from time to time someone would tinkle with a guitar. I just didn't like the vibes – it was very oppressive. So I stopped going." A loss of rapport between Kris and Peter followed naturally.

Sadly, Peter's divorce went through in the early 1980s. To this day he remains somewhat baffled by the fact that the lawyer who represented him throughout the settlement, to his knowledge, was a friend and associate of his ex-wife's Los Angelean lawyer. The first Peter knew of Margaret Bennett, he says, was at a rehearsal studio when she arrived and announced that she was his new lawyer.

CHAPTER 16

GREENBACKS: THE ROOT OF ALL EVIL

Peter Vernon-Kell bowed out of the business in 1981 after producing *Whatcha Gonna Do?* thus ending a four-year collaboration with Peter which was extraordinarily fruitful, especially in view of Peter's erratic health. He admired the guitarist's prodigious talent, with a pithiness that echoes his style of playing: "His gift was simple: he had a natural ability to always find the note he wanted, the note he could hear in his head."

One of Peter VK's greatest management skills in handling Peter's affairs was that he appeared not to be his manager; when the time came to make decisions he made the guitarist feel that he was in the driver's seat, which, in effect, he often was anyway. Then between 1980 and 1984 Jamaican percussionist Jeff Whittaker gradually took over Peter VK's role, although it must be said there was little love lost between the two. Jeff feels that Peter VK used him for his many musical contacts on the scene during the late 1970s and early 1980s in black London, while Peter VK reviles the succession of bands that played with Peter during that time – variously called White Sky, Kolors and Katmandu – who in his opinion were all milking the guitarist's legend for what it was worth.

Peter VK was in the audience when one such line-up played in north London: "I was disgusted. There was a blues legend fronting this cabaret band. I listened to about three numbers by which time I'd had enough. If I could have physically got to the front I would have got up on stage and chinned the one who kept reminding the audience that,

'Hey, man, this is Peter Green!'"

With the benefit of hindsight – which so often tends to be twenty-twenty – Jeff in a way now concurs with Peter VK that, during the four-and-a-half years that Peter and he collaborated, live performances and gigging were not a good idea for Peter at that stage in his career: "What I discovered quite soon with Peter was that although he wanted to work, he didn't want to work just because he had to. He wanted to work when he felt like it. We should have been in the studio, making records, but with the exception of drummer Godfrey Maclean, Peter and I were playing with second-rate musicians."

Whittaker, initially a dancer, had played in the early 1970s London musical *Catch My Soul* and was percussionist on Crosby, Stills And Nash's hit 'Love The One You're With'. He first bumped into Peter in the early 1970s during the *Gass* sessions. Jeff was working on a project in Germany while *Whatcha Gonna Do?* was being made and returned after Peter VK had departed. Peter, he says, at this point was once again disgruntled with the way the record company and accountants were interfering with the process of making music. When Jeff got back from Germany he learnt a bit more about the guitarist's business affairs: apparently after the divorce settlement and some steep fees from private clinics, Peter wasn't as comfortably off as he might have wished at the start of the 1980s. So, in a sense for the first time since his early days as a pro he now *had* to work. With the *White Sky* album finished by June 1981, the two musicians decided to go for a holiday in Barbados and plan their next move, forming a band. On this point Peter's eccentricities left Jeff in something of a quandary: "He wanted musicians around him who were financially independent and didn't put pressure on him to provide them with a wage. But as high calibre musicians wouldn't tolerate Peter's ways, the only musicians who would work with him were those who were struggling and eager to break through and make a name for themselves. So the players on the *White Sky* album were not the same as those who did the four gigs that everybody got upset about; they were Greg Brown, myself, Peter, Carlos Morela, Reg Isadore and when Carlos wasn't around, Reg's brother." Although many people close to Peter were saddened by what they saw at the *White Sky* Red Lion/Greyhound performances, not everybody regarded the music as the pitiful fiasco that mythology has made it.

In *The Guardian*'s arts pages of 18 January 1982, journalist Mick Brown reviewed White Sky's gig at London's The Venue: "After twelve years Peter Green seems committed to the idea of a comeback. He wrote some of the most memorable rock of the late 1960s. His current group, White Sky, is actually a black five-piece playing streamlined funk and rock which is a logical progression of the blues that was his main idiom. Inevitably perhaps, none of the newer songs carried quite the impact of those old ones, but there was enough craftsmanship, glimpses of the old skills, to make one optimistic for Green's renaissance. All he needs is more belief in himself." What with the ECT and medication, more self-belief was a very tall order.

After the famous four gigs, some promoters showed sufficient further interest to warrant putting a tour together and so rehearsals began at the hundred-pounds-a-day Orbis studios. Already though, Peter could smell a rat or, with his sensitivity, probably a plague of them. "We were rehearsing there," Jeff explains, "and Peter heard the tour organiser and some of the band arguing about money. Then, when Peter's lawyer came down everybody rushed towards her thinking she was going to give them generous advance wages for the tour. Peter saw this, looked at me and said, 'Let's go. I don't want this.' This totally freaked Greg Brown who regarded White Sky as his band. He could see it all falling apart. So I had to tell him and others there and then that, after some three days of rehearsals, Peter didn't want to go on with the band anymore."

The band had already cost Peter money: before the four gigs they had rehearsed for about a month, Peter's company paying each musician one-hundred-and-fifty pounds a week. Peter didn't like that, and wasn't happy about White Sky's live set either, which included some of his old hits which he sang because of Greg, an old friend. By that point what he really wanted to play was the material from *In The Skies,* which was more jazz-funk.

Peter's lifestyle was very much that of a blues musician: that is, one of stylish squalor in a small terraced-house, set in an incongruously bourgeois zone of beautiful Richmond. Incongruous because, according to some, it was as though the streetlife of the entire town used the *bijou* property as a crash-pad. Peter and his eldest brother Len both recall female visitors who persistently overstayed their welcome. One of them, Marie, Peter had met during one of his spells in hospital. "Marie used to sleep on the couch," Len explains, "when she stayed there. She came round whenever her social security money ran out and she needed drink. When we first met Marie she was a really nice plump girl. Then she became an alcoholic, dried out, went back on the booze again and her weight went down to five stone."

Another unwelcome hanger-on was a girl called Janine. "She just wouldn't get out of my house," recalls Peter. "She once brought a cheap Spanish guitar with her, which I also didn't really want in the house. So after I'd asked her to leave many times I lost my temper and smashed the guitar on her head. It was so cheap it just broke into three pieces. Perhaps I would have handled these things better if I hadn't been smoking weed but drugs turn you into a softy and you let things go on too long."

So it was in that kind of atmosphere that the Kolors project began to take off, rehearsing in Peter's front room. Kolors comprised Stefan Rene, Godfrey Maclean, Larry Steele, Jeff and Peter. Next door to Peter lived a guy called Zilch, who was in partnership with Knocker. They were like brokers connected with record companies and were good hustlers within the industry. Jeff arranged to meet Zilch, who although he had a Rolls Royce, was obviously broke. "When I told him about our line-up he said, 'Wow, with names like this we could make money!' So he took down all our names and went straight to Phonogram Records in Germany – where Peter was still a big name – to get us a deal. When he came back he had a sixty thousand pounds advance for us which we thought was great, but of course we'll never know how much of that he kept for himself. While Zilch was negotiating with Peter's lawyer, he gave us the opportunity and equipment to go into a studio and start work on the album."

Kolors went into the studio every day for over two months, Zilch paying for everything, but for some reason it just didn't come together. One of the band had a heroin habit and had turned to Buddhism for his salvation, which meant he thought he wasn't supposed to earn any money. In order to get any money Jeff had to form a company, Zilch paid him and he distributed six thousand pounds to each member of the band. Peter wanted it that way.

Not only did the original Kolors sessions not go well, but after a couple of months in the studio the band had little or nothing to show for it, although the Zilch company gave Jeff the impression that they were not really interested in seeing an album.

At the same time Jeff had an ongoing project in colleges and kindergartens in Cologne, Germany, and had some contractual obligations coming up. He had a brainwave: "I had to organise a finale concert of Afro-Caribbean music, due to take place in Cologne. So I thought the best thing to do was to get Peter down there to use him as an introduction. It also meant that we could get Kolors started."

Kolors' debut live performance took place on midsummer's day, 1982, on the famous Dom Plaza in front of the Cologne Cathedral. "I was quite well-known," says Jeff, "on the local arts scene in Cologne because I'd been working on that Kultur Stabil project for five years. I was due to do my last gig that day and I told the radio guys to expect a surprise – that I'd brought Peter Green with me and he was going to get up and play. Within five minutes I saw at least a thousand people gather in the square because of the radio announcement and as I went up to the microphone to start the gig I got all emotional and had to back off for a bit. Peter saw this and started dying with laughter."

But things turned very ugly with the Zilch company when they returned to England, as Jeff's wife Dee Whittaker recalls: "The records from the Phonogram deal didn't happen and Jeff arranged to meet Zilch's business partner Knocker in a pub in Richmond. Jeff wanted the masters of the original Kolors sessions back from Zilch because they weren't producing an album out of it. So Jeff went to the pub as arranged, and the next thing I knew at about half past eleven that night I got a telephone call from a man who said he had seen two men outside a pub in Richmond holding Jeff, and another guy beating him up. He reckoned they broke his jaw and his wrists because they didn't want him to play, and put him in hospital for three days. Knocker was annoyed that the band had got so many thousand pounds each – which was in fact Peter's idea – and then nothing had come out of it, even though that wasn't the band's fault. On reflection, if we'd have been sensible at the time then the members of the band wouldn't have actually got any of that money – it would have stayed in the bank and been used to carry things over and whatever else. But the whole thing with Peter was to share it out fairly, because of his attitude to money."

Dee, now a headteacher, eventually became Kolors' tour manager during school holidays.

For the following eighteen months the band toured intensively in Europe and Scandinavia. A television recording taken from the German *Rockpalast* programme shows a gig in Hamburg. Wearing flamboyant red headgear, Peter looks like a nomad just in from a trip through the desert; and as he plays an off-beat reggae version of 'Black Magic Woman', appears to be happily sharing a really good joke with himself. His playing is simple and sparse. "By that time," Peter points out, "I'd stopped bending strings and liked playing the guitar straight."

Life on the road during those tours was stressful for all concerned. Peter's health as ever was erratic and Jeff felt it was his responsibility somehow to curb Peter's appetite for nocturnal *frissons* of one kind or another: "After gigs in Europe, when the rest of the band went to sleep, Peter would go and walk the streets. Usually he'd bump into girls and once they knew he had money in his pockets they'd just put him into a room, lock him up and I'd have no idea where he was. So I soon learned that it was best to go with him everywhere – which meant I didn't get a lot of sleep for a year or two." Uncannily, this is borne out by the fact that in his forties Jeff actually does look younger than in shots taken of the band over ten years ago.

In 1983 Kolors toured Europe and Scandinavia once again and made the first of two trips to Israel. Shortly before Christmas, on 28 November, they played a high-profile London venue, the Dominion Theatre. Peter's performance here was rather inconsistent: most of the newer post-Mac material was good and funky, but some of the old numbers – most notably 'Love That Burns' – were so low-energy as to be comatose. Then a few minutes later, and probably when his powers of concentration luckily had returned for a while, he stunned the audience with 'Black Magic Woman', played as strongly as ever before. What all this added up to was a very unusual concert in which the mood of the crowd never stayed the same for more than a few minutes.

After the Dominion, Jeff and Peter decided it was time to go back to the drawing-board, to find really good musicians and start again. A mutual acquaintance had met Ray Dorset (of Mungo Jerry) at a party. Ray had enthused about how much he liked Peter Green, so Jeff suggested they went down to Ray's studio. Ray was running a video/commercials production company: "When we got down there and were having a jam one of Ray's clients from a Swiss company was there. He heard us playing and just said, 'I'll buy anything they do.' After that he put his money where his mouth was – with one-hundred-and-twenty thousand pounds. That's how Katmandu started up – as a studio band with Ray Dorset, Vincent Crane [of Atomic Roosters, now deceased], Peter and myself."

Recorded between December 1983 and January 1984 this album is an inspired combination of classic and original blues. The groove and mood has an urgency that is absent, perhaps deliberately so, from his other post-Mac releases. The album remains Peter's favourite of these, especially the track 'Who's That Knocking?'. But while making it gave Peter a boost, the business side of things increasingly left him cold. It seemed as though each new project, each fresh line-up of musicians, brought with it legal and financial complexities which Peter was more than happy to leave for his astute lawyer to sort out. It was as though his solo career was bringing him full circle, back to that same disdain he felt in the Fleetwood Mac days when the money-making always spoilt the music. Although Peter really enjoyed the Katmandu project, dividing the spoils – according to Jeff – marred the experience: "Peter realised very soon that Ray Dorset is a businessman and after we had done the album, which Peter thought was great, he wouldn't have him working with us. Too grabby."

Peter now feels that he was "over-encouraged" by Jeff during their four-year collaboration: but then again, he must have enjoyed it from time to time because he's not a guy who has ever remotely contemplated compromise or eating humble pie for a living. Jeff, perhaps more so than everybody else, is matter-of-fact about the extent to which Peter's health deteriorated during the time they worked together. As he sees it, the problems were there from the start in 1980 – mood swings, day-long silences and a fear of being alone – and the percussionist tried to make appropriate adjustments, particularly when they were on the road. Most probably, being an active travelling musician was better therapy than the institutions that held him in limbo for stretches during the 1970s. Nevertheless, towards the end of 1984 events conspired to make him want to give up being a professional musician and this time for good.

173

Two specific instances between 1982 and 1984 may well have led to this decision, although equally likely is the possibility that by then he was actually beyond caring. The first is the tackiest record release in his entire discography, the *Kolors* album. And the second was the cloak-and-dagger ending to his second visit to Israel in the summer of 1984.

The first track on *Kolors*, which shows a picture of Peter Green on the cover, is entitled 'What Am I Doing Here?'. Things wouldn't have been so bad were this opener an incredibly witty pun or conceit on behalf of the record company. The irony is that for the most part Peter in effect just isn't there: bad mixing often put his guitar to the back of beyond. The thinking behind this compilation of rejects and out-takes is shameless: that it was ever released is a great shame.

In the summer of 1984, Kolors went to Israel after an extensive European tour. A three-day world music festival was planned in Tel Aviv featuring names like Al di Meola and Billy Cobham. Sadly for the organisers and all concerned the money ran out on the first day and Kolors only played one of the three gigs they'd been contracted to play. For the next two weeks Peter and the band were holed up in the Carlton Hotel, Tel Aviv, in amongst some choice heavies and with slim prospects of getting out. As Jeff and Dee remember: "Peter spent the time working his way through the menu in the restaurant of the Carlton and swapping anecdotes with Billy Cobham. Meanwhile armed bodyguards were to be seen everywhere, as deals went on behind closed doors. The Carlton wasn't good enough for Al di Meola so they had to move him to the Hilton where he proceeded to get very lonely and ended up slumming it with us in the Carlton! In the meantime the Israeli promoter of the festival who went bust was holed up on the three top floors of the Carlton. Peter was on the floor below him. The promoter kept moving rooms, and wouldn't go anywhere without a bodyguard. After the first and only gig, we went back to the hotel and Jeff went to see this promoter. His armed bodyguard was standing outside his room, and you did get the feeling that something really heavy was going down. The promoter told Jeff he was really sorry, and that because it was Peter and he was loved by the Israeli people, we should stay as guests of the hotel until such time as the financial hassles were sorted out."

During the visit the band got talking to some of the promoters who were involved with the finance. One Dutch guy told them he was into electrical installation in Africa and that he'd invested all this money in the production: "He was hanging around to find out what had happened to it. What we gathered from him was that the organisers were groups of gun-runners who were selling arms round the international market. They had all come together to organise this festival. The contractors had done the work and erected the massive stage, the bands had arrived and suddenly there was no money upfront."

That Peter wasn't particularly surprised by these heavy business vibes is no surprise, nor was his gourmand's attack on the Tel Aviv Carlton's cuisine. But, as ever the money was getting in the way of his playing. "To tell you the truth," Peter emphasises, "why I don't play anymore is because I make too many mistakes. When I played for money with Kolors we played a lot of places like Scandinavia and Israel. All the time I was making a lot of mistakes, but when we got back to England and played for nothing at a Christian Aid charity thing I didn't make one mistake all night. So what am I meant to do? What am I meant to think?"

When they arrived back in England, some of the band members weren't too happy about not getting paid for the Tel Aviv debacle – the line-up was then Will Bath (bass), Alfred Bannerman (of Isaac Hayes, guitar), Emmanuel Rentzos (Osibisa and Johnny Nash, keyboards), Greg Terry-Short (Ozzy Osbourne, drums), Peter and Jeff. This mealymouthed attitude, Jeff says, got Peter down more then anything else: "Those guys made it clear that they were just after the money – if they didn't pick up their hundred pounds each night they didn't want to play." For the first time in four years Jeff had had enough, and as Peter didn't need much coaxing to hang up his touring boots, Kolors faded that autumn of 1984. The final gig – an on/off provisional booking at Harlesden's Mean Fiddler – never happened.

Peter retired to spend six bleak years living alone at Richmond and wrestling with his illness – the depressions, the lethargy induced by medication and intermittent voices from nowhere out to goad him into mischief.

Without a doubt this was Peter's darkest period. He still shudders when he remembers the persecution he felt from outside and from within. Children living nearby would taunt him about his scruffy tramp-like appearance; and living alone he now says that the voices were as bad as they had ever been for him. With the exception of two guardian angels – called Jan and Jill – who separately regularly would visit him, for the rest of the time he was vulnerable to life's myriad ne'er-do-wells. Sporadic bits of musical activity (eg the Enemy Within project) are thought to have taken place during those scary years but they remain so hazy for Peter that he can't even remember participating.

In 1991/2, eldest brother Len and his wife Gloria came to the rescue and he moved out to join them – and his mother – in the East Anglian peace of their house in Great Yarmouth. And so began a long, slow process of recovery. Peter was safer in the bosom of his family but it was also around that time that he was put on the medication he stopped taking just a couple of years ago. Again, the benefit of hindsight does strongly suggest that the time spent so heavily sedated were lost years passed in a kind of narcotic Rip Van Winkledom. Obviously, at the time people were doing what they thought was best. The family moved to Essex in 1993 and early the following year the author visited Peter for the first time. At first the guitarist refused to believe that tens of thousands of his fans out there wanted him back. "Nobody's going to want to buy a book which is about me," he said, quite seriously.

Call it strange coincidence or synchronicity, but in 1995, within months of the first edition of this book being published, two more album "tributes" to the work of Peter Green were released in addition to Gary Moore's *Blues For Greeny* – by Bernie Marsden and a various artists compilation. Thus the seeds for his comeback were being sown.

Another strange coincidence is that virtually one year to the day after Peter first got himself off the medication, he got back onto a British stage. Together with his black Gibson jazz semi-acoustic, he had a story to tell.

CHAPTER 17

ATTITUDE:
THE COMPLETE MUSICIAN

Peter Green prefers not to talk about music, and refuses to analyse it. If the language of music, he reasons, offers a far better means with which to express oneself, then why do anything other than play? Carlos Santana has said something similar – "My voice, is in my playing." Frank Zappa thought that talking about music is "like fishing about architecture". In a sense Peter is even more radical: "If someone asked me to play an F sharp in the studio I'd say, 'Why are you asking me? Why not ask him over there?'"

So the guitarist whose solos have been described by analysts as "the masterful interweaving of pentatonic major and blues scales" himself insists that he wouldn't recognise a pentatonic major scale if one had jumped up and turned his guitar pickup the right way round. This is also a musician who would listen to Mark Knopfler and be amazed how many "mistakes" he could hear in the playing.

Clearly Peter's feel and style is unique. What follows here is a pooling of ideas about the qualities that helped him to build on this feel, so that at his peak he "scaled the highest heights of music" – as guitarist Snowy White puts it – but did so with next to no musical theory to help him on the way up. Of course, Peter now sees it as luck: "I just got lucky when my knowledge of the fingerboard got good."

Right from the start Peter's natural inclination as a musician swayed from playing lead guitar to bass, and back again. He had a soloist's approach, and that of a rhythm man. As guitarist John Holmes puts it, "He seemed to effortlessly lay back with the rhythm section, to enhance with his lead lines what they are playing. So many 'blues' guitarists just blast away over the rhythm section, without adding anything to the overall feel of what is being played."

Switching between bass and lead also developed strength in his fingers. Roger Pearce points out how Peter as a bassist soon was able to play lead lines on bass that Roger struggled to get on lead. Guitarist and ex-Yardbird Top Topham remembers a similar thing a few years later at the Angel in Godalming while they recorded Duster Bennett's live *Bright Lights Big City* album: "We were on this tiny stage – the five of us – and my guitar was virtually right in Peter's face! What I found hard to believe was the voicing and precision of the notes he played on a six-string bass. Fast, but strong as well." So, even though Peter remains a lead guitarist to the vast majority of his fans, he was not solely devoted to that instrument during his formative years playing blues.

Whether with his own playing, or within a band context, the thing that counted was the complete feel. Although blues guitarists like Bukka White, BB King, Robert Johnson, Lightnin' Hopkins, Matt Murphy and Otis Rush all inspired him as he forged his own style from theirs, the one player that overawed Peter was a singer/harmonicist. "Junior Wells," laughs Jeff Whittaker, "has always scared Peter. He just couldn't believe how anyone could go from singing to playing, then back to singing, in the way that he did. Peter couldn't bear the thought of meeting him – he was so jealous!" Singing was central to Peter's approach to blues. Everything emanated from the words and the song.

Around the time Peter was developing in leaps and bounds, the guitar hero ethos was also firmly establishing itself on both sides of the Atlantic. He alluded to this disparagingly in his opening comment column in *Beat Instrumental* magazine in September 1968: "A point to clear up is that I don't call myself a great musician. Although people have made the 'wailing guitar' the blues trademark – usually ignoring the vocal lines – the guitar should be an extension of the song to help get across the way the singer feels."

The following month he wrote, "I've recently realised that I've been neglecting my own guitar playing while I've been worrying about good lyrics." And about a year earlier during his Mayall days he pointed out, "I've got a great admiration for harp-players Little Walter and Junior Wells, and guitarists Otis Rush, Muddy Waters, BB King and Buddy Guy, and I've studied their work. I seldom play harmonica these days but I do find myself playing a lot of harmonica lines on guitar."

So while Eric Clapton was knocking 'em dead with long guitar solos that often were the song, Peter's attitude was always to play in order to serve the song: instruments are there to talk to each other – the harmonica and the guitar for example – and take over where the voice leaves off. Top Topham sees this as the "call and answer" style that is the bedrock of most traditional blues: "That idea of the instrument being an extension of the voice is the whole black thing, really. Blind Willie Johnson is a great example of the guitar as a voice extension...Billie Holiday and Lester Young are other classic examples of a call-and-answering situation between the artist and soloist who's also the perfect accompanist. In Junior Wells this is all going on in one player because he had this tremendous fire in his voice and he could bend it rather like he could his harp playing – I remember Wells's 'Hoodoo Man Blues' [1966] was something Peter was really into around that time."

That Top cites Blind Willie Johnson indirectly relates to Peter. Johnson's eerie gospel singing along with the guitar (perhaps 'Dark Was The Night, Cold Was The Ground' is his best known piece in this style) appealed particularly to the late Duster Bennett with whom Peter frequently jammed and played impromptu pub gigs around Kingston in 1967/8. As Topham points out, "Peter always said that he felt evil when the evangelical Duster was around, and it was Duster who developed Peter's taste for gospel."

Also around this time guitarist Kevin Winlove-Smith would see Peter and the early Fleetwood Mac play whenever he could, and one thing in particular impressed him about Peter as a performer: "He would often stand there, just playing along with what he was singing and it was obvious that he could play note-for-note whatever tune came into his head...as it came into his head."

Given this natural ability to feel – not parody – black blues, Peter for some reason then seemed to see himself as an imposter playing alongside black musicians, and so gradually he moved on to other styles. Eddie Boyd, Otis Spann, and BB King musically regarded him as a brother, and yet – as he explained to journalist Chris Welch – Peter felt he could never be one of them, and so slowly edged out of the blues and into free form improvisation, via the rock ballad.

Drug experimentation must have had something to do with this change in direction, and the possibilities of free form initially – in that basement at the Munich commune – must have seemed limitless. But eventually Peter also saw that there can be constraints in boundless freedom: *End Of The Game* he judged to be a failure because listening back to hours and hours of tapes from this unstructured studio jam, there wasn't enough good stuff in his view even for a forty-minute album.

Zoot Money played on some of those sessions and has definite views on why, in effect, Peter hit a brick wall: "Musicians like Peter based their musical beliefs in a single blues format which is deep in its emotion, but doesn't hold any musical complexity that you can develop as in say, jazz. There is no room for expansion of ideas chordally or harmonically. If you've had formal musical training then the normal process is for you to chip away at bits of theory – cut away the harmonics and get it to be simple and bare. Peter and his kind of artist had to rely on musical simplicity because they are what I would call musically inept. I don't mean that in a derogatory way, it's just that their whole approach depends on emotion and three-chord simplicity. Now the problem is that if you want to develop, where do you go?"

Peter's direction after 1970 happily was that of a musical hobo. He would travel, meet up and jam with different musicians from different cultures and backgrounds, with varying results. Once he took a troupe of African drummers into the studio and was disappointed. "It didn't come together," Peter grins. "I felt they were drumming about the power of Africa and not really about the track we were doing at the time."

Throughout the 1970s, a shift from 'Green Manalishi' and its forcefulness to the reserve of *In The Skies* was accompanied by health problems and medication. With his powers of concentration lessened, delivery inevitably became less incisive; but his general attitude to playing also changed during this time, becoming more and more understated and self-critical. So understated in fact, that during most of his time with Kolors during the early 1980s he took to playing "clean" notes rather than bending strings for greater emotional impact.

Peter still considers himself a player who "scraped through", even at his peak and still dislikes the idea of playing for money. "It's purely luck," Peter explains. "When I play it isn't for anything but pleasure and, because it's for pleasure I can't always learn it – you know, look at the fingerboard to see what I just did. As my knowledge of the fingerboard got better I could usually get the note I wanted, but sometimes you can't find it and then you have to take it apart and see what's coming through, see what's forming. Sometimes there's nothing you can do about it if it's not happening – it's clearly just a bad night." And, of course, the bad nights had a habit of happening when business hassles cropped up.

Given his disdain about playing for money it's ironic that Peter's "last" gig was at a summer festival in Israel, 1984, which, as Jeff Whittaker understands it, may even have been funded by gun-runners. With backdrops like that no wonder he'd had enough of performing – which is not to say that he'd grown fed up with playing. Throughout the early 1980s he was still experimenting and trying for new feels to his music: guitarist Ronnie Johnson noticed this at the *White Sky* sessions in 1982 where Peter was looking for new sounds by plugging into a Marshall amp and a Leslie speaker ("something I'd heard Redbone do").

Looking back he's pleased with the *Katmandu* sessions (1983/84) which put him together in the studio with Ray Dorset and the late Vincent Crane. The track 'Who's That Knocking?' he stills sees as having "something fresh and creative about it".

If there were one Peter Green composition that encapsulates this musician/band leader's spirit, and his open attitude to music-making it would probably be 'Rattlesnake Shake'. The hook – Peter's vocal – comes in the track's opening second, and the power chords that follow are as simple and brutally direct as the lyrics – a song dedicated to Mick Fleetwood, and all about masturbation as a therapy. From the straight studio version on *Then Play On*, Peter developed the live version into a long jam with sudden changes to the beat and tempo. These would sometimes flummox drummer Mick Fleetwood. Peter didn't freak when this happened, but instead explored the musical confusion of such moments and turned them into a positive, as Mick explains: "When Peter got into doing all the jamming stuff that was all new to me and I'd be thinking to myself, 'What time are we meant to be playing?...Where's the "one"?' Pete would find out where I was on the beat and change his guitar lines around and basically save my ass! But in doing that we actually went off on some incredible journeys musically. We would go so far you'd think we were going to collapse any second and yet we never did, because Peter would always find a way of guiding me home. After a while that became habit and we could do it on purpose. A lot of those shuffle-jams on *Then Play On* are out of time if you really listen to them – in fact on one of the fades the drums are totally back the other way to the guitar playing. In those situations I would keep going and wait for Peter to resolve it. That's how I learnt my form of jazz I guess, because he was always there like a big safety net."

And what was Peter's musical inspiration for this "proto-heavy metal" song. Something by Led Zeppelin or Deep Purple? Wrong. "'Rattlesnake Shake' just kind of came to me when I heard The Who singing Martha And The Vandellas' 'Dancing In The Street'."

CHAPTER 18

UNDERWAY

The first edition of this book documented how Peter Green, over the past thirty years, has inhabited a House of Blues shared by demons and angels each trying unsuccessfully to evict the other. But on Sunday, 5 May 1996 the demons did finally get the boot and have been kept at a distance for most of the time ever since. It was on that fine spring bank holiday weekend that Peter stepped back on the boards at the opulent Buxton Opera House, after a quarter of a century's troubled absence from the world stage.

The occasion was the annual Alexis Korner Memorial Concert. At ten pm the twelve-hundred-strong capacity crowd see a portly figure with a worldly-wise gait saunter on stage – dressed in black and sporting a pork-pie hat – and the place erupts before the guitarist has played a note. It takes a full two minutes for the applause to fade, and then a mood of glad reverence fills this intimate theatre as The Splinter Group's five-number set gets into gear. "It's so good to see you, Peter!" "We love you, Peter!" – spontaneous cries from the audience continue throughout the thirty-minute performance.

Yet the man himself is nervous; frequently adjusting volume and tone controls on his coal black Gibson Howard Roberts Jazz Fusion guitar, seemingly never content with his sound. And of course, it's no surprise that he's nervous...here he is updating his own legend, and the high table of British blues is watching him from the wings: Paul Jones, Andy Fairweather-Low, Chris Farlowe, Mick Abrahams, Mike Sanchez and Bernie Marsden are just a few of the other names on the bill. Plus the

BBC cameras are there filming the whole thing for a half-hour arts documentary – *The Works* – due to be broadcast in the autumn.

The band – a four-piece featuring Nigel Watson on guitar, Cozy Powell on drums, and Neil Murray on bass – sounds tight but they're all obviously looking out for Peter. So while the evening's subtext for the crowd is "He's back!", the sentiment apparent from his co-musicians is more like "Will he cope?".

He does. Otis Rush's 'It Takes Time' is an appositely-titled opener and Green's vocal delivery throughout, though restrained and a tad apologetic, is a voice dripping with life's bitter-sweet experience. Blues buffs may remember a filmed interview with Muddy Waters back in the late 1960s: "If you wanna sing the blues like I sing the blues," bragged the first King of Chicago, resplendent in day-glo orange suit and axle-greased bouffant, "then you have to pay the cost out there. Maybe after another hundred years a white man will come along who can sing the blues like me..." McKinley Morganfield's clairvoyance back then did not see as far as Peter Greenbaum 1996: it's not that he now sings *like* a black man – weirdly, it's as though he sings *as* a black man.

The remainder of the Buxton set includes 'Black Magic Woman' (with Nigel Watson doing justice to the classic late 1960s Green guitar solos); Hank Marvin's 'Peace Pipes', where Peter coaxes the sweetest tones out of his red Strat; a big-beat Watson composition, 'The Indians', which has an Eagles-ish chorus; and finally a low-key version of 'Green Manalishi' showcasing Cozy Powell's flawless drumming.

In retrospect Buxton May 1996 perhaps is best viewed more as a spiritual, not musical turning point in this blues master's colourful career – putting it bluntly, he could have come out and played 'Popeye The Sailor Man' and the audience would have loved him, such is the esteem in which Peter Green, the man, is held.

That day's good atmosphere is recalled by Harry Lee of Stockport-based Active Promotions whose dream it was to be the man helping to bring about and promote Green's comeback gig. In the period leading up to it, Lee's task had been diplomatically to try and not straddle the fine line between well-meant enthusiasm and pushy ear-bending as he plotted. "On the afternoon of the gig the band did a long rehearsal," Harry points out, "and it was the most emotional thing just being there. The only people in the theatre were Peter's entourage and the BBC film crew. Peter came on and I was soon close to tears. The band was laid back and just let him do his thing and he played beautifully and I was really glad that the BBC was there filming the soundcheck.

"But the actual performance that night was another matter. He was obviously very nervous and musically it wasn't the greatest gig in the world – which, of course, nobody was expecting after such a long time away from audiences. Anyway, emotionally it was a wonderful evening and I'm sure that it took Peter back to the good times before things went wrong for him.

"But what the BBC then did was unforgivable – they only used the footage from the evening's performance and not one bit of the marvellous stuff at the rehearsal. Now that just wasn't fair. I haven't met one person who was there at Buxton and also saw the documentary who thought that it captured what was really going on that evening and I have to say that I think the guy who made it is an absolute shyster."

Harry Lee spent almost a year, on and off, bringing that gig about. During that time, he says, he noticed a big change for the better in Peter's appearance: "I first saw Peter after all these years at the memorial service for Rory Gallagher in London – which was November 1995 – and I remember thinking that he still looked fragile. As a great fan of Peter's as well as a promoter, this made me wonder if he was anywhere near ready for getting back up in front of an audience. But then a couple of months later I rang Mich Reynolds and she assured me that Peter did want to do the Alexis Korner Memorial in May. They were already scheduled to do a warm-up gig at the Frankfurt Music Fair in February."

The Splinter Group's co-manager, Stuart Taylor, remembers Frankfurt as a "qualified success". The reason it came about in the first place was because in the closing months of 1995, Peter had struck up an informal association with the Gibson guitar company. Gibson wanted him to collaborate in the development of a special edition Peter Green Les Paul. But Peter wasn't too comfortable with the whole idea of tributes or special edition guitars, mainly because they dwell too much on past glories: "Perhaps I'll help them with a special edition when I'm dead," he now points out drily.

The Frankfurt performance in February took place in front of a two thousand-strong audience and wasn't without its share of last-minute dramas backstage. These had nothing to do with the music but, alas, centred on business hassles. At the rehearsal, sponsors Gibson were more than a little miffed when they realised that on three of the five-number set (the same as at Buxton) Peter played a Fender Stratocaster and only used his Gibson Howard Roberts Fusion on 'It Takes Time' and 'Black Magic Woman'.

With thirty minutes to showtime the air was thick and heavy outside the band's dressing-room as agitated Gibson executives complained to management that, in effect, they'd been duped. Stuart mediated with tact and after a sticky ten minutes of confrontation in the end it was Peter who resolved the matter – he said that he had no problem swapping guitars at the last minute with the exception of one number – Hank Marvin's 'Peace Pipes', which demands a Fender Stratocaster sound.

The general feedback in England after the Frankfurt "dress rehearsal" for what was to become The Splinter Group, was that Peter's playing was much more together than people were expecting. What's more, there were occasional flashes of that old Green magic – enough, everyone agreed, to augur well for the future. Well, almost everyone...

From those very early days of The Splinter Group, drummer Cozy Powell never let nostalgia muffle his eardrums. Powell is the consummate professional muso and performer; he is also a huge admirer of Peter Green's legendary work. These two things combined have made him one of the harsher judges of the band's progress during 1996/97.

"From the very beginning," he explains, "I saw my role within this band as a supportive one. It's great that Peter is back playing and doing what he loves best, but my concern has always been that he is happy and doesn't feel any pressure."

After Frankfurt, Powell was not convinced that the band was ready to go out on the road, as Stuart Taylor well remembers: "Even a couple of months after Frankfurt Cozy was unsure because of the rawness of the raw material. So he said to us, 'Get yourself another bass player and drummer; get it finely honed up, and I'll rejoin the band.'

"Now I didn't find this all that satisfactory," says Taylor in a maelstrom of understatement, "and I told him as much. So Cozy stayed, but I'm sure he's never felt completely happy and relaxed about the situation." Backstage after the Buxton gig the BBC's cameras captured Powell's concern: as the others celebrated, he left the venue looking decidedly sceptical.

Nigel Watson agrees with Stuart that, in effect, from day one there was a splinter group within The Splinter Group. "At the beginning we were very grateful," Nigel emphasises, "for Cozy's professionalism combined with enthusiasm. But as time went on, him and the others clearly couldn't understand that dealing with Peter was a completely different thing. Their super-slick approach meant that they felt very uncomfortable when Peter took his time in between numbers to adjust his amp and so on. But then again, to them soundchecks before gigs were something to be got over with as quickly as possible whereas Peter liked to take his time, sorting out amp settings and stuff. Had the soundchecks been longer from the start, there might've been fewer gaps between numbers."

The next big date in the band's diary was headlining the Guildford Folk And Blues Festival. In between came two major blues festivals in Norway and Italy, and also the addition of keyboardist Spike Edney (ex-Queen). "It became clear," Stuart points out, "that the band was coming together and would obviously be playing to big audiences, so we brought Spike in not just for his musicianship and filling out the sound but also because we needed a frontman/MC-type who was totally relaxed handling crowds."

Guildford was a successful showcase outdoors in front of an estimated six thousand people. By now the set had extended to thirteen songs including two acoustic Robert Johnson numbers: 'Steady Rollin' Man' featuring Peter on harmonica and vocals, and Nigel Watson singing 'From Four 'Til Late' with Peter accompanying him on guitar and harmonica. The old hits included were 'Black Magic Woman', 'Rattlesnake Shake', 'Albatross', and 'Green Manalishi', plus Peter's calling card from his John Mayall days, 'The Stumble'.

From the very start, and as thoughts began to turn to a high-profile comeback in 1996, Peter never was comfortable playing the old hits. He made this quite clear to Cliff Jones in an interview for *The Guitar Magazine* (February 1996) – which, to this author's knowledge, is the most illuminating feature ever to be written about the man's approach to making music. "Yeah," he tells Jones about recycling the old stuff, "but I was persuaded to do them. I won't do any of the old stuff but I was persuaded to do it for just one show [Frankfurt]. It's past tense to me. Those are old, dusty songs. I did it enough times in the olden days and I should be allowed to move on. I shouldn't have to do the old songs – I shouldn't and I won't."

This fighting talk comes from an artist who is not, and has never been, shackled by thoughts of box office take and the bottom-line. Yet, it also says something about his generosity when you realise that since that interview took place in early 1996, the "just one show" extended to nearly one-hundred-and-fifty.

Significantly, doing the old hits in a sense was the making of The Splinter Group for their 96/97 British and European "comeback" tour – that's what audiences by the thousand wanted to see and hear once again...the exquisite nostalgia of seeing Green back on stage after so many lost years, and playing 'Albatross'.

But, at the time of writing in early October 1997, doing the old hits has also turned out to be the breaking of that original line-up. Three weeks before The Splinter Group are to appear as special guests on a BB King six-date UK tour of the arenas, Cozy Powell and Spike Edney have left the band. "The problem," explained Cozy shortly before going onstage for what was to be his final Splinter Group gig at the Rory Gallagher Memorial concert in Buxton, "is that Peter is getting very reluctant to do his old hits anymore. And if you try and explain to him that the old hits are what punters pay to come and hear, then he'll say something like, 'Well, they'll have to learn to enjoy the other stuff.'"

There is a dollop of irony in Peter's attitude because, if anything, the mid 1990s versions of 'Albatross', 'Green Manalishi' and 'Rattlesnake Shake' are far more polished – if more sedate – than live versions of those songs back in the late sixties. Is this surprising? Not really, when you think about it. It is no slight whatsoever on the original Fleetwood Mac rhythm section to assert that Cozy Powell and ex-Whitesnake bassist Neil Murray, aged in their forties, technically are far more accomplished musicians than were Fleetwood and McVie as young, rock 'n' rolling twenty-somethings.

You can never please everyone, of course. For instance, while at Guildford, a happily anonymous and fit-looking Eric Clapton later commented how Peter's playing was "better than I was expecting", the view of producer Mike Vernon, standing next to him, was less diplomatic – both about the choice of songs, and the backing band. "My overall impression," Mike said afterwards, "I have to say was one of disappointment. I was trying very hard not to be too mawkish and reverential about the memory of Peter as I remember him, in the hope that he would come back and be able to do the same thing again which I think is unrealistic. What I was concerned about – and saying this I am trying to bear in mind that Peter has been through the mill backwards ten times more than any of us would in ten lifetimes – was that despite the sound musicianship of the people involved, I felt that the band around Peter was inappropriate. Cozy is a distinguished drummer but like a fish out of water in this environment.

"And I don't think Nigel Watson does Peter any favours in as much as he's playing all the licks and all the solo passages that Peter made famous. Now this may be because Peter can't play them anymore, then I ask myself the question: 'Why?' And if Peter's going to offer the excuse, 'Well, I don't want to play them', then, to me as a producer that's not acceptable because that's what the people want to see and hear. I don't want to hear somebody else playing note-for-note like Peter Green when Peter himself is standing three feet away. I want to hear Peter Green...and at the end of the day I think that's what the public will want."

Vernon is right about one thing, as Nigel Watson confirms: "I play those solos mostly like the original because that is the song...and the reason Pete doesn't play them is because he's played them thousands of times in the past and no longer wants to do them – he's moved on."

Mike Vernon continues: "At Guildford, even when I did get to hear Peter Green playing an instrumental I originally produced for him – 'The Stumble' – I have to say that whilst the performance was okay, it wasn't a patch on what he was able to play twenty-five years ago. All right, even Freddie King [who wrote 'The Stumble'] made mistakes, but what I'm looking for is fluidity and some fire.

"The reality is that there are so many guitar players that have created new and far more diverse styles which encompass more melody and improvisation...and are far more upfront as personalities, that Peter is just going to become another has-been."

Strong words indeed. Peter Green – soon to be a has-been? Bearing in mind that Mike Vernon is notorious for only airing views which have their master volume set on overdrive, does this well-meaning devil's advocate have a point about Peter's future career? No, is the answer, for when it comes to legends, the music and technical prowess are only part of the story. To compare, as Vernon seems to want to, Peter Green with a new-generation guitar gunslinger such as Yngwie Malmsteen is to completely miss the point.

That very point in question – ie what makes for "legend appeal" – can be illustrated by reference to a different, extreme and sad example of the "legendary comeback" which is mentioned in Charles Keil's classic book *Urban Blues*. Keil remembers a concert in London in the early 1960s where once-famous American bluesmen, some by now over seventy, played before a British audience – many for the first time. "The event featured an array of elderly bluesmen," Keil writes, "doing all they could do to stave off the effects of acute alcoholism. Aside from an impassioned but slobbery harmonica solo by Sonny Boy Williamson, a couple of numbers in which Howlin' Wolf coerced the dilapidated rhythm section into a more cohesive state, and an all too brief display of artistry from Lightnin' Hopkins, the concert might be best described as a third-rate minstrel show.

"The thousands of Englishmen assembled for the event in awed silence; the more ludicrous the performance, the more thunderous the applause at its conclusion. The high point of the evening came when Willie Dixon, the bulky bassist, picked up an unamplified guitar and sang his own ballad on peace, love and brotherhood in the Appalachia tones of Joan Baez. The applause was deafening and justifiably so. Considering this utterly sincere ballad, specially composed for the occasion, and the hundreds of lyrics Dixon has created for his fellow bluesmen, I could not help feeling genuine awe in the presence of a genius."

Of course, Keil's example of this tacky "comeback" – where some of the rediscovered artists probably had no interest in playing but were coaxed into it by the promoter's promise of a fast buck and endless supply of whiskey – has nothing in common with Peter Green's current artistic reawakening. What it does show, though, is that audiences feel a need to appreciate the past as well as the present. The term blues legend (or "leg-end", as Green self-mockingly sometimes pronounces it) amounts to a part-true, part-mythical life story in which the artist's music plays a leading role, but not the only role.

And so Keil's astonishment over the apparently OTT applause, like Vernon's technical critique of The Splinter Group at Guildford, betrays a blinkered attitude by focusing exclusively on the music. 'The Stumble' in 1996 isn't a patch on the original? Mike is welcome to his view, but on an emotional level he's not seeing nine-tenths of the bigger picture that guitarist and Peter's old sparring partner, Snowy White, obviously has in full view: "If Mike's just looking at what notes Peter plays all the time, or what it sounds like, then he's not going to be particularly impressed. But what I sensed when I saw Pete in Sardinia [this was a month or so before Guildford] was a far more positive attitude coming from him. His playing at that point was rough round the edges but when he did 'The Stumble' he had this solid attitude which made me think that he's now playing because he wants to. Back in the late 1970s I got the impression that his heart wasn't in it and he'd been pushed by others."

Snowy saw Peter play again in Brighton and at the Shepherd's Bush Empire at Christmas, shortly after the live album had been recorded. "I'd already noticed," says Snowy, "he was far more confident as a person at the end of the summer compared to that Sardinia gig; but his playing was much, much stronger in Brighton." Snowy also watched Peter from the soundboard at a blues festival in Norway during summer 1996, and says he himself felt tearful when some fans wept as Green began to play the Freddie King classic he made his own.

Strong emotions also came from a young fan at Dublin's Mean Fiddler – during the band's second sell-out tour of Ireland in May 1997 – who sent the following words to him backstage, written, where else, but on the back of an empty fag-packet: "Look Peter, I don't want to do the dramatic, but the happiest memories in my life are listening your records with my father (who died two years ago). I would love to meet you."

Then there was the mother and daughter backstage at the Manchester Ritz who looked like something out of the TV comedy *Absolutely Fabulous* – mum with wild punk hair; teenage daughter prim by comparison. Having been introduced to the man, the daughter – who knew Peter's music inside out because, thanks to mum, it was always on in the house during her childhood – soon had to back away, starstruck and speechless. As she left the room a couple of minutes later all she could say time and time again was, "I've just met Peter Green!"

Of course, all this is just mawkish nostalgia to Mike Vernon who judged Peter's performance in Guildford "wearing my producer's hat" and possibly on the look-out to make a better Peter Green record than the last one he produced with him (*Man Of The World*) and ideally sell more records than last time. But what Mike couldn't see at Guildford were expressions on the faces of hundreds in the crowd right by the stage and therefore close enough to feel Green's presence as opposed to spectating a band's performance from a distance.

Here, Charles Keil's Willie Dixon reference to "awe in the presence of a genius" springs to mind. And especially so whenever Peter sings and plays harmonica on Robert Johnson's 'Steady Rollin' Man': the sight of any musician totally absorbed in his playing is an interesting one, but when that musician's legacy over the past thirty years still is contributing to part of what's going on right now in the music world, then audiences are captivated perhaps for reasons which go beyond the notes being played at that very moment.

In 1997, the Green sphere of influence among a new generation of musicians and listeners even includes a Brixton dance-techno act called Alabama 3 who this year were signed to the almighty Geffen label in America. Their music is innovative fusion that combines techno with blues and country and western: surprise, surprise, they cite Peter Green as a guiding light when leaders Rob and Wayne were first developing their ideas for the band. And it's not just his old hits and *Then Play On*'s innovation that inspired them; certain tracks on Peter's 1970 solo project *End Of The Game* – 'Bottoms Up', for instance – they see as prototype techno. Of course, as mentioned earlier in this book, that solo project was derided at the time as indulgent space-cadet musical gobbledygook.

Then there's Aerosmith's Joe Perry, who lauds Peter as the guitarist who took Hank Marvin's sound into the 1970s; and then there's contemporary US blues maestro Ronnie Earl who has recently composed a tribute to Peter – an instrumental called 'Heart Of Glass'. Pithily, Earl describes Green as "the greatest guitarist of any style ever...ever". Billy Gibbons and Tinsley Ellis would agree with Earl, and the list goes on and on.

And yet all this worldwide tub-thumping about Green's legacy falls on deaf ears as far as Peter himself is concerned, and this probably only serves to empower his reputation still further. Why? Because this combination of greatness and humility is the stuff from which legends – the long-term ones that forever fascinate, and not the comeback variety – are made.

He articulates some of the reasons for this humility in an incisive and stylishly-shot thirty-minute TV documentary about him filmed by director Neil Rawles for Anglia TV. Titled *Peter Green – Back For Good?*, it was screened in October 1997, though regrettably only in the Anglia region.

"I have to watch out," Peter warns, "for people paying me false compliments – trying to see if they can make you go up on a cloud. That's what happened to me now I think about it...I went up on a cloud and I thought I was better than I was. I kind of went up on success and I accepted their compliments – and see where I ended up," he adds ruefully.

What's more, in an interview with the author for *The Sunday Telegraph* published the week after the Guildford showcase he said quite snappily, "If I'm their guitar hero then who's gonna be my hero?" This remark does hint at the loneliness and alienation he increasingly may have felt back in the 1960s as his fans – mostly male – deified him. And, alas, some still do and presumably always will.

For instance in September 1996 a seemingly unremarkable incident in the hotel foyer on the afternoon before the first of four nights at Ronnie Scott's in Birmingham, gives an idea of just how weird this kind of hero-worship must have been back in the 1960s. Two men in their mid-to-late forties – presumably the type Peter now remembers as "funny blokes that would go 'eeeee!'" – had been lurking there for hours, albums and CDs under their arm ready to be autographed. When Peter appeared they approached him and the guitarist obliged, pen in hand. As patiently he signed away, one guy kept saying to the other – and within earshot of Peter, "God, it's him...it is him!" as he ogled his hero in the strangest way, like he was some kind of alien or apparition.

Minutes later the next "funny bloke" waiting there in that foyer for an autograph felt it wasn't enough when Peter went on to sign about four different Fleetwood Mac CDs and albums for him. Instead he then took from his bag a large format rock encyclopaedia in which on consecutive pages there were numerous photos of Peter with his old band. This obsessive in all seriousness thought it reasonable to ask Peter to sign each individual photograph...in other words up to three signatures per page. He looked put-out when politely Peter declined. (Witnessing the encounter close-up and also sensing this autograph-hunter's creepily furtive demeanour throughout, the thought occurred that there is really little difference in the mind-set of this fan and the young Beatlemaniacs back in the early 1960s who snipped off locks of hair from the Fab Four; not to mention the not-so-young Beatlemaniac who in 1980 thanked John Lennon for signing his album by assassinating him later the same day.)

Stacking this kind of eerie fanatical interest alongside the Manchester and Dublin backstage greetings does suggest that, broadly speaking, there have always been two kinds of Greenophiles: supporters who in essence want to give – give thanks to their idol; secondly, there are fanatics who have to take – take some form of relic away from their saint. And looking back to the stardom days, we understand more about the price Green paid for his fame, when night after night for two to three years an essentially shy artist was forced to run the gauntlet of what was often rather scary sycophancy.

"Sick-ophancy" perhaps is a better way to describe the ultra-weird posturings of an Essex farmer called Patrick Harper. Harper secured his Warholian fifteen minutes of fame between 1993-94 as a ridiculously accomplished Peter Green impostor before he was exposed as a fraud by journalist Dean Nelson of *The Observer* newspaper. From then on he earned himself the nickname the "Egg and Potato Man".

It beggars belief that this six-out-of-ten lookalike managed to con the music industry to the brink of securing a respectable record deal as "Peter Green" – but he did. With his hippie-speak ramblings about being hassled by the "spaghetti-eaters" (music-biz mafia), and his *Stars In Their Eyes*-type devotion to mimicking the classic 1960s clipped, nasal guitar tones typified by the genuine Peter's playing on 'Need Your Love So Bad', he fooled people who rightly should have known better.

The author first got wind of "Peter Green" when he was sighted at the 1992 London Music Show in Wembley, north London. Looking "tidy" and showing his young daughter Gibson Les Pauls on the various exhibition stands, when asked for his autograph he signed as Peter Green and chatted freely about the old times in Fleetwood Mac. Because the author, only a few days previously, had spoken over the phone to Len Green in Great Yarmouth, he knew for certain that the real Peter Green was many miles from Wembley...and, at that point, a million miles from wishing to make semi-public appearances and check out the latest Gibson guitars. The real Peter Green was taking strong medication that meant he spent up to sixteen hours per day asleep, passing his few waking hours watching MTV, eating and going for the occasional bracing walk along the seafront.

Even so, despite this clear first-hand evidence that a fraudster was on the loose, certain editors on certain music magazines became hostile if their view – that Harper was Green, as it were – was challenged. After a few very heated telephone conversations the author decided it was best to walk away from the fiasco – having learned from it an important lesson for his forthcoming Peter Green biography: namely, that most myths which have built up about Peter Green – the Munich drama; the shotgun incident; to name but two – self-perpetuate themselves and are impervious to the truth. Nine times out of ten the music business and the media still have Peter Green down as the rock star who got spiked with bad acid in Munich and soon after quit music to become a gravedigger. The truth – he left because in essence Fleetwood Mac wanted to make money more than they wanted to make new music – is dull by comparison.

Myths endure because people actually want to believe them, as a part of the legend. The "Egg and Potato Man" story is a variation on this theme: perhaps it was because the industry so badly wanted Peter Green to return from the wilderness that they were even prepared to be duped in order to up the chances of it actually happening.

But back in the 1960s it was more scaled-down and contained versions of Patrick Harper that partly were the making and breaking of Peter Green. What we now know, again with the huge benefit of hindsight, is that for the first year of that heady period of success – 1968-70 – he managed to keep his feet firmly on the ground. He could handle fronting Britain's number one blues band with a Top Ten album in the charts for months on end: "Right from the start I kind of always saw Fleetwood Mac," Peter now remembers, "as being on the same level as Jethro Tull in this country, but then they got big in America and we thought we wanted to do and could do the same."

As we already know (Chapter 4), with America came drugs, and with 'Albatross' came a quite different level of fame to anything he'd experienced before – plus a feeling of "exaltation" as Peter has described it. Then on that second late 68/early 69 US tour drugs, adulation and 'Albatross' topping the charts, all came at the same time. The outcome was that the guitarist/songwriter, in his own words, floated up on a cloud.

In November 1996 – and in the middle of a very hectic UK and European tour schedule – Peter once again said he felt he could float, but this time in a much less sinister sense of the word. The venue in question was the Irish Centre in Liverpool. "When we went on stage to start our set," says Peter, beaming at the memory, "I just couldn't believe what was coming up from the audience...there was so much warmth there I felt like it was solid enough for me to be able to walk out on it over them."

Throughout that autumn and winter a schedule of intensive gigging for The Splinter Group in Britain, Ireland, Germany, Poland, Switzerland, Austria, Greece, Spain and France was productive in several ways: firstly, a live album was recorded – taken from four UK gigs in December. *Peter Green The Splinter Group* was released in May 1997 to positive critical acclaim. Secondly, touring for the most part was very therapeutic for Peter, keeping him stimulated, whereas off the road he's much more laid-back. His lifestyle at home near Croydon is eccentric – many times he's the last one to go to bed, falling asleep in front of the telly watching one of the satellite music channels with an unplugged electric guitar in his lap; and then often not rising until the early afternoon. His daily schedule on the road is another matter.

Arriving in an interesting new town he's the first to want to check out the street life. For instance, having booked into the hotel at Belfast on the opening night of their second Irish tour in May, most of the entourage wanted to venture no further than the ground-floor restaurant. "Come on," Peter urged some of them, "we can be a bit more more adventurous. Let's meet some Belfast people and see what the girls are like." On the ten-minute walk to a cafe at the university end of the city, no fewer than four people spotted him and stopped just long enough to shake hands and welcome him. Peter visibly was pleased by these gestures.

Another time, his natural curiosity and interest in people from other cultures meant that when the band played Bradford's St George's Hall in February, he was the first one up and about the next morning walking round the city centre before breakfast "just looking at faces" in this multi-cultural town. The gig the previous night had been truly a concert with an acutely attentive audience of serious Bradfordians – something that Green much prefers to muffled chatter and hubbub coming from some noisy clubs. At one point someone briefly broke the reverent hush in between numbers with a reverent heckle: "Eric Clapton, eat your heart out..." Once again, Peter looked encouraged by the remark, yet it was clear to all that he didn't for a moment take it seriously.

Everything points to The Road being a good thing for Peter's well-being; but over the past two years crucial changes have taken place in other areas which have played and continue to improve his quality of life. Firstly, new legal representation – formally appointed in early 1996 – is ensuring that Peter is now properly consulted on all matters concerning his estate. This may seem like stating the obvious but in mid 1995 The Splinter Group's managers Reynolds and Taylor were surprised when they discovered his previous lawyer's modus operandi. "I was amazed," explains Mich Reynolds, "how little Peter seemed to know about his own financial affairs and it soon became clear to me that decisions were being taken by his old lawyer on his behalf and he was being kept in the dark." Peter was introduced to his new lawyer, Cathy Fehler, in the summer of 1995, and months of complex legal wrangles followed, many of which have yet to be resolved.

A second massive improvement to Peter's quality of life was set in motion by Peter himself in the spring of 1995: it was then he stopped taking the tranquillisers that he'd been prescribed some four years earlier whilst living with brother Len and his family, first in Great Yarmouth and then in Essex. When Mich Reynolds first went to visit Peter in March 1995 his physical appearance came as quite a surprise:

"I hadn't seen Peter in years and when this old man with grey hair came to the door I was shocked. We went out for a drive and Pete told me how he was on strong medication and spent most of his time either asleep or feeling tired. Later I found out that he'd been prescribed the tranquillisers several years earlier and that nobody had checked up in the meanwhile whether he still needed to take such large dosages or anything.

"Then a couple of months later he came to visit me just after he'd got back from a short holiday in the Lake District. The first thing he said was, 'Guess what...I've stopped taking the medication.' And my first reaction was that perhaps it would be a good idea if he went to see a doctor just to check whether stopping so suddenly was wise."

Peter stayed off the stuff and mostly it was Nigel Watson who helped him through the transition. "There were a few bad nightmares he told me about and he said he still sometimes heard voices," says Nigel. "Now my attitude to that was not to say, 'Don't be stupid, Peter, you know they're not really there.' Instead, I tried to get to the bottom of it by asking him, 'Well, who is it...what are they saying...do you agree with them?'"

Gradually, day-by-day Peter learned to live with his new unsedated and aware frame of mind and now compares his years on medication to "living like a worm – even a worm has more of a life than I had on tranquillisers. You just about know your name but that's about it."

Peter re-establishing contact around that time with his old friends Mich Reynolds and Nigel Watson in fact led to his first public appearance in years, at the Shepherd's Bush Empire. To the complete surprise and delight of an unsuspecting audience there to see and hear Gary Moore promote his *Blues For Greeny* thank you album, Mich and Nigel persuaded him to walk onstage after Gary's gig and take a bow. "It took a lot of persuading him before he would even agree to go along and watch Gary from backstage," Mich remembers. "And even when he did finally say okay, I remember as Nigel and I drove him into town he kept asking me, 'You're not taking me in to do *This Is Your Life*, are you?' But then when we got there he said he was pleased he'd come along."

At that gig Nigel began to sow the seeds which over the spring and summer months of 1995 led to a minor miracle, namely Peter changing his mind about not ever picking up a guitar again: "It was obvious that

Pete was enjoying being back in that whole environment, and at one point I just looked over to him and said, 'It should really be you out there playing your songs.' He just smiled but, knowing Pete, I could see that he knew I was right and that he might just be beginning to think things over."

For the following nine months Peter stayed mostly with Nigel and his wife near Croydon, spending some weekends at Mich's place. "After work in the afternoon I would go straight back and some days we'd go fishing which he always enjoyed," says Nigel. "Other times I'd pick up a guitar in our kitchen, but he once said, 'Sorry Nige but I've got long fingernails so I can't play guitar.' I kept on trying to encourage him saying if you don't wanna do it for yourself play something for me as a friend. Eventually he picked up a guitar but at first you could see that that when he played his mind wanted to do more than his hands could and so he fumbled a little. But with time – maybe three or four weeks – that went.

"Because I've known Pete for a long time I know that he has always lived for music. So that same summer my wife Sandra – who'd not met him until then – worked on reminding him about table manners and personal hygiene in front of the children; and he and I also did a lot of talking. I would say things like, 'What are you going to do for the rest of your life? For your own good you've got to work...and your job is playing guitar, and loads of people love what you do.' Then Pete would run himself down by saying that it was all a long time ago and so I'd say, 'Music you love it...everyone can see that it's in you buzzing away – let's just channel some of it.' Eventually he decided to give it a try but before he could do that Sandra had to cut his fingernails. And then the two of us would play Robert Johnson's 'Steady Rollin' Man' sitting at the kitchen table."

Watson's achievement was no less than a miracle. For years if anyone made the faintest suggestion that Green might, let alone should, ever play again then he looked troubled and even haunted, admitting that, "Playing the guitar ended up breaking my heart and I can't let that happen anymore." But thanks to his friend's gentle handling, within a couple of months Peter was back in the studio with Nigel demoing the latter's 'The Indians' and rehearsing a slightly slower and Santana-esque 'Black Magic Woman'.

Despite how he feels about living off past glories, Peter now says it was Santana's version of 'Black Magic Woman' that in summer 1995 encouraged him to think about going back on the road. "'Black Magic Woman'," he explains, "I always love playing because we do it a bit differently each night. The Splinter Group version is somewhere between the old Fleetwood Mac one and Santana's. To tell you the truth, I didn't especially like Santana's version when I first heard it but then I grew used to it. But I've always felt very grateful about Carlos doing a cover because Santana made me much more well-known in America – none of my other records did well over there."

For Nigel Watson the happiest and most rewarding moment in Peter's return was on one of those demo sessions: "I looked over at Peter in the studio at one point and for the first time could see that he was getting a real buzz from his playing – that was a great moment."

A similar glad instant was witnessed by the author, who has been lucky enough to be a guest at about two dozen Splinter Group performances throughout the 1996/97 European tour. At the Colne Municipal Hall last December the band – and Peter in particular – warmed to a crowd who had immediately warmed to them. During the opening few bars of Freddie King's classic 'Goin' Down', Peter tried out his own seven-note phrase over King's familiar intro of staccato hammering (sadly, he didn't do it on the nights the Fleetwood Mobile recorded the band's live album). This decoration worked, Peter knew it, and he beamed across to Nigel. It was a beam on a par with his happiest times in Fleetwood Mac in 1968.

Thankfully there were plenty of other moments to make Peter's return to The Road worthwhile – although he says he'd do some things differently next time. "Poland was my favourite concert," he smiles, "the one where they ended up jumping up and down to the music. But I'm not sure I want to do as much gigging as last year...it takes it out of you driving on motorways all the time. I kind of like the idea of just gigging at weekends.

"Right now [October/November 1997] me and Nigel are doing a Robert Johnson album we've both been wanting to do for some time now. It's going well and the thing I'm trying to get right is the wildness in his playing. But, in the future I'd also like to try stuff by Fred McDowell, Mississippi John Hurt, and Memphis Minnie – they all play that kind of controlled blues."

Work on the Robert Johnson sessions at KD's studio in Acton, London, has seen both men try to recapture and update Johnson's raw, animal passion. "Pete and I have always shared this love and respect for animals," explains Nigel. "Animals don't tell lies; they live on their wits and instincts; and often it's in a dangerous environment. Those are the kinds of things Robert Johnson's music and guitar playing mean to me."

The first edition of this book ended with the big question – will he ever play guitar again? The equivalent question for this second edition is – will he ever take up songwriting again? For the moment, it doesn't feature in Peter's plans. "After the Robert Johnson tribute we're going to do a Splinter Group studio album," he says, "with Nigel's songs on it."

On will he/won't he himself write songs again the jury is still out. Literally. For, as Peter sees things, only a jury of musicologists might be able to help remove one major obstacle which presently is inhibiting his songwriting. "For years now I've been getting messages that I should give back part of my songwriting royalties to the blues musicians who inspired me to write certain songs."

Even though ex-Led Zeppelin singer Robert Plant has described the world of blues musicians through time as "one big family of beggars and thieves" when it comes to using other people's ideas, evidently Peter Green now wants to be a cut above. Which means that until his conscience about plagiarising old blues is soothed it is highly unlikely that his innovative talents as a songwriter will be tested out to see whether they have matured over time.

The Splinter Group's bass player Neil Murray has strong views about this: "I think a crucial part of Peter's comeback – as well as a crucial part of the development of The Splinter Group – is that at some point he sits down either on his own or with another musician and starts working on some new and original material."

Peter himself sees that his main priority now is to "practise and learn more ways of playing more notes well". One way of doing this involves hooking up with his past, in the sense that he has always thrived on jamming and exchanging ideas with other guitarists. Bernie Marsden – who in the autumn of 1995 came up with the freshest of the three "thank you Greeny" covers albums – remembers a recent after-gig hotel room jam: "We just played a couple of unplugged electric guitars and did Peter's old stuff but in different ways. In that kind of relaxed situation Peter's playing has much of the fire he had in the old days."

Peter's family in Southend and Brighton reportedly are pleased to see him back up on stage and playing guitar once again. Interestingly, the room he had at brother Len's house until spring 1995 still has some of Peter's things there and is kept exactly as it was when he lived there.

That the future looks promising for the guitarist is echoed by The Blues Band's harp player, actor and broadcaster Paul Jones who sat next to Peter on the flight to a summer 1997 blues festival in Hell, Norway. Jones was nicely surprised by Peter's obvious progress since he last spoke to him at Buxton two years earlier: "I think everybody there at Buxton a couple of years ago felt that musically Peter had a steep hill in front of him, although it was great to see him attacking it in the first place. He's gone a long way up that hill which is great, and makes me think how well it augurs for the future.

"But on that flight he said one thing that I really wanted to delve deeper into, but felt that there and then was not quite the moment. Peter said, 'You see, Jewish people don't go for too much in the way of spontaneity, adventurousness and ground-breaking.' And as he said it I thought, 'That's him really...very much working within a rigid format – blues – but then again who took that format further ahead than he did?'"

But the final word on Peter's return to the spotlight goes to blues expert, Jimi Hendrix biographer, and *Daily Telegraph* album reviewer, Charles Shaar Murray. A couple of Murray quotes tell Peter Green's followers that we have much for which to be grateful, and also suggest to Peter that he has a lot to look forward to. In his indispensable blues encyclopaedia *Blues On CD The Essential Guide* first published in 1993, Murray's appreciation of Green's legacy in effect was also an epitaph. Back then he wrote: "The power of the blues can destroy those who tap it if the physical and mental vessel is unequal to the task of containing that power. Peter Green burned astonishingly bright before he burned out."

Four years on in May 1997, reviewing The Splinter Group's live album Murray told *Daily Telegraph* readers: "Way back then, Green was the greatest of the sixties' British Blues Guys. And guess what? He still is."

SOUND EQUIPMENT
THROUGH THE YEARS

- *Guitars* -

GIBSON LES PAUL STANDARD

Peter Green's 1959 sunburst Gibson Les Paul Standard has become a logo for his blues playing. It is now owned by Gary Moore, albeit with a new neck. Readers wanting chapter and verse on this guitar's history should refer to *Guitarist* magazine's Gary Moore interview in the April 1995 issue. Its unique "nasal" sound resulted from a happy accident Peter had when he put back one of the pick-ups upside-down, in effect ensuring the sound was permanently out-of-phase. This tone is particularly evident on two tracks he recorded in 1968 – 'Need Your Love So Bad' and 'Love That Burns'.

GIBSON HOWARD ROBERTS FUSION

This coal-black 1995 semi-acoustic jazz guitar is an interesting choice since it is a quiet guitar to have within a rock band. But bearing in mind the kind of players Peter is now listening to and learning from – as much Kenny Burrell as Jimi Hendrix or Freddie King – it may be indicative of his intended direction in the future. When he first tried it he immediately took to the guitar's "jazzy mellow sound".

FENDER STRATOCASTER

On stage with The Splinter Group his other mainstay, along with the Howard Roberts Fusion, is a new, sonic blue Strat used in particular for the blues-rock repertoire, for example 'Rattlesnake Shake' and 'Goin'

Down'. (The March 1997 issue of *Guitarist* magazine carried an illustrated feature about Peter's ever-burgeoning guitar collection. Since that was published, his most notable acquisition has been a new National Resophonic steel guitar he bought in Germany.)

Lack of space is the only thing that stops Peter buying many more interesting old guitars from shops he always visits while on tour. His room at Mich Reynolds' house now is crammed with guitars, CDs and tapes of rare blues guitar masterpieces.

HARMONY METEOR

In Peter's second band, The Tridents, guitarist Brian Durney gave Peter his Harmony Meteor when he traded up to a Gretch Country Gentleman. Peter promptly converted the Meteor into a four-string bass. When Peter joined The Muskrats, his brother Michael helped him to buy a Star bass and, as he began to get back into playing lead guitar, Peter restored the Meteor to a six-string.

DALLAS TUXEDO

Peter's Dallas Tuxedo was "for home use", although he can be seen playing it on the promo film for 'Man Of The World'.

MICHIGAN (WOODEN-BODIED) RESONATOR

The opening riffs of 'Oh Well Part 1' are played on his Michigan wooden-bodied resonator.

RAMIRES FLAMENCO GUITAR

Peter played his Ramires Flamenco model on 'Oh Well Part 2' for the classical parts. The guitar has tuning pegs, as opposed to machineheads.

FENDER SIX-STRING BASS

During this time Peter also owned a Fender six-string bass with a Jazzmaster-shaped body, which he used in the studio.

ZEMAITIS ACOUSTIC

Peter took a custom-made Tony Zemaitis acoustic to the US in the late 1970s.

FENDER JAGUAR

Peter used a Fender Jaguar on the *In The Skies* album.

FRAMUS NASHVILLE

During Peter's years with Kolors his main guitar was a Framus Nashville. This guitar was unfortunately stolen from the doorway of his house in Richmond when he popped out to buy some cigarettes.

ARIA LES PAUL, IBANEZ & USA STRATOCASTER

Peter replaced the Framus Nashville with a black Aria Les Paul which had "clouds" inlayed along the fretboard. For some gigs he also used a yellow Ibanez, and a rosewood neck sunburst USA Stratocaster. He still owns the Strat.

- Amplifiers -

FENTON WEILL FIFTEEN-WATT AMP

Peter's first amp was a Fenton Weill fifteen-watt bass amplifier.

VOX FOUNDATION FIFTY-WATT AMP

After the Fenton Weill, Peter moved on to a Vox Foundation Bass fifty-watt amp with an eighteen-inch speaker.

MARSHALL FIFTY-WATT

During his Bluesbreakers days Peter mostly used a fifty-watt Marshall and single 4x12 cabinet.

ORANGE AMPLIFICATION

In November 1968 Fleetwood Mac were kitted out with Orange amplification. Peter used a hundred-watt amp head (GT120 model) and two 2x12 speaker cabinets. In addition he also had a separate Orange valve reverb unit. Although Mac's road manager at the time, Dinky Dawson, rated Orange highly, Peter now says that both he and Danny Kirwan were "uncertain" about the gear.

FENDER BANDMASTER

Peter eventually changed from the Orange gear to a Fender Bandmaster with a Tremolux 2x10 and 1x12 cabinet.

FENDER TREMOLUX "PIGGY-BACK" AMP

Around the same time Peter also owned a Fender Tremolux "piggy-back" amp and 2x10 cabinet.

MESA/BOOGIE HUNDRED-WATT

With Kolors Peter's main amp was a hundred-watt Mesa/Boogie, but he also used a Marshall and a Leslie Speaker Cabinet.

FENDER BLUES DE VILLE

Until autumn 1997 Peter's main amp on stage with The Splinter Group was a Fender Blues De Ville sixty-watt 4x10 combo he sometimes used together with a Fender Twin Reverb. He now also uses a mahogany special edition Vox AC30 called The Collector.

For practising he is trying out a special edition Green Matamp V-14 hundred-and-twenty-watt combo, made by the company that manufactures Orange amplification.

DISCOGRAPHY

By RJ Greaves

SOLO ALBUMS

1970	End Of The Game	Reprise RSLP 9006	(Reissue K44106)
1979	In The Skies	PVK PVLS 101	(Creole RNCD 1001)
1980	Little Dreamer	PVK PVLS 102	(Creole RNCD 1002)
1981	Whatcha Gonna Do?	PVK PET1	(Creole RNCD 1006 Castle CHC7017)
1981	Blue Guitar	Creole CRX 5	(Creole RNCD 1003)
1982	White Sky	Headline HED 1	(Creole RNCD 1004)
1983	Kolors	Headline HED 2	(Creole RNCD 1005)
1988	Legend	Creole CRX 12	(Creole CRXCD12)
1990	A Case For The Blues	Nightflite NTFL 2001	

COMPILATIONS BASED ON SOLO ALBUMS

Peter Green	Backtrackin'	TRKLP101 (2LP) TRKCD101 (2CD)
Last Train	Frogg	FGI 801 (FG2 801)
Baby When The Sun Goes Down	Castle	CBC 8026 (2CD)

(Creole Material plus two tracks from Nightflite album)

DECCA YEARS COMPILATION

Peter Green   Profile   (German Teldec 6.24778)
11 tracks taken from John Mayall era including rare singles.

OTHER ALBUMS FEATURING PETER GREEN

Raw Blues (Various Artists)	Ace Of Clubs SCL 1220
Eddie Boyd And His Blues Band	Decca LP4872
World Of Blues Power Vol 1 (Various Artists)	Decca SPA14
World Of Blues Power Vol 2 (Various Artists)	Decca SPA63
History Of British Blues (Various Artists)	Sire SAS 3701
7936 South Rhodes (Eddie Boyd)	Blue Horizon 7–63202. BGOCD195.
Long Overdue (Gordon Smith)	Blue Horizon 7–63211
Smiling Like I'm Happy (Duster Bennett)	Blue Horizon 7–63208
Blues From Laurel Canyon (John Mayall)	Decca SKL 4972 (Decca 820539)
Biggest Thing Since Colossus (Otis Spann)	BH.7–63217 Columbia 4759722
Bright Lights Big City (Duster Bennett)	Blue Horizon 7–63221
Jeremy Spencer (& Fleetwood Mac)	Reprise RSLP 9002 (Reprise K44105)
Trackside Blues (Brunning Sunflower)	SagaEros 8132 Appaloosa AP031
Wish You Would (Brunning Sunflower)	SagaEros 8150 Appaloosa AP035
Rarities (Brunning Sunflower Tramp)	Appaloosa AP052
The Answer (Peter Bardens)	Transatlantic TRA 222
Vintage 69 (Peter Bardens)	Transatlantic TRA SAM 36

Blue Memphis Suite (Memphis Slim)	Barclay 920.214 W
	Bros (WB1899)
Dave Kelly (& Brunning Sunflower)	Mercury 6310001
Gass (Gass)	Polydor 2383 022
BB King In London	Probe SPB 1041
	(ABC LP730)
Penguin (Fleetwood Mac)	Reprise K44235
Tusk (Fleetwood Mac)	Warner Bros K66088
A Dark Horse (Brian Knight)	PVK BRY1
Blue Eyed Slide (Brian Knight)	Lost Moments
	LMLP 022
The Visitor (Mick Fleetwood)	RCA RCALP 5044
Touch Of Sunburn (Enemy Within)	Red Lightnin' RL0067
Two Greens Make A Blues (Enemy Within)	Red Lightnin'
	RLCD 0087
Out In The Blue (Duster Bennett)	Indigo IGOCD 2018
Twang! A Tribute To Hank Marvin And The Shadows (Various Artists)	
Knights Of The Blues Table (Various Artists)	Viceroy 54189-2
Peter Green And The Splinter Group	Artisan SARCD 101

PETER GREEN SINGLE RELEASES IN UK

Heavy Heart b/w No Way Out	June 1971	Reprise
Beasts Of Burden b/w Uganda Woman	January 1972	Reprise
The Apostle b/w Tribal Dance	June 1978	PVK
In The Skies b/w Proud Pinto	July 1979	PVK
Walkin' The Road b/w Woman Don't	April 1980	PVK
Loser Two Times b/w Momma Don'tcha Cry	June 1980	PVK
Give Me Back My Freedom b/w Lost My Love	March 1981	PVK
Promised Land b/w Bizzy Lizzy	July 1981	PVK
The Clown b/w Time For Me To Go	June 1982	Headline
Big Boy Now b/w Bandit	1983	Headline

THE MAYALL AND FLEETWOOD MAC UK ALBUMS

John Mayall's Bluesbreakers
(Re-releases in brackets)
A Hard Road – Decca SKL 4853 (CD 820 474)
With Paul Butterfield EP – DFE-R 8673
Looking Back – Decca SKL 5010 (CD 820 331)
World Of John Mayall – Decca SPA 47
World Of John Mayall Vol 2 – Decca SPA 138
Thru' The Years – Decca SKL 5086

Fleetwood Mac
(Re-releases in brackets)
Peter Green's Fleetwood Mac – Blue Horizon 7-63200
(Embassy EMB 31036; CD Columbia 4773582)
Mr Wonderful (Essential ESSCD 010)
The Pious Bird Of Good Omen – Blue Horizon 7-63215
Then Play On – Reprise RSLP 9000 (Reprise 7599 27448)
Blues Jam At Chess – Blue Horizon 7-66227 (Columbia 474613-2)
The Original Fleetwood Mac – CBS 63875 (Essential ESSCD 026)
Castle Classics – CLACD 344) (Columbia 475979)
Fleetwood Mac Greatest Hits – CBS 69011
Live In Boston – Shanghai HAI 107
Cerulean – Shanghai HAI 300 (2 LP)
London Live 68 – Thunderbolt THBL 1.038
Original Fleetwood Mac/English Rose – CBS 22025 (2LP)
History Of Fleetwood Mac
Fleetwood Mac Collection – Castle Communications CCSCD 157
Like It This Way – Elite 008CD (20 Blue Horizon tracks)
Fleetwood Mac, The Blues Years – Essential ESBCD 138 3 CD Set with booklet
Live At The BBC – Essential EDF CD 297; 2 CD set culled from the various radio sessions listed in the Sessionography

SESSIONOGRAPHY

Peter Green compositions are marked #

THE PETER B'S – FEBRUARY 1966

If You Wanna Be Happy b/w Jodrell Blues
Released March 1966 Col DB7862
Peter Green gtr; Peter Bardens org; Dave Ambrose bs;
Mick Fleetwood dms

JOHN MAYALL'S BLUESBREAKERS WITH PETER GREEN –
30 SEPTEMBER 1966

Looking Back b/w So Many Roads
Decca F 12506,SKL 5010 (Out Oct 66)
Peter Green gtr; John Mayall v/p/gtr; John McVie bs;
Aynsley Dunbar dms; Henry Lowther tpt; John Almond,
Nick Newell sax

BLUESBREAKERS – 11 OCTOBER 1966

Sitting In The Rain b/w Out Of Reach
Decca F12545, SKL 5010 (Released Jan 67)
Peter Green gtr; John Mayall v/gtr; John McVie bs;
Aynsley Dunbar (drumsticks on guitar case)

BLUESBREAKERS – 11, 12, 19, 24 OCTOBER, 11 NOV

A Hard Road (Decca SKL 4853)
It's Over
You Don't Love Me (-1)

The Stumble
Another Kind Of Love
Hit The Highway
Leaping Christine (-2)
Dust My Blues
There's Always Work (Mayall solo)
The Same Way # (-1)
The Supernatural #
Top Of The Hill
Someday After A while (-2)
Living Alone
Not On Album:
Mama Talk To Your Daughter (Decca SKL 5086)
Out Of Reach # (-1)(Decca F12545; SKL 5086)
Alabama Blues (-1, Green solo) (Decca SKL 5086)
Peter gtr (v on -1), John Mayall v/hca/p/gtr; John McVie
bs; Aynsley Dunbar dms; plus John Almond & Ray
Warleigh sax (on -2)

JOHN MAYALL & PETER GREEN – AUTUMN 1966

Evil Woman Blues # (A of C SCL 1220)

**BLUESBREAKERS WITH PAUL BUTTERFIELD EP –
26 NOVEMBER 1966**

All My Life (Decca DFe-R 8673)
Riding On The L&N
Little By Little
Eagle Eye
Peter Green gtr; John Mayall v/p/hca; Paul Butterfield
v/hca; John McVie bs; Aynsley Dunbar dms

RADIO 1 SESSION – Winter 1967

Riding On The L&N (Invasion Unlimited 9303-1)
Sitting In The Rain (Invasion Unlimited 9303-1)
Dust My Blues (on bootleg)
Curly # (on bootleg)
Top Of The Hill (on bootleg)

Peter Green gtr; John Mayall v/gtr; John McVie bs;
Aynsley Dunbar dms

BLUESBREAKERS – 16 FEBRUARY 1967

Curly # b/w Rubber Duck (Decca F12588;
SKL 5086. Released March 67)
Greeny # (Decca SKL 5086; SPA14)
Missing You # (-1)
Peter Green v (-1) gtr/hca; John McVie bs; Aynsley
Dunbar dms

BLUESBREAKERS – 8 MARCH 1967

Please Don't Tell (Decca SKL 5086)
Your Funeral My Trial (Decca SKL 5086)
Personnel as 16 Feb

EDDIE BOYD AND HIS BLUES BAND – 14 MARCH 1967

Letter Missin' Blues (Decca LP 4872)
Unfair Lovers
The Big Bell
Steak House Rock
Night Time Is The Right Time
Rock 'Em Back
Too Bad Pt 2
Peter Green gtr; Eddie Boyd v/p; John Mayall hca; John
McVie bs; Aynsley Dunbar dms

EDDIE BOYD AND HIS BLUES BAND – 17 MARCH 1967

Ain't Doin' Too Bad (Decca LP 4872)
Vacation From The Blues
Key To The Highway
Pinetop's Boogie Woogie
Blue Coat Man
The Train Is Coming
Too Bad Pt 1 (-1)
As above plus Albert Hall tpt; Rex Morris sax; Bob
Efford sax; Harry Klein sax (-1 only)

21 MARCH 1967

Dust My Broom (-1) (Decca LP4872)
Save Her Doctor (-1) (Decca LP 4872)
Empty Arms (-2) (BH 1009)
So Miserable To Be Alone (-2) (BH 1009)
Personnel as above plus Tony McPhee gtr (-1) omit John Mayall

BLUESBREAKERS – 19 APRIL 1967

Double Trouble b/w It Hurts Me Too (Decca F12621;
SKL5010–alternate mix. Out June 67)
Fleetwood Mac # (CBS 63875)
First Train Home # (CBS 63875)
Peter Green gtr; John Mayall v/p/org/gtr; John McVie bs; Mick Fleetwood dms

AYNSLEY DUNBAR RETALIATION – SUMMER 1967

Stone Crazy (Sire SAS 3701)
Peter Green gtr; Rod Stewart v; Jack Bruce bs; Aynsley Dunbar dms

LIVE AT THE MARQUEE – 15 AUGUST 1967

Talk To Me Baby (Sunflower CD SF104)
My Baby's Sweet
Looking For Somebody #
Evil Woman Blues #
Got To Move
No Place To Go
Watch Out For Me Woman #
Mighty Long Time
Dust My Blues
I Need You, Come On Home
Shake Your Moneymaker
Peter Green v/gtr/hca; Jeremy Spencer v/gtr; Bob Brunning bs; Mick Fleetwood dms/wbd

PETER GREEN'S FLEETWOOD MAC – SEPTEMBER 1967

I Believe My Time Ain't Long (BH 3051; 7-63215)
Rambling Pony # (BH 3051; 7-63215)
Rambling Pony No 2 # (CBS 63875)
Long Grey Mare # (BH 7-63200)
Personnel as above

RADIO 1 SESSION – 7 NOVEMBER 1967

Broadcast 12 November 1967

Long Grey Mare # (Early Years CD 3316)
Baby Please Set A Date (Early Years CD 3316)
Looking For Somebody #
Got To Move
John McVie replaces Bob Brunning on bs

PETER GREEN'S FLEETWOOD MAC – NOVEMBER/DECEMBER 1967

My Heart Beat Like A Hammer (BH 7-63200)
Merry Go Round #
Hellhound On My Trail (Spencer v/p)
Shake Your Moneymaker
Looking For Somebody #
No Place To Go
My Baby's Good To Me
I Loved Another Woman #
Cold Black Night
The World Keeps On Turning # (Green v/gtr)
Got To Move

Also from same sessions:

Leaving Town Blues # (CBS 63875)
Watch Out #
A Fool No More #

Can't Afford To Do It
Mean Old Fireman (Spencer v/gtr)
Allow Me One More Show (Spencer v/gtr)

Both Spencer tracks are out-takes from earlier session in 1967
Peter Green v/gtr/hca; Jeremy Spencer v/gtr/p; John McVie bs; Mick Fleetwood dms

WITH JOHN MAYALL – 4-5 DECEMBER 1967

Jenny b/w Picture On The Wall (Decca F12732; SKL 5010)
Peter Green gtr and slide; John Mayall v/p/gtr; Keef Hartley dms

RADIO 1 SESSION – 16 JANUARY 1967

Broadcast on *Top Gear* 21 Jan 1968 and 24 Mar 1968

Can't Hold Out (Koine K890104)
Sweet Little Angel (Koine K890104)
Don't Be Cruel (Koine K890104)
The World Keeps Turning (Koine K890104)
Bee-I-Bicky-Bop-Blue-Jean-Honey-Babe-Meets-High-School-Hound-Dog-Hot-Rod-Man (Track Unissued)
Where You Belong (Track Unissued)
The Sun Is Shining (Track Unissued)
The Stroller (-1) (Track Unissued)
Blue Coat Man (-1) (Track Unissued)
Personnel as above plus Eddie Boyd v/p (-1)

AT DUSTER BENNETT'S HOME IN KINGSTON – EARLY 1968

Trying So Hard To Forget # (-1) (-4) Indigo IGOCD 2018
Kind Hearted Woman (-1)
Coming, I'm Coming(I'm Coming On Home) # (Peter's instrumental)
I'm Thinking About A Woman
Untitled Instrumental (-4) (-2)?

*Peter Green gtr v (-1) hca (-2); Duster Bennett v (-3)
hca (-4) /gtr/perc*

7936 SOUTH RHODES EDDIE BOYD – 25 JANUARY 1968

You Got To Reap (BH7–63202)
Just The Blues (BH7–63215)
She's Real
Back Slack
Be Careful
Ten To One
The Blues Is Here To Stay
You Are My Love
Third Degree
Thank You Baby
She's Gone
I Can't Stop Loving You
The Big Boat (BH 57-3137; 7-63215)
Sent For You Yesterday (BH 57-3137; 7-63215)
*Peter Green gtr; Eddie Boyd v/p; John McVie bs; Mick
Fleetwood dms*

FLEETWOOD MAC BLACK MAGIC WOMAN – 22 FEBRUARY 1968

Black Magic Woman # b/w The Sun Is Shining (-1) (BH
57–3138; 7–63215)

*From same sessions personnel as above plus Christine
Perfect p on*

Worried Dream (CBS 63875)
Love That Woman (Spencer p)
Drifting #

RADIO 3 SESSION – 26 FEBRUARY 1968

Broadcast on Radio 3 *Blues In Britain*

Peter Green v/gtr; Jeremy Spencer v/gtr (-1); John McVie

bs; Mick Fleetwood dms

RADIO 1 SESSION – 9 APRIL 1968

Broadcast on *Saturday Club* 13 April

Worried Dream
Please Find My Baby
Peggy Sue Got Married
Black Magic Woman

RADIO 1 SESSION – 16 APRIL 1968

Broadcast on *Night Ride* 17 April

How Blue Can You Get
My Baby Is Sweet
Long Grey Mare #
Buzz Me
I'm So Lonesome And Blue
Personnel as above

FLEETWOOD MAC MR WONDERFUL SESSIONS – APRIL 1968

Stop Messin' Round # (BH57-3139)
Stop Messin' Round (alternate take) (BH7-63205; 7-63215)
Coming Home
Rollin' Man #
Dust My Broom
Love That Burns #
Doctor Brown
Need Your Love Tonight
If You Be My Baby #
Evenin' Boogie
Lazy Poker Blues #
I've Lost My Baby
Trying So Hard To Forget # (-1)
As above plus Christine Perfect org; strings added
Need Your Love So Bad

Personnel as above plus Steve Gregory and Dave Howard alto sax; Johnny Almond Roland Vaughan tenor sax; Christine Perfect p; Duster Bennett hca on (-1)

LONDON "LIVE" PETER GREEN'S FLEETWOOD MAC – APRIL 1968

Got To Move (Thunderbolt 1038)
I Held My Baby Last Night
My Baby's Sweet
My Baby's A Good 'Un
Don't Know Which Way To Go
Buzz Me
The Dream
The World Keep On Turning # (Green v/gtr)
How Blue Can You Get
Bleeding Heart

RADIO 1 SESSION – 27 MAY 1968

Broadcast *Top Gear* 2 June and 7 July

That Ain't It (I Need Your Love) (Moby Dick MDCD 004; Koine K890104)
Mean Mistreatin' Mama
Intergalactic Musicians Walking Walking On Velvet
Dead Shrimp Blues
Sheila

WITH GORDON SMITH – AUGUST 1968

Diving Duck Blues (BH7-63211)
Peter Green hca; Gordon Smith v/gtr

DUSTER BENNETT SMILING LIKE I'M HAPPY – 8, 9 JULY AND 8 SEPTEMBER 1968

My Lucky Day (BH7-63208)
My Love Is Your Love
Shady Little Baby

Peter Green gtr; Duster Bennett v/hca/gtr/bass drum and p as 'Ham Richmond' John McVie bs; Mick Fleetwood dms; Stella Sutton v

JOHN MAYALL BLUES FROM LAUREL CANYON – 26-28 AUGUST 1968

First Time Alone (Decca SKL 4972)
Peter Green gtr; Steve Thompson bs; Colin Allen dms; Mick Taylor gtr; John Mayall v/keys

RADIO 1 SESSION – 26-27 AUGUST 1968

Broadcast *Top Gear* 1 Sept, 13 Oct, 24 Nov

Need Your Love So Bad (Early Years CD-3316)
Shake Your Moneymaker (Early Years CD-3316)
Stop Messin' Round # (Early Years CD-3316)
A Mind Of My Own (Koine K890104)
I Have To Laugh (Mean Old World) (Koine K890104)
(Moby Dick MDCD004)
Preachin' Blues
You Need Love (Whole Lotta Love)
A Talk With You
Wine, Whiskey, Women (Unissued)
Crutch And Cane (Unissued)
If You Be My Baby # (Unissued)
Crazy For My Baby (Unissued)
Peter Green v/gtr/hca; Jeremy Spencer v/gtr; Danny Kirwan v/gtr; John McVie bs; Mick Fleetwood dms; Christine Perfect v/keys

ALBATROSS SESSIONS – OCTOBER 1968

Albatross # b/w Jigsaw Puzzle Blues (BH 57-3145; 7-63215)
Something Inside Of Me (CBS 22025)
One Sunny Day (CBS 22025; Reprise RSLP9000)
Without You (CBS 22025; Reprise RSLP9000)
Personnel as above less Jeremy Spencer

RADIO 1 SESSION – 9 OCTOBER 1968

Like Crying
Albatross # (Moby Dick MDCD004)
Hang On To A Dream (Koine K890104)
Baby Don't You Want To Go (Koine K890104)
Personnel as above plus Jeremy Spencer

RADIO 1 SESSION – 1 NOVEMBER 1968

Broadcast on BBC World Service *Rhythm & Blues 26*

Presenter Alexis Korner
Sweet Home Chicago
Crazy About My Baby
Baby Please Set A Date
Personnel as above

FLEETWOOD MAC BLUES JAM AT CHESS – 4 JANUARY 1969

Watch Out # (BH 7-66227)
Ooh Baby (less Danny Kirwan)
Last Night (-2)
South Indiana (Take 1)
South Indiana (Take 2)
I Need Your Love
Horton's Boogie Woogie
I Got The Blues (Unissued)
Untitled Instrumental x 2 (Unissued)
Have A Good Time (Unissued)
Rock Me Baby (Unissued)
Fleetwood Mac less Jeremy Spencer plus Walter
"Shakey" Horton hca on (-2) (Add Otis Spann p; SP
Leary dms; less Mick Fleetwood)

Red Hot Jam
My Baby's Gone (less JT Brown) (Unissued)
Peter Green gtr; Buddy Guy gtr; Honeyboy Edwards
gtr; JT Brown sax; Willie Dixon upright bs; Mick

Fleetwood dms

Rockin' Boogie
Above less Buddy Guy, add Jeremy Spencer

World's In A Tangle (-1)
Talk With You
Like It This Way
Sugar Mama
Homework
Ain't Nobody's Business (Otis Spann v)
Someday Soon Baby
Hungry Country Girl
Fleetwood Mac less Jeremy Spencer; add Otis Spann p;
SP Leary dms (-1)

WITH OTIS SPANN COLOSSUS SESSIONS – 9 JANUARY 1969

No More Doggin' (BH 7-63217)
I Need Some Air
Walkin' (57-3155)
My Love Depends On You (PR45/46)
Blues For Hippies (Excello 2329)
It Was A Big Thing (Bh 7-63217)
She Needs Some Loving
Dig You
Someday Baby
Temperature Is Risin' (100.2¯F)
Temperature Is Risin' (98.8¯F) (57–3155)
Ain't Nobody's Business
*Fleetwood Mac less Jeremy Spencer and Mick
Fleetwood; plus Otis Spann v/p and SP Leary dms*

MAN OF THE WORLD SESSIONS – JANUARY 11-12 1969

Man Of The World # b/w Somebody's Gonna Get Their
Head Kicked In Tonite (Immediate IM 080)
*Fleetwood Mac less Jeremy Spencer on A-side; plus
Jeremy Spencer on B-side as "Earl Vince And The*

Valiants"

RADIO 1 SESSION – 10 MARCH 1969

Broadcast *Top Gear* 16 March and 11 May

You'll Never Know What You're Missing Till You Try
(Unissued)
Heavenly (Unissued)
I Can't Believe You Want To Leave (Unissued)
Early Morning Come (Unissued)
Blues With A Feeling (Moby Dick MDCD 004)
Tallahassie Lassie (Moby Dick MDCD 004)

RADIO 1 SESSION – 17 MARCH 1969

You'll Be Mine
Roll Along Blues
Peggy Sue Got Married
Albatross # (Moby Dick MDCD 004)

RADIO 1 SESSION – 17 MARCH 1969

Pt 2 Broadcast on *Symonds On Sunday* 30 March 1969

Shady Little Baby (-1) (Koine K890104)
Hot Rodding (-2)
New Worried Blues
*Peter Green gtr; Alexis Korner v (-1) gtr; Duster Bennett
v (-2) hca; Christine Perfect p; John McVie bs; Mick
Fleetwood dms*

FLEETWOOD MAC LIVE IN AMSTERDAM – APRIL 1969

Merry Go Round # (Discurios DIS 113CD)
One Sided Love
Dust My Broom
Got To Move
Sugar Mama
Can't Hold Out
Stop Messin' Round #

San Ho Zay
Albatross #
Blue Suede Shoes

WITH DUSTER BENNETT – LIVE AT THE ANGEL, GODALMING – 15 APRIL 1969

Bright Lights Big City b/w Talk To Me (BH 7-63221; 57-3154)
Peter Green six-string bs; Duster Bennett v/hca/gtr/bass drum; Top Topham gtr; Tony Mills bs; Stella Sutton v

FLEETWOOD MAC THEN PLAY ON SESSIONS – APRIL-JULY 1969

Coming Your Way (Reprise RSLP 9000)
Fighting For Madge
When You Say
Show-Biz Blues #
Under Way #
Although The Sun Is Shining
Rattlesnake Shake #
Searching For Madge
My Dream
Like Crying
Before The Beginning #
Oh Well (Parts 1 & 2) #
Less Jeremy Spencer on all tracks

RADIO 1 SESSION – 14 MAY 1969

Broadcast on *World Service R&B* 2 June 1969
Talk With You (Moby Dick MDCD 004; Koine K890104)
Just Want To Tell You

JEREMY SPENCER SOLO ALBUM – JUNE 1969

Stringalong (Reprise RSLP 9002)
Fleetwood Mac plus Peter Green on banjo

RADIO 1 SESSION – 10 JUNE 1969

Broadcast 15 June

Coming Your Way
Man Of The World # (Moby Dick MDCD 004; Early Years
CD3316)
Jumping At Shadows (Moby Dick MDCD 004; Early Years
CD3316)
Linda (Moby Dick MDCD 004; Early Years CD3316)

RADIO 1 SESSION – 6 OCTOBER 1969

Broadcast 12 October
Oh Well (Part 1) #
Although The Sun Is Shining

WITH BRUNNING SUNFLOWER BLUES BAND – OCTOBER 1969

Ride With Your Daddy Tonight (-2) (Saga 8132;
Appaloosa 052)
Simple Simon (-1)
It Takes Time
If You Let Me Love You
Ah! Soul/Uranus (Take 1)
Uranus (Take 2) (Saga 8150)
Peter Green v/gtr; Bob Hall p; Bob Brunning bs/v (-1);
Pete Banham dms; plus Colin Jordan gtr (-2)

WITH CLIFFORD DAVIS – SEPTEMBER 1969

Before The Beginning # b/w Man Of The World #
Peter Green all instruments; Clifford Davis v

WITH PETER BARDENS – OCTOBER 1969

The Answer (Transatlantic TRA SAM 36)
Don't Goof With A Spook
I Can't Remember
I Don't Want To Go Home
Homage To The God Of Light
Let's Get It On (Transatlantic TRA 222)
Peter Green gtr; Peter Bardens v/p/org; Andy Gee gtr;
Reg Isadore dms; Bruce Thomas bs; Rocky congas;

Linda Lewis, Steve Ellis, Alan Marshall, David Wooley backing v

FLEETWOOD MAC LIVE AT THE BOSTON TEA PARTY – 5-7 FEBRUARY 1970

Oh Well # (Shanghai HAI 107)
Like It This Way
World In Harmony
Only You
Black Magic Woman #
Jumping At Shadows
Can't Hold Out
Madison Blues (Shanghai HAI 300)
Sandy Mary #
Stranger Blues
Great Balls Of Fire
Jenny Jenny
Got To Move
Oh Baby
Teenage Darling
Loving Kind
Tutti Frutti
Rattlesnake Shake #
Keep A Knocking
Red Hot Mama
Green Manalishi #

PETER GREEN WITH ERIC CLAPTON ALSO AT BOSTON TEA PARTY

Instrumental Jam (Gold Standard BLU 883)

APRIL 1970

Green Manalishi # b/w World In Harmony RS 27007

RADIO 1 "IN CONCERT" FEATURING FLEETWOOD MAC – 9 APRIL 1970

Broadcast 19 April 1970

Rattlesnake Shake/Under Way # (TAKRL 1906; Early
Years CD3316)
Tiger (TAKRL 1906; Early Years CD3316)
Green Manalishi # (TAKRL 1906; Early Years CD3316)
Stranger Blues
World In Harmony
Great Balls Of Fire/Twist And Shout

RADIO 1 SESSION – 27 APRIL 1970

Broadcast *Top Gear* on 23 May 1970
Sandy Mary #
World In Harmony
Tiger
Only You
Leaving Town Blues #
Peter Green plus Nick Pickett violin

FLEETWOOD MAC AND CLIFFORD DAVIS – MAY 1970

Come On Down And Follow Me b/w Homework
(Reprise R27008)
Peter Green all instruments

END OF THE GAME SESSIONS – MAY-JUNE 1970

Bottoms Up (Reprise K44106)
Timeless Time
Descending Scale
Burnt Foot
Hidden Depth
The End Of The Game
*Peter Green gtr; Zoot Money p; Nick Buck p/org; Alex
Dmochowski bs; Godfrey Maclean dms/perc*

WITH MEMPHIS SLIM – 3, 5, 6, 18 JUNE 1970

The Blue Memphis Suite (Barclay 920.214)
Born in Memphis Tennessee
Chicago

Me And My Piano
Handy Man
Feel Like Screamin' And Cryin'
Riding On The Blues Train
I Started Moving (Freedom Bound)
Wind Gonna Rise
(Plus Chris Spedding gtr; Ray Dempsey gtr; Duster
Bennett hca; Pete Wingfield p/org; Trisan Fry perc)
Youth Wants To Know
Boogie Woogie 1-9-7-0
Mason-Dixon Line
(Plus Stephen Thompson bs)
Otis Spann & Earl Hooker
Chicago Seven
*Peter Green gtr; Memphis Slim v/p/clav; John Paul
Jones org; Pete Wingfield p/org/celeste; Johnny Dean
chimes; Larry Steel bs; Conrad Isadore dms; Henry
Lowther, Harry Beckett, Kenny Wheeler tpts; Nick
Evans, John Manfred tbnes; Carl Jenkins, Brian
Smith, Stan Saltzman, Jerry Gibbs and Peter King
sax*

WITH GASS – AUGUST 1970

Juju (Polydor 2383 022)
Black Velvet
*Peter Green gtr; Bobby Tench v/perc; Derek Austin
keys/flute; Michael Piggott vio/gtr; Delisle Harper bs;
Godfrey Maclean dms*

WITH DAVE KELLY – SEPTEMBER 1970

Gotta Keep Running (-1)(–3) (Mercury 6310001)
You Got It (-1)(–2)
Green Winter
*Peter Green gtr; Dave Kelly v/gtr; Bob Brunning bs;
Barry Guard dms plus Alan Hawkshaw p/org (-1); Bob
Hall p (-2); Jo Ann Kelly v (-3)*

SOLO SINGLES SESSIONS – JANUARY 1971

Heavy Heart b/w No Way Out (Reprise 14092)
Released June 1971
Beasts Of Burden b/w Uganda Woman (Reprise 14141)
Released Jan 1972
*Peter Green gtr; Nigel Watson congas; Clifford
Chewaluza perc; Snowy White gtr*

WITH BB KING LIVE IN LONDON SESSIONS – 9-16 JUNE 1971

Caledonia (ABC LP 730)
*Peter Green gtr; BB King v/gtr; Jim Price tpt; Ollie
Mitchell tpt; Chuck Findley tbne; Bobby Keys sax; Bill
Perkins sax/clar; Gary Wright org; Rick Wright el p;
Klaus Voorman bs; Jim Gordon dms; Duster Bennett
hca*

WITH FLEETWOOD MAC PENGUIN SESSIONS – JAN-FEB 1973

Nightwatch (Reprise K44235)
*Peter Green gtr; Dave Walker v; Bob Welch gtr; John
McVie bs; Christine McVie p/keys; Mick Fleetwood
dms*

IN THE SKIES SESSIONS – AUTUMN 1977

In The Skies # (PVK PVLS 101) PV24
Slabo Day #
Fool No More #
Tribal Dance #
Seven Stars
Funky Chunk#
Just For You #
Proud Pinto#
Apostle#
Apostle (acoustic) (PVK PV 16)
All songs composed by Peter Green. 'In The Skies',
'Seven Stars' and 'Just For You' co-written by Jane
Samuel

Peter Green v/gtr; Snowy White gtr; Pete Bardens keys;
Kuma Harada bs; Reg Isadore dms; Lennox Langton
perc; Godfrey Maclean dms

FLEETWOOD MAC TUSK ALBUM – EARLY 1979

Brown Eyes (WB K66088)
Peter Green gtr; Lindsey Buckingham gtr; Christine
McVie keys; John McVie bs; Mick Fleetwood dms

LITTLE DREAMER – LATE AUTUMN 1979

Loser Two Times (PVK PVLS 102)
Momma Don'tcha Cry
Born Under A Bad Sign
I Could Not Ask For More
Baby When The Sun Goes Down
Walkin' The Road
One Woman Love
Crying Won't Bring You Back
Little Dreamer #
Peter Green v/gtr; Ronnie Johnson gtr; Paul Westwood
bs; Roy Shipston org; Dave Mattacks dms; Morris Pert
perc; David Wilkey p; Peter Vernon-Kell p; John
Edwards bs; Kuma Harada bs

WHATCHA GONNA DO? – AUTUMN 1980

Got To See Her Tonight (PVK PET1)
Promised Land
Bullet In The Sky
Give Me Back My Freedom
Last Train To San Antone
To Break Your Heart
Bizzy Lizzy PV112
Lost My Love PV103
Like A Hot Tomato
Trying To Hit My Head Against The Wall
Peter Green v/gtr; Paul Westwood bs; Roy Shipston keys;
Dave Mattacks dms; Lennox Langton perc; Mo Foster

bs; Jeff Daly sax

WITH BRIAN KNIGHT & DARK HORSE – AUTUMN 1980

Boogie Beat (BRY 1)
Going Down Slow
Bring Your Corn To Me
Trouble In Mind
Honey Bee
Blues Is Rock And Roll
Mannish Boy
Got The Blues 4 U
Good Morning Blues
Cabin In The Sky
Bright Lights, Big City
Peter Green gtr; Brian Knight v/gtr/hca: Geoff Bradford gtr: Ian Stewart p; Dick Heckstall-Smith sax; Art Theman sax; Geraint Watkins acc; Charlie Hart bs; Charlie Watts dms

WITH MICK FLEETWOOD VISITOR SESSIONS – JAN-FEB 1981

Rattlesnake Shake # (RCA RCALP 5044)
Super Brains
Peter Green v/gtr; George Hawkins bs; Mick Fleetwood dms; Todd Sharp gtr; Lord Tiki & Ebaali Gbiko hand drums

WHITE SKY – MAY 1981

Time For Me To Go (Headline HED1)
Shining Star
The Clown
White Sky (-1)
It's Gonna Be Me
Born On The Wild Side
Fallin' Apart
Indian Lover
Just Another Guy
Peter Green v/gtr; Webster Johnson keys; Larry Steel

bs; Reg Isadore dms; Jeff Whittaker perc; Mike Green
v (-1)

KOLORS COLLECTION – OUT-TAKES 1981-82

What Am I Doing Here? (Headline HED2)
Big Boy Now
Black Woman
Bandit
Same Old Blues
Liquor And You
Gotta Do It With Me (-1)
Funky Jam
Personnel as above plus Bob Bowman slide gtr; Trevor
Orton pan-pipes

THE LEGEND COLLECTION – OUT-TAKES 1981-82

Touch My Spirit (Creole CRX12)
Six-String Guitar
You Won't See Me Anymore
Long Way From Home
Rubbing My Eyes
Corner Of My Mind
Carry My Love

KATMANDU SESSIONS – DECEMBER 1983 – JANUARY 1984

Dust My Broom (Nightflite NTFL2001)
One More Night Without You
Crane's Train Boogie
Boogie All The Way
Zulu Gone West
Blowing All My Troubles Away
Stranger Blues
Sweet Sixteen
Who's That Knocking

The Case
Peter Green v/gtr/hca/dms; Ray Dorset v/gtr/bs/hca;
Vincent Crane v/keys; Len Surtees bs; Greg Terry-Short
dms; Jeff Whittaker v/perc/dms

WITH THE ENEMY WITHIN – 1986

Chinese White Boy (Red Lightnin' RL0067; RLCD0087)
Peter Green gtr bs; Lawrie Gaines (The Raven)
v/gtr/sax/synth; Mick Green gtr; Ed Deane gtr; Gypsie
Mayo gtr/bs; Gary Peters gtr

TWANG! – HANK MARVIN/SHADOWS TRIBUTE – JULY 1996

Midnight
Peter Green gtr; Nigel Watson gtr; Spike Edney keys;
Neil Murray bs; Cozy Powell dms; plus session
musicians

KNIGHTS OF THE BLUES TABLE – OCTOBER-DECEMBER 1996

Travelling Riverside Blues (Viceroy 54189-2)
plus two others unissued
Peter Green v/gtr/hca; Nigel Watson v/gtr

PETER GREEN/SPLINTER GROUP – DECEMBER 1996

Hitch-Hiking Woman (Artisan SARCD 101)
Travelling Riverside Blues
Peter Green v/gtr; Nigel Watson v/gtr

PETER GREEN/SPLINTER GROUP – DECEMBER 1996

Look On Yonder Wall (Artisan SARCD 101)
Homework
The Stumble
Help Me

Watch Your Step
From Four Till Late
Steady Rollin' Man
It Takes Time
Dark End Of The Street
Goin' Down
*Peter Green v/gtr/hca; Nigel Watson v/gtr; Spike Edney
keys; Neil Murray bs; Cozy Powell dms*

BIBLIOGRAPHY

Fleetwood Mac – Behind the Masks
Bob Brunning (New English Library 1990)

Fleetwood: My Life And Adventures With Fleetwood Mac
Mick Fleetwood with Stephen Davis (Sidgwick and Jackson 1990)

My Twenty-Five Years In Fleetwood Mac
Mick Fleetwood (Weidenfeld & Nicholson 1992)

Fleetwood Mac – Rumours 'N' Fax
Roy Carr and Steve Clarke (Harmony Books, New York 1978)

The Authorised History – Fleetwood Mac
Samuel Graham (Warner Bros Publications 1978)

Blues On CD – The Essential Guide
Charles Shaar Murray (Kyle Cathie Ltd 1993)

Crosstown Traffic: Jimi Hendrix And Postwar Pop
Charles Shaar Murray (Faber and Faber 1989)

Survivor – The Authorised Biography Of Eric Clapton
Ray Coleman (Sidgwick and Jackson 1985)

Keith Richards – The Biography
Victor Bockris (Hutchinson 1992)

White Boy Singin' The Blues
Michael Bane (Da Capo Press, New York 1982)

Musicians In Tune
Jenny Boyd (Simon & Schuster 1992)

On a final note there are many interesting, obscure Peter Green recordings freely available to supplement this brilliant legit collection. Search long and hard, and you will find.

INDEX

ALSO AVAILABLE FROM
SANCTUARY MUSIC LIBRARY

MIND OVER MATTER – THE IMAGES OF PINK FLOYD
£30.00/$39.95   by Storm Thorgerson   1-86074-206-8
DEATH DISCS – AN ACCOUNT OF FATALITY IN THE POPULAR SONG
£14.99/$19.95   by Alan Clayson   1-86074-195-9
BORN UNDER THE SIGN OF JAZZ
£16.99/$22.50   by Randi Hultin   1-86074-194-0
SERGE GAINSBOURG – VIEW FROM THE EXTERIOR
£12.99/$19.95   by Alan Clayson   1-86074-222-X
LONELY TEARDROPS – THE JACKIE WILSON STORY
£14.99/$19.95   by Tony Douglas   1-86074-214-9
LET THEM ALL TALK – ELVIS COSTELLO
£12.99/$19.95   by Brian Hinton   1-86074-197-7
JONI MITCHELL – BOTH SIDES NOW
£12.99/$19.95   by Brian Hinton   1-86074-160-6
GEORGE GERSHWIN – HIS LIFE & MUSIC
£9.99/$14.95   by Ean Wood   1-86074-174-6
THE QUIET ONE – A LIFE OF GEORGE HARRISON
£9.99/$14.95   by Alan Clayson   1-86074-184-3
RINGO STARR – STRAIGHT MAN OR JOKER?
£9.99/$14.95   by Alan Clayson   1-86074-189-4
CELTIC CROSSROADS – THE ART OF VAN MORRISON
£9.99/$14.95   by Brian Hinton   1-86074-169-X
SEVENTEEN WATTS? THE FIRST 20 YEARS OF BRITISH ROCK
GUITAR, THE MUSICIANS AND THEIR STORIES
£19.99/$34.95   by Mo Foster   1-86074-182-7
HAMBURG – CRADLE OF BRITISH ROCK
£12.99/$14.95   by Alan Clayson   1-86074-221-1
THE KINKS – WELL RESPECTED MEN
£9.99/$14.95   by Neville Marten & Jeffrey Hudson   1-86074-135-5
HAPPY BOYS HAPPY – THE SMALL FACES, FACES & HUMBLE PIE
£9.99/$14.95   by Uli Twelker & Roland Schmitt   1-86074-197-5

For more information on titles from Sanctuary Publishing Limited, please contact Sanctuary Publishing Limited, 82 Bishops Bridge Road, London W2 6BB Tel: +44 (0) 171 243 0640 Fax: +44 (0) 171 243 0470. To order a title direct, please contact our distributors: (UK only) Macmillan Distribution Limited Tel: 01256 302659. (US & Canada) Music Sales Corporation Tel: 1 800 431 7187. (Australia & New Zealand) Bookwise International Tel: 08268 8222.